Haunted historiographies

Manchester University Press

Haunted historiographies
The rhetoric of ideology in postcolonial Irish fiction

MATTHEW SCHULTZ

Manchester University Press
Manchester and New York
distributed in the United States exclusively by Palgrave Macmillan

Copyright © Matthew Schultz 2014

The right of Matthew Schultz to be identified as the author of this work has been asserted by him in accordance with the Copyright, Designs and Patents Act 1988.

Published by Manchester University Press
Oxford Road, Manchester M13 9NR, UK
and Room 400, 175 Fifth Avenue, New York, NY 10010, USA
www.manchesteruniversitypress.co.uk

Distributed in the United States exclusively by
Palgrave Macmillan, 175 Fifth Avenue, New York,
NY 10010, USA

Distributed in Canada exclusively by
UBC Press, University of British Columbia, 2029 West Mall,
Vancouver, BC, Canada V6T 1Z2

British Library Cataloguing-in-Publication Data
A catalogue record for this book is available from the British Library

Library of Congress Cataloging-in-Publication Data applied for

ISBN 978 0 7190 9092 9 *hardback*

First published 2014

The publisher has no responsibility for the persistence or accuracy of URLs for any external or third-party internet websites referred to in this book, and does not guarantee that any content on such websites is, or will remain, accurate or appropriate.

Typeset in Sabon by
Koinonia, Manchester
Printed and Bound in Great Britain by
TJ International Ltd, Padstow

Contents

Acknowledgements   *page* vii

Introduction: Textual spectrality and *Finnegans Wake*   1

Part I: Famine

1 The persistence of Famine in postcolonial Ireland   23
2 The specter of Famine during World War II   67

Part II: Revolution

3 Ancient warriors, modern sexualities: Easter 1916 and the advent of post-Catholic Ireland   97
4 Gothic inheritance and the Troubles in contemporary Irish fiction   129

Conclusion: Famine and the Western Front in Samuel Beckett's *Waiting for Godot*   164

Bibliography   183
Index   200

For my wife,
Jayme

Acknowledgements

This book is partially funded by a Susan Turner Fund Endowment Grant from the Research Committee at Vassar College. I am grateful to Ellen Crowell, Jennifer Rust, and Joya Uraizee for their invaluable, extensive, and expert support, to Joe Webb and Christopher Dickman for their magnanimous feedback on various drafts of this work, and to Natalie Friedman and Sue Mendelsohn from whose wisdom and friendship I have profited greatly. I would also like to thank my colleagues in the American Conference for Irish Studies who helped me think through many of these ideas at numerous meetings.

Portions of the 'Introduction' to this work were originally published as '"Arise Sir Ghostus": Textual Spectrality and *Finnegans Wake*,' in *James Joyce Quarterly* (2013). Portions of Chapter 1 originally appeared as 'Narratives of Dispossession: The Persistence of Famine in Postcolonial Ireland,' in *Postcolonial Text* 7.2 (2012). Chapter 4 was first published in *The Irish Journal of Gothic and Horror Studies* 10 (2011) as '"Give it Welcome": Gothic Inheritance and the Troubles in Contemporary Ireland.'

Introduction:
Textual spectrality
and *Finnegans Wake*

'Why this hunt for ghosts?' (Jacques Derrida, *Specters of Marx*)

The October 2010 special issue of *PMLA* – Literary Criticism for the Twenty-First Century – assembled a collection of shorter essays that forecast possible paradigm shifts in literary criticism. In the introductory essay, Jonathan Culler aptly notes a salient feature appearing throughout the issue: 'the motif of return: return to rhetoric, a return to thematics, a return to textual criticism...'[1] As it mines contributors' varied attempts to sketch this 'return' in what Meredith McGill and Andrew Parker call 'the future of the literary past,'[2] *Haunted historiographies* entertains Richard Klein's suggestion from the above-mentioned issue of *PMLA* that literary critics (re)turn to Derridean textual analysis, and explore Gayatri Spivak's assertion that a deliberate 'loss of control' is central to learning in the contemporary world of globalization.[3] Further, I extend Shelly Rambo's observation that the ghostly 'may point to something missing,'[4] while developing Werner Hamacher's understanding that 'Repetition ... not only repeats; it releases itself from repetition and dissolves it.'[5] In short, I argue that the textual specter – a non-present presence, a dual being and non-being – precisely symbolizes, for postcolonial Irish writers, the overlap between Irish myth and Irish history.

I want to begin by offering a reconsideration of James Joyce's *Finnegans Wake* (1939) that forecasts Jacques Derrida's notion of spectrality as a viable theoretical lens for the twenty-first century, even as the spectral figure aids our reinterpretation of Joyce's text.[6] For Joyce's corpus, central to Irish literary tradition, celebrates this impurity and offers us insight into contemporary postcolonial novelists' motivations for and methods of reinvention.

In a 1940 letter to Fritz Vanderpyl, James Joyce wrote, 'The title of [*Finnegans Wake*] signifies at once the wake and the awakening of Finn, that is, of our legendary Celto-Nordic hero.'[7] Joyce's biographer Richard Ellmann explains, '[Joyce] conceived of his book as the dream of old Finn, lying in death beside the river Liffey and watching the history of Ireland and the world – past and future – flow through his mind like flotsam on the river of life.'[8] Ellmann characterizes *Finnegans Wake* as a textual river, where mythology and history contaminate one another, where past and present overlap. Joyce places the mythological Finn MacCool within the historical space of mid-twentieth-century Ireland: the heroic leader of the legendary Fianna lies below Dublin, ready to reawaken and defend Ireland in the hour of its greatest need.[9] Joseph Campbell, observing Finn's textual presence in *Finnegans Wake* as a figure lying present beneath modern Dublin, notes, 'Mythological heroes and events of remotest antiquity occupy the same spatial and temporal planes as modern personages and contemporary happenings.'[10] In this way, Joyce's text reflects Ireland's historical narrative, which is, as Vicki Mahaffey has observed, 'so richly storied and ancient, so heavily inflected with folklore, that it should perhaps be rechristened 'mythstory' (a lisping enunciation of 'mystery'), in which myth and history are hopelessly intertwined.'[11]

Earlier, in 1927, Joyce wrote to Harriet Shaw Weaver about the architecture of his *Work in Progress*: 'I am making an engine with only one wheel. No spokes of course. The wheel is a perfect square.'[12] According to Ellmann,

> [Joyce] meant that the book ended where it began, like a wheel, that it had four books or parts, like the four sides of a square, and that *Finnegans Wake* contained *doubles entendres* of wake (funeral) and wake (awakening or resurrection), as well as of Fin (end) and again (recurrence).[13]

Joyce constructed *Finnegans Wake* upon the historical theories of Giambattista Vico (1668–1744), a Neapolitan philosopher who understood history as an endless repetition of four stages: the mythic-theological, the heroic-aristocratic, the human-democratic, and the chaotic *ricorso*.[14] While the cyclical framework of *Finnegans Wake* is conspicuous, its cycle is not merely repetitive; it is multifarious. In other words, the narrative architecture of *Finnegans Wake* can be understood in terms of spectrality.[15] Joyce uses spectral tropes – resurrection, contamination, apparition of the inapparent, and omnipresence – throughout the *Wake* to evoke and conflate multiple spaces, temporalities, and languages so that individual words and sentences, as well as the text as a whole, always mean at least 'two thinks at a time'.[16] The result is a protean text that exhibits the characteristics of a specter defined by Jacques Derrida in *Specters of Marx* (1994): 'The specter is ... what one imagines, what one thinks one sees and which one projects – on an imaginary screen where there is nothing to see.'[17] It would seem, then, that Joyce's working title for *Finnegans Wake* during its serialization (1923–1938), *Work in Progress*, does not refer merely to Joyce's labor as its author, but also to our labor as its readers. Joyce produced a text whose spectral design invites 'performative interpretation,' an interpretive mode that is similarly employed by Derrida for the examination of ghosts: 'that is, an interpretation that transforms the very thing it interprets.'[18] *Finnegans Wake* sheds some light on Derrida's pluralistically malleable method of interpretation. While my own reading of the *Wake* focuses on the specters of Irish history and nationality, others may identify ghosts of different compelling forces, for *hauntology* allows us to problematize the ghost, to see it as 'two thinks at a time.'[19]

The ghost of 'Faun MacGhoul'[20] is the bedrock upon which Joyce constructs the text's spectral architecture. MacCool is lying below Dublin, and the imminent return of his ghost, reflects Irish history's particularly spectral structure – an ever-present past that, like a 'piously forged palimpsest,'[21] is not erased, but written over. *Wake* scholar John Bishop has located and examined textual references to Finn MacCool in order to reinforce Joyce's assertion that the book's omnipresent specter is in fact the dreaming ghost of that legendary Celto-Nordic hero:

> Since 'Finnegan,' by associative 'sound sense' [109.15], modulates through 'Finnagain' into 'Finn again' [5.10, 628.14], and since Joyce erratically conceived of the *Wake* as 'the dream of old Finn lying in death beside the river Liffey' [Ellmann, *James Joyce*, 544], we might momentarily regard the man lying 'dead to the world' at the *Wake* as the 'sleeping giant,' 'Finn MacCool' [540.17, 139.14][22]

I add to Bishop's explication that since the title of Joyce's work is not punctuated – the assumed noun does not contain an apostrophe; it is not in the possessive – the word *wake* can be read as a command verb. If read as such, Joyce's command conjures the specter of Finn MacCool to haunt his text: Finnegans, wake! Or, 'Arise, Sir Ghostus!'²³

In the relatively self-contained, and comparatively comprehensible, sixth chapter of *Finnegans Wake*'s Book I, Shem constructs a twelve-question quiz in which he asks his twin brother, Shaun, to identify a number of the text's recurring characters. The first, and most detailed question, charges Shaun with the task of identifying Finn MacCool.²⁴ Buried within a sentence that spans thirteen pages is Shem's haunting clue – 'go away, we are deluded, come back, we are disghosted.'²⁵ This hunt for Finn's ghost – a *revenant*, that which comes back – enacts Samuel Beckett's assertion that in *Finnegans Wake* 'form *is* content, content *is* form.'²⁶ In other words, Finn's specter is both a character ubiquitous throughout the text and the text itself: an omnipresent *revenant* of 'circular design, of which every part is beginning, middle, and end.'²⁷

In a gesture of positive conjuration – one that convokes specters from the past not to evoke fear and cause recoil, but to represent complexity and ambiguity – Joyce calls forth, translates, and coalesces ancestral voices from disparate moments in Ireland's 'marryvoising moodmoulded cyclewheeling history.'²⁸ The invocation, 'go away, we are deluded, come back, we are disghosted'²⁹ calls attention to the importance of communing with these ancestral voices. Joyce's portmanteau word, *disghosted*, emphasizes the negative connotations of the prefix *dis*: 'in twain, in different directions, apart, asunder, to separate or distinguish, implying negation or reversal of action.'³⁰ *Dis* is a deconstructive morpheme; it negates. And when attached to the stem *ghosted*, a term synonymous with *haunted*, it implies a negation of ghosts – a loss. Joyce's request, 'come back,' begs for spectral reinstatement. But of what, and to what end?

In his 1892 lecture, 'The Necessity for De-Anglicising Ireland,' Douglas Hyde, who later served as the first president of Ireland (1938–1945), insisted,

> We must strive to cultivate everything that is most racial, most smacking of the soil, most Gaelic, most Irish, because in spite of the little admixture of Saxon blood in the north-east corner, this island is and will ever remain Celtic at the core.³¹

In the early twentieth century, a number of Irish writers and republican politicians – including W.B. Yeats, J.M. Synge, and Eamon de Valera – did set out to Celtcize (if not de-Anglicize) Ireland.³² That is, they invented a romanticized historical narrative in order to (1) go beyond sectarian politics *to unify Ireland under a single national identity*, (2) present a strong interest in Irish culture and life including an interest in origins of Irish culture to be found in folklore and Celtic mythology, (3) show that Ireland was not the home of buffoonery and easy sentiment as suggested by the stage Irishman of the Victorian period (4), create Irish art that is distinctly non-English, and (5) see life through Irish eyes.[33]

Joyce, however, rejected the methods of Revivalist artists, in which he saw a gross oversimplification and misrepresentation of Irish history, and in 1907 delivered a lecture concerning the mutability of Irish identity to a group of Trieste residents at the Poplare University. The lecture, originally given in Italian and later translated into English as 'Ireland, Island of Saints and Sages,' began by comparing individual and national identity construction: 'Nations, like individuals, have their egos. It is not unusual for a race to wish to attribute to itself qualities or glories unknown in other races.'[34] As in his lecture, Joyce's fiction from *Stephen Hero* through *Finnegans Wake* encourages the reinvention of Ireland via an imagined history. To be sure, at the end of *A Portrait of the Artist as a Young Man* (1916), Stephen Dedalus famously goes forth 'to forge in the smithy of [his] soul the uncreated conscience of [his] race.'[35] What Joyce does seem to challenge, though, is the assertion that Irish history and culture conform to any single, forged ideal. As Gregory Castle maintains,

> Joyce's struggle against history (which is, more precisely, a struggle against the master narratives of history which determine social conventions of all kinds) is not a rejection of history per se but rather an agonistic relation with history whenever it functions as a monological, authoritarian legitimation of social power.[36]

In the Poplare lecture Joyce definitively rejects monological, authoritarian representations of Irish history and identity: 'Our civilization is an immense woven fabric in which very different elements are mixed ... In such a fabric, it is pointless searching for a thread that has remained pure, virgin and uninfluenced by other threads nearby.'[37] A century later, in 2008, the Irish playwright and novelist Sebastian Barry similarly observed, 'The fact is, we are missing so many threads in our story that the tapestry of Irish life cannot but fall apart. There is nothing to hold it together.'[38] The evolution of this tapestry metaphor signals the shift in national identity politics from a debate about the necessary or unnecessary homogeneity of Irish civilization to a program that establishes ambiguity as the one crucial characteristic of Irishness in the twenty-first century: 'There is nothing to hold it together' but webbings of contradiction, ambivalence, and equivocation of language – specters. Drawing upon two key ideas from *Specters of Marx* that I find useful as ways into the *Wake* – positive conjuration and imaginative reconstruction – shows how Joyce's plea, 'come back, we are disghosted', invites 'the ghost of resignation [to diffuse] a spectral appealingness' throughout his text.[39] For 'If you let it, the ghost can lead you toward what has been missing, which is sometimes everything.'[40] In short, the ghost can reconstruct, or re-signify, common pitfalls of historical representation: misremembering, misperceiving, and the 'necessary falsification' of the past.[41] To explain how acts of borrowing can reverse dominant conceptions of 'haunting' as something terrifying that is to be escaped and forgotten, we can turn to Derrida's meditation on Karl Marx's *Eighteenth Brumaire* (1852). In it, Marx proposes a theory of revolution that illustrates how the more one tries to create a new identity – for instance, a de-Anglicized Irishness – the more one has to borrow from the past those elements that are missing, the more one has to conjure ghosts. Derrida thus quotes Marx's observation of the 1848 French Revolution:

> Just when they seem engaged in revolutionizing themselves and things, in creating something that has never yet existed, precisely in such periods of revolutionary crisis they anxiously conjure up the spirits of the past to their service and *borrow* from them *names*, battle-cries and costumes in order to present the new scene of world history in this time-honoured disguise and this *borrowed language*.[42]

Marx's identification of the possession of 1848 rebels by the specters of 1789–99, and the haunting of the 1789–99 rebels by the specters of the Roman Republic and the Roman Empire, offers a model by which to view Joyce's contention with Revivalists' Romanticized borrowing from the Celtic past. While self-invention, both individual and national, was central to the spirit of the Celtic Revival, Joyce did not simply dismiss what he saw as the Revivalists' uncomplicated 'borrowed language.' Rather, he deconstructs and re-employs this language in *Finnegans Wake* via portmanteau words, avant-garde mythology, and kaleidoscopic history. His most direct attack on the Revivalist program occurs at moments when Shem and Shaun conjure not Finn MacCool, but the specter of that hyphenated '*Celto-Nordic* hero,'[43] thereby significantly complicating early twentieth-century political and cultural debates that seemed staunchly dichotomous. The presence of Finn MacCool's specter in *Finnegans Wake* challenges the Irish Free-State's 'devil era'[44] program of defining itself against Britain by reinscribing an ancient Gaelic ideal upon the Irish present. Take, for instance, the revenant 'Fingool MacKishgmard Obesume Burgearse Benefice,'[45] who embodies both HCE and the treacherous barman Sockerson in Book II, chapter 3.[46] Philip Kitcher helpfully observes that 'HCE, "dour douchy," is linked to Sackerson (whom he will become [530.22])' via song,[47] but it is my contention that HCE's metamorphosis is more forcefully preordained in this tavern brawl scene by the ghost of Finn MacCool. And it is *hauntology* that signals this dual possession thereby blurring the distinction between past and present (primeval Finn, contemporary HCE, future Sackerson); all three temporalities are paradoxically incorporated into this particular moment of possession. 'Fingool' phonetically becomes Finn's ghoul, a spectral rendering of MacCool, or 'MacKishgmard,' which associates with Kish Merari, a member of the landless Levite tribe.[48] The Levite tribe's lack of physical place reinforces Finn's non-present presence – that is, his specter – throughout the *Wake*. 'Obesume' translates easily to 'absume' (waste away), which in turn reminds us of Tim Finnegan/Finn MacCool's fall. And by deconstructing 'Burgearse' to reveal the words 'urge' and 'arse' (backside) we are reminded that Finn has been urged back ('come back, we are disghosted' [136.7]), and therefore his return should be read as 'Benefice[nt].' Dual possession by Finn's ghoul (a hyphenated Celtic-Nord) serves, in turn, to hyphenate Sockerson (an indigenous Dubliner) and HCE (a Scandinavian immigrant), in the process undermining both political and cultural attempts to define Irishness as homogenous. Read through the lens of spectrality, *Finnegans Wake* is (ironically) less obfuscating than *Ulysses* in its assumption that contemporary Ireland is the future of Ireland's past – with the compulsion to reinvent old national myths for a postcolonial culture – even as Joyce's present is simultaneously and consciously the past of some other imminent future, itself destined to be similarly reinvented.[49]

Finn's specter is a particularly keen figure for examining the complex postcolonial process of historical reinvention because of its ontological inconsistencies. 'Neither soul nor body, and both one and the other,' the specter not only defies identification, it also blurs the distinction between being and non-being and transgresses the boundary between past and present.[50] This is precisely the ghost that haunts modern Ireland: an ever-present and seemingly ever-changing historical narrative that, like a palimpsest, brings together past and present moments to bear upon one another.

Those familiar with the *Wake's* fluidity (of space, time, and language) can begin to notice how the patterns of return and repetition in the individual chapters are analogous to the estuary of Irish history. If we take, for instance, Chapter 1 of Book I, in which our narrative gaze is compelled by the flow of the Liffey's 'riverrun' through Dublin, and time's 'recirculation' through history, we observe the fall and wake of Tim Finnegan, enjoy a tour of contemporary, historic, and legendary 'Howth Castle and Environs'[51] before returning to the wake scene at the mention of whisky: '*Usqueadbaugham!*'[52] We are not simply returned to the wake, however, for the chapter ends with the synthesis of HCE and the primeval Finnegan. Such is the ghosting upon which Joyce's text insists. Consider, as an example of its historical parallel, Jonathan Stevenson's 1996 study of the Northern Irish Troubles in which he attempts to discern the origin of Ireland's violent history in hopes of locating an end. Stevenson provides a select chronology that elucidates Ireland's haunted/ haunting history in which every moment of violence both justifies and is justified by each subsequent act of violence.

The island's heritage is speckled with violent events, which serve as justifications for more violence. Depending on the context, republicans and loyalists will assert that relevant history [of the Troubles] starts at the Norman conquest (1171), the Irish rebellion in Ulster against Protestants (1641), Oliver Cromwell's evangelistic terror against Catholics (1649), King William's victory at the Battle of the Boyne (1690), Wolfe Tone's United Irishmen rebellion (1798), the Easter Rising (1916), partition (1921), the founding of the new UVF (1966), the Catholic civil rights movement (1968), the August riots in Belfast (1969), or the IRA split (1970).[53] These events are not easily defined, autonomous moments, nor are they simple recurrences. Like Finnegan's 'metamorphoseous'[54] into HCE, the spirit of 1798 imbues the 1916 Easter Rising even as 1916 prefigures the 1969 August riots in Belfast.

In the *Wake,* Joyce's conjuration of the ghost of Finn MacCool prepares his readers for precisely these sorts of more ambiguous renderings of Irish history, and by extension Irish identity. MacCool is the heroic Everyman of Fenian folklore who stands in stark contrast to Cuchulainn, the lone champion of the Ulster myth cycle. He represents a wide-spectrum of Celtic traditions from Ireland, Scotland, and the Isle of Man; his multiple lineages challenge the modern notion of a definitive Celtic stock. Len Platt observes, 'all attempts to assert the Self by denying the Other are problematized as unstable in the multipleness of *Finnegans Wake*.'[55] In fact, the Self/Other binary is problematized to the point that an authentic Self or an authentic Other 'is ridiculed, not just through "allusions," but as a product of the *Wake*'s monstrous language, the inveterate, hopeless confusion of its storytelling, and the disastrously uncertain identification of its characters.'[56] Joyce summons the specter of Finn MacCool to remind us not only of MacCool's various lineages, but also his multiple manifestations throughout Celtic folklore; Finn's specter comes back as a representation of Ireland's conflicted national identity.

The spectral design of *Finnegans Wake*, wherein multiple meanings and layers of history are present in every line, operates as a textual 'cracked looking-glass'[57] that reflects modern, fragmented Irish identity, and that represents the 'reamalgamerge in that identity of undiscernibles.'[58] Consider the multiple identities of any character in the *Wake*: HCE, in addition to being named by thousands of 'h.c.e.' constructions – from 'Howth Castle and Environs'[59] to 'a man of hod, cement, and edifices'[60] and from 'Here Comes Everybody'[61] to Humphrey Chimpden Earwicker[62] – also takes on the roles (among others) of Adam, Noah, Moses, the Flying Dutchman, Persse O'Reilly, Charles Stuart Parnell, Tim Finnegan, and Finn MacCool. As Declan Kiberd observes of Joyce's *Ulysses* (1922), *Finnegans Wake* similarly suggests that a singularly envisioned Irish identity and Irish history encourages a one-dimensional, isolated, and provincial present, a present that does not allow for the sociopolitical complexities of a postcolonial, globalizing nation:

> The problem seems clear enough: the narrow-gauge nostalgia of the Irish revival, whose adherents fail to realize that a cracked mirror, like a cubist painting, projects a multiple, not a singular, self. Fragmented, maybe, but also authentic. Instead of sincere devotion to a single self-image, [the cracked looking-glass] calls for a recognition that every person has several selves, which it is the labor of a lifetime to be true to. In being true to a single image, the romanticist is inevitably being false to several others.[63]

It is therefore appropriate that Joyce would evoke the 'Celtic-Nordic hero,' Finn (whom Fargnoli and Gillespie identify as having the ability to communicate with the dead),⁶⁴ in the title of his mythstoric masterwork, and conjure his spirit to haunt the text, symbolizing a past working to expose misinterpretation and omission.⁶⁵

To this end, Joyce's ghost is *re*constructive, and so – I argue – is Derrida's *hauntology*. The omnipresence of Finn's specter disturbs our perception of a singular, unimpeachable past. The coordinated resurrection stories of Tim *Finnegan* and *Finn* MacCool challenge the homogenous narratives of Irish history Kiberd identifies. In the words of Derrida, therefore, 'time is out of joint.'⁶⁶ Early on in *Specters of Marx*, Derrida calls into question time's linear trajectory in these very words borrowed from Shakespeare's Prince Hamlet. Past, present, and future become – for both Derrida and Joyce – unreliable temporal markers, and the twinned resurrection narratives provide us with one example of spectral time, emphasizing the necessary *re*construction of the past as far more complex than previously rendered. In short, the obfuscated and fragmented nature of spectrality (as well as the narrative of *Finnegans Wake*, and formal experimentation throughout late Modernism more generally) compels us to seek out and challenge moments of assumed certainty.

An early exchange between Mutt (a Dublin native) and Jute (the perennial invader)⁶⁷ serves as a particularly salient example of Joyce's reconstructive specter. Mutt, presumably an ancient permutation of the contemporary tour guide who ushered us through a museum exhibit as well as the Irish countryside, continues in his role by informing Jute about local points of historic interest – including his participation in the Battle of Clontarf.⁶⁸ Joyce's spectral vision, the overlapping in his text of a present-day tour guide and an ancient warrior, allows us to read Joyce's contemporary moment as a palimpsest lying over ancient Ireland. By bringing these two seemingly disparate moments into contention, Joyce challenges all claims of historical authenticity and ethnic purity. The period during which Joyce wrote *Finnegans Wake* (1922–1939) coincided with the founding and development of the Irish Free State, and was thus marked by a prevailing republican creed of self-sufficient Irish independence, supported by claims of Gaelic Irish distinctiveness. Mutt's history lesson contends with such notions of Irish distinctiveness. His story returns to a site of impurity, where 'Mearmerge two races, swete and brack.'⁶⁹ And, of course, Mutt is himself a mongrel: the specter of our previously mentioned tour guide as well as a version of Shem, 'a constant, if often timid, critic of the rigidity, lack of imaginative freedom and intolerance that characterizes his brother [Shaun/Jute].'[70]

In a meta-textual moment, Mutt announces that the 'Countlessness of livestories [that] have netherfallen by this plage, flick as flowflakes, litters from aloft, like a waast wizard all of whirlworlds. Now are all tombed to the mound.'[71] The countless life stories previously omitted from the tapestry of Irish history are now included in this very tome – a potentially comprehensive survey of Irish history and culture. Joyce's textual ambiguity ensures a *hauntologically* couched 'performative interpretation' of *Finnegans Wake* ('the wholeborrow of rubbages' [17.4–5]) that significantly complicates the 'wrongstor[ies]' of Irish history.[72]

In *Finnegans Wake*, we've witnessed how Joyce calls upon Ireland's historical ghosts to establish Irish history and national identity as far more complex and convoluted than popular conceptions of Ireland's historical narrative have previously admitted. But, as in any undertaking of exploration, one important piece of work remains to be completed – for while discovery is generally valuable, it is of far greater value to find use for such discoveries. This essay offers two potential uses to the reader armed with this new understanding of the specter imbuing Joyce's fiction.

The discovery of this spectral register in *Finnegans Wake* at minimum sharpens one's reading of the text. The specter, which Derrida defines as, among other things, 'what one imagines, what one thinks one sees and which one projects – on an imaginary screen where there is nothing to see,'[73] highlights the wide-ranging imaginative reinvention of postcolonial Ireland and Irishness. Joyce's text illustrates how Ireland's competing histories might be used in collaboration to reinscribe the intricacies and contradictions and tragedies of colonial Ireland that have been falsified and oversimplified by ideologically motivated historical writing. In this way, *Finnegans Wake* moves beyond the pale of Irish literature to challenge the reliability of any narrative (historical or fictional), which assumes authority.

Furthermore, spectrality, as a theoretical lens, can also heighten our awareness of reemergent cultural factors (colonial trauma, religious discrimination, political insularity) that originally led to the Irish artist's dual aesthetic and political identity during the late nineteenth and early twentieth centuries, and give us a glimpse into how

Joyce turned to fiction in order to respond to the longstanding identification of the Irish artist as politically vested. *Finnegans Wake* highlights the reciprocity between historical events and literary discourse, thereby influencing the ways in which we remember Ireland.

Ultimately, by illustrating that Joyce uses spectrality and the specter to blur the boundaries between past and present Ireland, historical and fictional representations of Irish history, and the political and religious debates over the 'true' nature of Irish identity, I've suggested that *Finnegans Wake* is more meta-textual and meta-historiographical in its treatment of questions about history and representation than other modernist texts, which tend to treat historical narrative more obliquely. By recognizing patterns of historical reinvention in the novel, we can see how Joyce takes on the dual role of novelist and historiographer. Doing so, he exposes the overt constructedness of Ireland's undead past, while also introducing a new critical paradigm for readers and writers following in his wake.

In the following chapters, we will encounter contemporary Irish writers who call upon historical ghosts in order to recalibrate the national narrative. We will come to recognize their specters, 'what one imagines, what one thinks one sees and which one projects,'[74] as both a literary and a historical trope – as well as a model for other postcolonial Irish writers seeking to imaginatively reconstruct Irish history. Spectrality, therefore, proves a useful lens through which to read these more complex renderings of the past as reinventions of Irish cultural identity in the present.

The four chapters of *Haunted historiographies* are divided into two sections: Famine and Revolution. Part I groups four contemporary, Post-Celtic Tiger novels that explore the consequences of social and political uses of the Famine throughout much of the twentieth century, and that draw upon the Famine's legacy to urge Irish participation in international humanitarian efforts at the turn of the twenty-first century. Part II juxtaposes another group of four recent novels that re-mythologize Ireland's revolutionary history, in the process liberalizing the nation and calling for greater tolerance among its citizens in the emerging post-Catholic Irish culture.

The first chapter demonstrates the ways in which two thematically and structurally similar novels, Nuala O'Faolain's *My Dream of You* (2001) and Joseph O'Connor's *Star of the Sea* (2002), complicate popular uses of the Famine narrative in arguments on both sides of the debate over Irish independence. By calling forth ghosts from the nineteenth century to expose both intentional and unintentional misrepresentations of the Famine (imagery, ideological meaning, and political mandate), O'Faolain and O'Connor redefine modern Ireland in terms of hunger and dispossession, revealing a more complex national narrative and a more cosmopolitan national identity.

Chapter 2 builds upon representations of this foundational moment of trauma to emphasize a spectral blending of Famine and World War II imagery in Sebastian Barry's novel *The Whereabouts of Eneas McNulty* (1998), which argues against Irish neutrality. I define and measure the effect of spectrality in Barry's fiction by focusing on the ghostly (tropes, modes, themes, and forms that bring multiple histories and fictions into dialogue with one another) to trace the way in which Barry crafts a Famine subtext that functions as a critique of Ireland's non-engagement. *Eneas McNulty* employs imagery that conjures the history of the Famine into the historical space of World War II, and can therefore be read as invoking that nineteenth-century Irish trauma as rationale not for neutrality, but for engagement.

Chapter 3 marks the transition from Famine narratives to revolutionary fictions. In it, I analyze two novels that seek to reestablish 'forgotten' elements of Irish history: Roddy Doyle's *A Star Called Henry* (1999) and Jamie O'Neill's *At Swim, Two Boys* (2001). Both novels excavate feminist and queer narratives that have been hidden behind the façade of Ireland's conservative national narrative by establishing the prominence of such narratives during the 1916 Easter Rising. Reading both novels through the lens of spectrality – a narrative mode that conflates temporalities, events, and peoples – and in the context of Ireland's waning conservatism at the end of the twentieth century offers a clearer notion of how both texts reconsider the founding mythology of Irish culture. *At Swim, Two Boys* places gay lovers and ideals of homosexuality at the absolute core of the Easter Rising, thereby implying the revolutionary notion that the Irish Republic was in fact founded upon the principles of queer politics. *A Star Called Henry*, while certainly invested in acknowledging class divisions in early twentieth-century Dublin, also seeks to recover feminism as a logical extension, or corollary, to nationalism.

In the final chapter, I juxtapose Seamus Deane's *Reading in the Dark* (1996) and Anna Burns's *No Bones* (2002), novels in which child narrators relate their personal accounts of the Northern Troubles using the Gothic's spectral modes and tropes. I then argue that this common narrative choice highlights recurrent psychological damage caused by transgenerational acts of retributive violence stemming back through the Easter Rising to the Great Famine. The Gothic mode in contemporary, postcolonial Irish writing generally serves to shadow the progress of Irish modernity. Narratives like *Reading in the Dark* and *No Bones* expose the underside of postcolonial Irish nationhood: the ongoing struggle for a thirty-two county Republic and recurring debates about whether Protestantism or Catholicism constitutes the 'True' national character. By reimagining ancestral voices that speak of absolution rather than retribution, Deane and Burns break from popular political and social discourses that draw upon Ireland's ghosts as a way of justifying recurrent political violence. Both authors employ the familiar trope of the past-haunted present from Celtic folklore, but reverse typical outcomes: haunting is imagined as a productive vehicle for moving the nation out of the past rather than for keeping it there. By focusing on the domestic consequences of the Troubles, specifically trauma experienced by children, both authors imagine a new generation of Irish individuals struggling to regain self-possession while remaining dedicated to a more egalitarian vision of Northern Irish society.

Each chapter juxtaposes two works that employ spectral tropes and themes to represent Irish historical ambiguity. The specter's anomalous state (to borrow a term from Irish literary and cultural critic David Lloyd)[75] – its non-present presence, its dual being and non-being – precisely symbolizes, for these novelists, the overlap between Irish myth and Irish history. James Joyce's oeuvre, central to Irish literary tradition, celebrates this impurity in *Finnegans Wake*, and offers us insight into contemporary novelists' motivations for, and methods of, reinvention:

> Whether it is Stephen in *Portrait* resisting the various voices that would tie him down like nets, or whether it is the different styles of *Ulysses* or whether it is the babel of voices in *Finnegans Wake*, the aim seems to be identical: to avoid the imperialism of the Cyclopean or one-eyed view, to encourage parallax or the second look.[76]

In *Finnegans Wake*, Joyce established the specter, that figure of uncontrollable and uncanny repetition, as a narrative device for (re)inventing a more nuanced version of Irish history. In *Haunted historiographies*, we'll see how contemporary authors adopted the specter in his wake as a symbol for Irish complexity.

Notes

1 Jonathan Culler, 'Introduction: Critical Paradigms,' *PMLA*, 125.4 (2010): 908.
2 Meredith L. McGill and Andrew Parker, 'The Future of the Literary Past,' *PMLA*, 125.4 (2010): 959–967.
3 See Cathy Caruth, 'Interview with Gayatri Chakravorty Spivak,' *PMLA*, 125.4 (2010): 1020–1025.
4 Shelly Rambo, 'Haunted (by the) Gospel: Theology, Trauma, and Literary Theory in the Twenty-First Century,' *PMLA*, 125.4 (2010): 936–941.
5 Werner Hamacher, 'From 95 Theses on Philology,' *PMLA*, 125.4 (2010): 994–1001.
6 My reading of *Finnegans Wake* builds upon the work by others who have paired Derridean *hauntology* and James Joyce's fiction in order to locate the specter and spectrality as the central motif in *Finnegans Wake*: Maud Ellmann's 'The Ghosts of *Ulysses*'(1990), Derek Attridge's edited collection of Derrida's essays *Acts of Literature* (1991), Thomas Hofheinz's *Joyce and the Invention of Irish History* (1995), Roughly's *Reading Derrida Reading Joyce* (1999), Christine van Boheemen's *Joyce, Derrida, Lacan, and the Trauma of History* (1999), and Peter Mahon's *Imagining Joyce and Derrida: Between Finnegans Wake and Glas* (2007). I am also indebted to foundational work on Joyce and Race Theory by Vincent Cheng in *Joyce, Race, and Empire* (1995) and Len Platt in *Joyce, Race, and* Finnegans Wake (2007), in which Platt links early twentieth-century race theory and Theosophy in the *Wake* as overlapping components of a larger discourse on Modernism. For an annotated list of theosophical references in the *Wake*, see Len Platt's 'Madame Blavatsky and Theosophy in *Finnegans Wake*: An Annotated List' published in *James Joyce Quarterly*, 45.2 (2008): pp. 281–300.
7 James Joyce, *Letters of James Joyce*. Vol. 3. Ed. Richard Ellmann (New York: Viking Press, 1966), p. 437.
8 Richard Ellmann, *James Joyce*. Rev. edn (New York: Oxford University Press, 1982), p. 544.
9 It is supposedly Joyce, in fact, who extended this belief by suggesting that Finn's head forms Ben of Howth and his feet form two hills near Phoenix Park: see A. Nicholas Fargnoli and Michael Patrick Gillespie, eds., *James Joyce A–Z: The Essential Reference to His Life and Writings* (Oxford: Oxford University Press, 1995), p. 74.

10 Joseph Campbell and Henry Morton Robinson, *A Skeleton Key to Finnegans Wake*. Ed. Edmund L. Epstein (Novato, CA: New World Library, 2005), p. 3.
11 Vicki Mahaffey, *States of Desire: Wilde, Yeats, Joyce, and the Irish Experiment* (Oxford: Oxford University Press, 1998), p. 184.
12 James Joyce, *Letters*, p. 251.
13 Ellmann, *James Joyce*, p. 597.
14 James Joyce, *Letters*, pp. 117–118, 463 and 480.
15 Throughout this essay I draw upon Jacques Derrida's notion of spectrality and the specter as representative of historical ambiguity. Derrida explains, 'The subject that haunts (whether it be an object, spirit, or concept) is not identifiable, one cannot see, localize, fix any form, one cannot decide between hallucination and perception, there are only displacements' (*Specters of Marx: The State of the Debt, the Work of Mourning, and the New International*, 1993. Trans. Peggy Kamuf [New York: Routledge Classics, 2006]). p. 136. The specter not only defies identification, it also blurs the distinction between being and non-being, and transgresses the boundary between past and present. Derrida insists, 'The specter is a paradoxical incorporation, the becoming-body, a certain phenomenal and carnal form of the spirit. It becomes, rather, some "thing" that remains difficult to name: neither soul nor body, and both one and the other' (*Specters of Marx*, p. 6).
16 James Joyce, *Finnegans Wake* (New York: Penguin, 1999), p. 583.7. I will include parenthetical references to *Finnegans Wake* that include both the page and line numbers from this edition.
17 Derrida, *Specters of Marx*, p. 125.
18 Derrida, *Specters of Marx*, p. 63.
19 Joyce, *Finnegans Wake*, 583.7.
20 Joyce, *Finnegans Wake*, 354.6.
21 Joyce, *Finnegans Wake*, 182.2.
22 John Bishop, *Joyce's Book of the Dark: Finnegans Wake* (Madison, WI: University of Wisconsin Press, 1993), p. 146.
23 Joyce, *Finnegans Wake*, 532.2–4. This command, which pluralizes the name Finnegan, would also include Tim Finnegan, the resurrected prehistoric hod-carrier from the popular ballad, 'Finnegan's Wake,' which provided Joyce his title. For the music and lyrics of the song, see Ruth Bauerle, ed., *The James Joyce Songbook* (New York: Garland Publishers, 1982), pp. 553–557.
24 While Edmund L. Epstein (see n. 10) claims that Joyce himself insists that the twelve questions are asked by Shem of Shaun, others (such as Fargnoli and Gillespie, in *James Joyce: A to Z*, pp. 80–81) suggest the first eleven questions are asked by Shem of Shaun, but the final twelfth question is asked by Shaun.
25 Joyce, *Finnegans Wake*, 136.7.

26 Samuel Beckett, 'Dante ... Bruno. Vico ... Joyce,' *Samuel Beckett: The Grove Centenary Edition*, Vol. 4. Ed. Paul Auster (New York: Grove Press, 2006), p. 503. 'Here form is content, content is form. You complain that this stuff is not written in English. It is not written at all. It is not to be read – or rather it is not only to be read. It is to be looked at and listened to. His writing is not about something; it is that something itself' (503).
27 Campbell and Robinson, *Skeleton Key*, p. 3.
28 Joyce, *Finnegans Wake*, 186.2.
29 Joyce, *Finnegans Wake*, 136.7.
30 'Dis, prefix.' Def. *The Oxford English Dictionary Online*. 3rd edn. 2009. www.oed.com. 28 August 2010.
31 Douglas Hyde, 'The Necessity for De-Anglicising Ireland.' *Language, Lore and Lyrics: Essays and Lectures by Douglas Hyde*, Ed. Breandán Ó Conaire (Dublin: Irish Academic Press, 1986), p. 169. Douglas Hyde (1860–1949) founded the Gaelic League in 1893, and served as the first president of Ireland from 1938–1945.
32 Poet W.B. Yeats (1865–1939) was a co-founder of the Abbey Theatre in 1897, was awarded the Nobel Prize in literature in 1923 and served as a senator for two terms (1922–1928); Dramatist J.M. Synge (1871–1909) was another co-founder of the Abbey Theatre in which his best known play, *The Playboy of the Western World* (1907) instigated riots over a perceived slight on the virtue of Irish womanhood; Eamon de Valera (1882–1975) played a significant role in Ireland's struggle for independence from Britain; he served multiple terms as head of government and head of state, and he is credited with authoring the 1938 Constitution of Ireland.
33 The single most concise narration of these ideals was presented in the statement of the Irish National Theatre, which was founded by W. B. Yeats, Lady Augusta Gregory, and Edward Martyn in 1897. See Lady Gregory's 'Our Irish Theatre,' *Modern and Contemporary Irish Drama*, Ed. John P. Harrington. 2nd edn (New York: W.W. Norton, 2009), pp. 401–407.
34 James Joyce, 'Ireland, Island of Saints and Sages,' *James Joyce: Occasional, Critical, and Political Writing*. Oxford: Oxford University Press, 2000. p. 108.
35 James Joyce, *A Portrait of the Artist as a Young Man*. Ed. John Paul Riquelme (New York: W.W. Norton, 2007), p. 224.
36 Gregory Castle, 'Ousted Possibilities: Critical Histories in James Joyce's Ulysses,' *Twentieth Century Literature* 39.3 (1993): p. 307.
37 Joyce, 'Ireland, Island of Saints and Sages,' p. 118.
38 Sebastian Barry, *The Secret Scripture* (New York: Viking, 2008), p. 183.
39 Joyce, *Finnegans Wake*, 56.16–17.

40 Quoted in Rambo, 'Haunted (by the) Gospel,' p. 939.
41 See Raphael Samuel's 'Ancestor Worship,' *Island Stories: Unraveling Britain, Theatres of Memory*, Volume 2. Ed. Alison Light et al. (London: Verso, 1999), pp. 272–275.
42 Quoted in Derrida, *Specters of Marx*, p. 135.
43 Recall Joyce's 1940 letter to Fritz Vanderpyl quoted on page 2.
44 Joyce, *Finnegans Wake*, 473.8. 'Devil era' likely refers to the political career of Eamon de Valera (President of Dáil Éireann, 1919–1921; President of the Executive Council of the Irish Free State, 1932–1937; Taoiseach, 1937–1948, 1951–1954, 1957–1959; and President of Ireland, 1959–1973).
45 Joyce, *Finnegans Wake*, 371.22.
46 Joyce, *Finnegans Wake*, 370.30. In *Joyce and Hagiography: Saints Above!* (Gainesville, FL: University of Florida Press, 2000), p. 46, R.J. Schork identifies this recurring string of names as a reference to Oscar Wilde (46.22; 371.22), which is equally valid since, as Thomas Hofheinz observes, 'Joyce's play of Irish voices can easily be perceived as an echo-chamber of extinct cultural identities, a garbled set of broadcasts from the Irish dead': Hofheinz, *Joyce and the Invention of Irish History:* Finnegans Wake *in Context*. Cambridge: Cambridge University Press, 1995, p.50.
47 See Phillip Kitcher, *Joyce's Kaleidoscope: An Invitation to* Finnegans Wake (Oxford: Oxford University Press, 2007), p. 176. HCE, 'Dour Douchy was a sieguldson'(FW 371.6). Kitcher seems to identify 'Sieguldson' with 'Sackerson.' Later, the two become one: 'Seckersen, magnon of Errick. Sackerson! Hookup!'(530. 21–22). At this late stage in the text, Seckerson is no longer identified as an indigenous Dubliner, but the cro-magnon of Earwick, which conflates him (hooks him up), at least in name, with Humphrey Chimpden Earwicker.
48 See the Holy Bible, 1 Chr. 23:21; 24:29. Upon entering the land of Canaan, the Levite tribe was excluded from owning land 'because the Lord the God of Israel himself is their inheritance' (Deuteronomy 18:2). Michael D. Coogan et. al., eds. *The New Oxford Annotated Bible with Apocrypha: New Revised Standard Version*. 4th edn (New York: Oxford University Press, 2010).
49 In *Ulysses and Us*, Declan Kiberd observes, 'The whole thrust of Ulysses suggests that as we are the future of the past, with the right to remake the old for a new order, we also are the past of someone else's future, ourselves bound to be remade.' Declan Kiberd, *Ulysses and Us: The Art of Everyday Living* (London: Faber & Faber, 2009), p. 308.
50 Derrida, *Specters of Marx*, p. 6.
51 Joyce, *Finnegans Wake*, 3.1–3.
52 Joyce, *Finnegans Wake*, 24.14. The Gaelic 'usquebaugh', meaning 'Water of Life', phonetically became 'usky' and then 'whisky.'

53 Jonathan Stevenson, 'We Wrecked the Place': Contemplating an End to the Northern Irish Troubles (New York: The Free Press, 1996), p. 6.
54 Joyce, Finnegans Wake, 190.31.
55 Len Platt, '"No Such Race": The Wake and Aryanism,' Joyce, Ireland, Britain. Eds. Andrew Gibson and Len Platt (Gainesville: University Press of Florida, 2006), p. 26.
56 Vincent J. Cheng, Joyce, Race, and Empire (Cambridge: Cambridge University Press, 1995), p. 158.
57 James Joyce, Ulysses. Ed. Hans Walter Gabler (New York: Vintage, 1986), 1.146.
58 Joyce, Finnegans Wake, 49.36–50.1.
59 Joyce, Finnegans Wake, 3.3.
60 Joyce, Finnegans Wake, 4.26.
61 Joyce, Finnegans Wake, 32.18–19.
62 Joyce, Finnegans Wake, 33.38.
63 Kiberd, Ulysses and Us, p. 45.
64 See Fargnoli and Gillespie, James Joyce A–Z, p. 74.
65 For references to Finn MacCool, see 3.3: 'Howth Castle and Environs'(Dublin Landmark where Finn MacCool's sentinels stood guard against sea invasion); 79.27: 'Kate Strong, a widow'(Kathleen na Hoolihan, Old Mother Ireland, widow of Finn MacCool); 125.6: 'Diremood is the name is on the writing chap of the psalter, the juxtajunctor of a dearmate and he passing out of one desire into its fellow.'(Diarmait [Dermot] was the captain who abducted Grainne, the bride of Finn MacCool); 139.14: Finn MacCool!; 201.27: 'How many aleveens had she in tool?'(aleveen can be translated as 'young fish,' specifically a newly hatched salmon. 'The strong play on the salmon theme throughout Finnegans Wake corresponds to the importance of the salmon in Irish myth and folklore. It was from the taste of the flesh of the great, wise salmon that Finn MacCool, according to the ancient tale, acquired his "Tooth of Knowledge"' [Campbell 133n]); 310.31–2: 'just a tug and a fistful as for Culsen' (Campbell translates 'Culsen' as 'Coolson MacCool': Finn MacCool); 322.1: 'Take off thatch whitehat' (according to MacCulloch, Finn MacCool was brought to a hurling match at age fifteen, and the King asked 'Who is that fin cumhal ("white cap")?' Finn's grandmother responded 'Fin mac Cumhal will be his name'); 354.6: 'Shurenoff! Like Faun MacGhoul!' (it is interesting that Joyce defines him spectrally here); 367.28–9: 'where coold by cawld breide lieth langwid' (Campbell translates this as 'where MacCool by his cauled bride lieth languid'); 371.22: 'Fingool MacKishgmard Obesume Burgearse Benefice'; 374.21: Finnish Make Goal!; 375.29: 'Fummuccumul with a graneen aveiled'; 532.2: 'Search ye the Finn!'; 532.33: 'she was romping off on Floss Mundai out of haram's way round Skinner's circusalley first

with her consolation prize in my serial dreams of faire women'(Epstein points out that this is Grainne's legendary face for Finn: Liffey's race, p. 105); 617.9–12: 'Who would pellow his head off to conjure up a, well, particularly mean stinker like funn make called Foon MacCrawl brothers, mystery man of the pork martyrs?'
66 Derrida, *Specters of Marx*, p. 61.
67 See Campbell and Robinson's *Skeleton Key*, p. 46.
68 Joyce, *Finnegans Wake*, pp. 8–18.
69 Joyce, *Finnegans Wake*, 17.24.
70 Fargnoli and Gillespie, *James Joyce A–Z*, p. 202.
71 Joyce, *Finnegans Wake*, 17.26–29.
72 Joyce, *Finnegans Wake*, 17.3. Recall my earlier assertion that 'hauntology allows us to problematize the ghost, to see it (like the Wake itself) as "two thinks at a time"' (FW 583.7) (4).
73 Derrida, *Specters of Marx*, p. 125.
74 Derrida, *Specters of Marx*, p. 125.
75 David Lloyd, *Anomalous States: Irish Writing and the Post-Colonial Moment* (Dublin: Lilliput, 1993).
76 Trevor Williams, 'Mr. Leopold Bloom, Staunch Britisher: The Problem of Identity Under Colonialism,' *Joyce, Imperialism, & Postcolonialism*. Ed. Leonard Orr (Syracuse, NY: Syracuse University Press, 2008), p. 85.

Part I
Famine

1

The persistence of Famine in postcolonial Ireland

The Great Famine is often referred to as the most haunting event in modern Irish history and the memory of the Famine continues to inform one of the more contentious debates about both the Irish historical narrative and the Irish national character. Few dispute that approximately one million people died as a result of malnutrition and starvation, and nearly one million more emigrated during the Famine years. There is, though, a bitter argument over the actual cause of famine (agricultural practices or inept or belligerent government practices), which has continued to rage since the late nineteenth century. Arguments have largely played out in historical representations of the Famine, which typically adhere to one of two ideological perspectives: the Irish nationalist argument that British mismanagement of the potato blight caused the Famine, and the British loyalist argument that Ireland's underdeveloped social and economic structures simply collapsed when one-third of the population's only food source was destroyed by disease.

Irish nationalists denounced British mismanagement of the potato blight to justify their increasingly adamant resistance to British rule in Ireland. This critical historical perspective continued to gain traction following John Mitchel's 1860 declaration that 'The Almighty, indeed, sent the potato blight, but the English created the Famine.'[1] In *History of the Great Irish Famine* (1875), John O'Rourke maintained, 'The deaths resulting from it, and the emigration which it caused, were so vast, that, at one time, it seemed as if America and the grave were about to absorb the whole population.'[2] Nationalist authors in the twentieth century continue to argue that the British and Anglo-Irish aristocracy systematically wiped out the peasant Irish Catholic population during the mid-nineteenth century.[3] In *The Great Hunger: Ireland 1845–1849* (1962), Cecil Woodham

Smith (née Fitzgerald)[4] maintains that the British actually promoted a policy of starvation in Ireland; both Liz Curtis in *Nothing but the Same Old Story: The Roots of Anti-Irish Racism* (1984) and L. Perry Curtis Jr. in *Apes and Angels: The Irish in Victorian Caricature* (1996) insist that the Famine was the result of Anti-Irish racism.

For those arguing from a decidedly loyalist perspective, on the other hand, all blame for the catastrophe is diverted away from the British crown and the Anglo-Irish landlords and is instead placed on Ireland's underdeveloped social and economic structures. This argument was promulgated by politicians, historians, and landlords such as Lord Dufferin, who wrote in *Irish Emigration and the Tenure of Land in Ireland* (1867) that 'There can be no doubt that agriculture in Ireland is in a backward condition,'[5] thus leading to the Famine. Subsequent arguments made by R.D. Edwards and T.D. Williams in *The Great Famine: Studies in Irish History 1845–1852* (1956), Mary Daly in *The Famine in Ireland* (1986), and Roy Foster in *Modern Ireland* (1988) defend British organization and administration of relief efforts, claiming any amount of aid would have been insufficient in 'conditions whose severity made such expedients irrelevant.'[6] According to these historians, the problem was not simply food shortage but also the antiquated agrarian system. Echoing Dufferin's assessment of Irish farming in the nineteenth century, Roy Foster maintains that '[Ireland's] agriculture was in many areas (not all) conducted at a fairly backward and unproductive level.'[7]

Despite the active historiographical debate over who or what caused the Famine, the Famine is conspicuously absent from much of Ireland's canonical literature. In *Heathcliff and the Great Hunger: Studies in Irish Culture* (1995) Terry Eagleton points to the deficiency of literary material dealing with the Irish Famine prior to 1995. He asks,

> Where is the Famine in the literature of the Revival? Where is it in Joyce? There is a question here, when it comes to the Revival, of the politics of form: much of that writing is programmatically non-representational, and thus no fit medium for historical realism, if indeed any fit medium for such subject matter is conceivable ... If the Famine stirred some to angry rhetoric, it would seem to have traumatized others into muteness.[8]

Eagleton may have overstated the absolute drought of Famine imagery in Irish literature – Maud Gonne uses famine as a backdrop for her 1904 play *Dawn*; Liam O'Flaherty directly engages with the event in his novel *Famine* (1937); and Patrick Kavanagh indirectly engages with it in his long poem 'The Great Hunger' (1942). But Eagleton is not too far off the mark: his call for a realist depiction of the event received attention from contemporary Irish novelist Joseph O'Connor, who claims that he wrote his historical novel *Star of the Sea* (2002) in direct response to Eagleton's question. O'Connor maintains that 'When I first read [*Heathcliff and the Great Hunger*], I felt it implicitly threw down a challenge.'[9] O'Connor's novel, in turn, throws down a challenge of its own, illustrating both the limits of historical realism and the misrecognition of the Famine as an event that can only incite 'angry rhetoric' or 'traumatize others into muteness.'[10]

At the turn of the twenty-first century two thematically and structurally similar novels, Nuala O'Faolain's *My Dream of You* (2001) and Joseph O'Connor's *Star of the Sea* (2002), complicate popular uses of Famine narratives in arguments on both sides of the debate concerning the Irish troubles. By exposing both intentional and unintentional misrepresentations of the Famine, *My Dream of You* and *Star of the Sea* establish an expanded sense of how the Famine might be used in new ways, to new ends.

O'Faolain and O'Connor are among a number of recent novelists such as Jane Urquhart (*Away*, 1993), Helen Humphreys (*After Image*, 2001), and Peter Behrens (*The Law of Dreams*, 2007) as well as a host of writers across the disciplines who have shown a renewed interest in depictions of the Famine, and have begun to blur the distinctions between its historical and esthetic representations. Famine scholar Christine Kinealy observes that the surge in Famine-related scholarship coincides with its 150-year anniversary in 1995:

> The anniversary of the Great Famine has demonstrated a massive interest in that defining event in Irish history. Apart from historians – who ignored the Famine for so long – the Famine has started to attract the interest of folklorists, geographers, demographers, linguists, political activists, and Third World specialists.[11]

Among these Irish intellectuals who have renewed interest in the Famine are a number of contemporary political figures and novelists writing after 1995 who complicate both extremist lines of argument.

Countering politically influenced writers who have used references to the Famine as definitive support for ideological arguments,

O'Faolain's *My Dream of You* and O'Connor's *Star of the Sea* claim the Famine as a site of uncertain complexity. These Dublin-born novelists, writing at the outset of the twenty-first century, craft their novels as frames that (re)collect several interrelated yet diverse famine narratives that transgress the traditionally accepted congruence between national boundaries and cultural identities as well as boundaries between past and present Ireland. In doing so, these novels offer new interpretations of the Famine as the founding moment of modern, dispossessed Ireland, and pose attendant questions about Ireland's (inter)national identity.

O'Faolain and O'Connor complicate dominant ideological renditions of Ireland's Famine narrative by challenging oversimplified historical 'facts.' Both novels construct a spectral architecture by layering disparate historical moments and spaces over one another to produce a narrative effect in which contemporary events are recognized as the reappearance of previous occurrences, but which have also been complicated to the point where they can no longer be definitive. This structure, wherein contentious ideological perspectives of the Famine are organized into a cooperative and collaborative narrative, urges the reader to apprehend the ways in which ambiguous representations of the Famine (its causes and outcomes) yield a more nuanced and complex literary vision of the Irish national condition than that offered by historical records.[12]

In *My Dream of You* and *Star of the Sea*, each protagonist is a historian who has set out to write a definitive account of a local event that took place during the Famine years. Kathleen de Burca, in *My Dream of You*, researches and writes about the alleged Talbot affair in Roscommon, Ireland (O'Faolain draws upon the actual divorce case document, *A Judgment of Talbot v. Talbot*, 1856).[13] In *Star of the Sea*, G. Grantley Dixon documents the lives of passengers aboard the titular fictional transatlantic cargo ship. Each protagonist's research uncovers diverse, and often antagonistic, accounts of the events they are trying to record. Both protagonists come to realize that writing an 'accurate' or 'definitive' account of these events would be impossible; therefore, they ultimately turn to historiographical fiction as a more appropriate medium for authentically representing historical complexity.

By systematically breaking down and overturning perceived truths about the Famine, both novels resist widely accepted and wildly oversimplified historical depictions of the nineteenth- and early twentieth-century Irish as fundamentally poor, senseless, and anti-colonial, by establishing the Irish population – both during and after the Famine – as something more economically motivated, socially aware, and politically complex. To this end, the various narrative structures and convoluted plotlines in *My Dream of You* and *Star of the Sea* parallel the haunted landscape of a physically disjointed, and psychologically dispossessed, Irish nation. In undertaking this important task of commenting on divisive historical debates, Irish novelists like O'Faolain and O'Connor were answering the call of a new political generation.

On 2 February 1995, Mary Robinson, then President of Ireland, delivered an address to the Houses of the Oireachtas entitled 'Cherishing the Irish Diaspora: On a Matter of Public Importance.'[14] Her address focused on sesquicentennial Famine commemorations in both Ireland and abroad, and asked that those commemorations resist traditional ideological bias that had previously led to physical and psychological violence in Ireland. She began by pointing to the value in retaining and increasing Irish diversity:

> Four years ago I promised to dedicate my abilities to the service and welfare of the people of Ireland. Even then I was acutely aware of how broad that term the people of Ireland is and how it resisted any fixed or narrow definition. One of my purposes here today is to suggest that, far from seeking to categorize or define it, we widen it still further to make it as broad and inclusive as possible.[15]

Robinson maintained that Ireland must embrace dispossession as a diversifying yet unifying element of Irish identity. The aim of this lecture was to call for stronger ties to the global community through participation in transnational humanitarian efforts – especially in nations suffering from Famine.

Robinson calls into question historical oversimplifications of the Famine narrative by both nationalist and loyalist propagandists and attempts to move beyond simply reimagining the Irish past for some political gain, towards finding a meaning for that past in the present:

> We cannot want a complex present and still yearn for a simple past. I was very aware of that when I visited the refugee camps in Somalia and more recently in Tanzania and Zaire. The thousands of men and women and children who came to those camps were, as the Irish of the 1840s were, defenseless in the face of catastrophe … We cannot undo the silence of our own past, but we can lend our voice to those

who now suffer. To do so we must look at our history ... with a clear insight which exchanges the view that we were inevitable victims in it, for an active involvement in the present application of its meaning ... One of the common bonds between us and our diaspora can be to share this imaginative way of re-interpreting the past.[16]

Robinson's comparison between dispossessed victims of the Irish Famine in the 1840s and victims of more recent famines in Somalia, Tanzania, and Zaire asks artists to engage with the Famine narrative in new ways that do not fall back upon tired generalizations, 'angry rhetoric,' or 'traumatized muteness.'[17]

A prime example of ideologically driven fiction that relies heavily on angry nationalist rhetoric is Maud Gonne's 1904 one-act play, *Dawn*. According to Angela Bourke, Gonne wrote the play in response to waning nationalist fervor in the Irish theater. Gonne was deeply invested in nationalist theater from 1900 when she founded Inghinidhe na hEireann, played the title role in W.B. Yeats's and Lady Gregory's co-written play, *Cathleen ni Houlihan* (1902), and served as vice-president of the National Theatre Society before resigning over its staging of J.M. Synge's *The Shadow of the Glen* (October 1903) which she saw as a withdrawal from nationalist interests.[18] In *Dawn*, Gonne identifies English occupation and Famine evictions as the origin of Irish troubles, and advocates violent insurrection for what she sees as malicious evictions of poor Irish farmers by wealthy English landlords. During the period in which *Dawn* was composed, Irish artists often cultivated direct relationships between literary texts, revolutionary political events, and constructions of Irish national identity. In her play, which echoes Yeats's and Lady Gregory's nationalist drama, *Cathleen ni Houlihan*, Gonne argues that the Famine created the modern Irish condition: desolate, poor, and anti-British. During the Literary Revival, many authors and politicians worked to promote Irish Republican nationalism, and hoped to influence revolutionary resistance to British imperialism by drawing upon past colonial abuses.

Though there is no record of it ever being staged, *Dawn* was published on 29 October 1904 in the *United Irishman*, the very paper in which – upon Queen Victoria's final visit to Ireland in 1900 – Gonne had written, 'However vile and selfish and pitiless her soul may be, she must sometimes tremble as death approaches when she thinks of the countless mothers who, shelterless under the cloudy Irish sky, watching their starving little ones, have cursed her before they died.'[19] As we will see, contemporary authors, writing in a postcolonial environment, complicate such rigid ideological reactions to the Famine.

One method by which O'Faolain's and O'Connor's novels highlight ambiguity within the Irish historical record is the prominent addition of spectrality to the Famine narrative. In *Specters of Marx* (1994), Jacques Derrida explains that reality, and the historical writing that attempts to document past reality, follows a logic of the specter, meaning that reality is comprised of nothing but contradiction and ambivalence. Derrida maintains:

> If we have been insisting so much since the beginning on the logic of the ghost, it is because it points toward a thinking of the event that necessarily exceeds a binary or dialectical logic, the logic that distinguishes or opposes *effectivity or actuality* (either present, empirical, living – or not) and *ideality* (regulating or absolute non-presence).[20]

For our purposes, Derrida's 'logic of the ghost' illuminates the ways in which *My Dream of You* and *Star of the Sea* employ a similar spectral logic that subverts clear repetitive binaries in favor of more genuinely complicated historical representation. It follows that if the Irish historical narrative is bereft of certainty, national identity based upon that narrative would remain equally dispossessed and protean.

Mary Robinson, looking back at that period of hunger, insists upon imaginatively re-interpreting the Famine at later commemorations. She calls for debating historians and politicians to acknowledge that the act of assigning blame for Famine-related hardship stands in stark contrast to her contemporary understanding of Irishness (via famine) as fundamentally diasporic. In short, she argues that contemporary Irish identity is the product of dislocation and uncertainty. For Robinson, and indeed for the historian-protagonists in *My Dream of You* and *Star of the Sea*, the Irish diaspora personifies such dispossession, and offers insight into appropriate Irish responses to similar present-day suffering throughout the world:

> I am certain that [our diaspora], too, will feel that the best possible commemoration of men and women who died in that famine, who were cast up on other shores because of it, is to take their dispossession into the present with us, to help others who now suffer in a similar way. Therefore I welcome all initiatives being taken during this period of commemoration, many of which can be linked with those abroad, to contribute to the study and understanding of economic

vulnerability. I include in that all the illustrations of the past which help us understand the present.[21]

Robinson's address builds upon her recognition that the Irish nation transcends the geographical space of Ireland (largely because of the Famine) to draw an explicit connection between mid-nineteenth-century Irish and late twentieth-century Somali hunger. She insists that the most appropriate commemoration for those who suffered during Ireland's Great Famine in the nineteenth century is to offer relief to those affected by the Somali drought at the end of the twentieth century. Her address, therefore, establishes dispossession as a defining theme for international Famine commemorations, thereby introducing a third dimension to the otherwise reductive representations of the Famine produced by politically influenced historians and literary authors. Robinson calls for these simplifications to be reevaluated, urging commemorators to move beyond socially and politically reductive divisions in order to organize cooperative international famine relief efforts.

In *The Great Irish Famine: Impact, Ideology and Rebellion* (2002), Christine Kinealy reinforces the timeliness of Robinson's address. She maintains that after the peace process had begun in the North, historical writing became decidedly less vested in 'British versus Irish' debates since each side had at least begun to come to terms with the other politically. She explains,

> The relations between the two islands have now reached a maturity which allows us to look at our history objectively and to tell the story as it was ... After all, the Famine is not just an Irish event, it was just as much a British event, a shared experience.[22]

Robinson's address comes on the heels of the Provisional Irish Republican Army's (PIRA) 31 August 1994 ceasefire in Northern Ireland.[23] Kinealy suggests, therefore, that lingering effects of the trauma caused by political divisions that may or may not have contributed to the Famine, but certainly intensified because of it, continue to haunt the contemporary Irish understanding of what it meant to be England's Other during the Famine.

Mary Robinson's reference to Ireland's diaspora affords the opportunity to both hear with a new perspective the echoes of Irish history and speak with a new significance of Ireland's proper place in the contemporary global landscape. Because of Ireland's turbulent past and the widespread dispersion of those who claim

Irish heritage, Robinson maintains that Ireland's place is at the fore of international humanitarian and globalization efforts; therefore, Irish intellectuals must move beyond narrow definitions of what it means to be Irish. The Great Famine serves as an ideal backdrop for narratives seeking to de-essentialize definitions of Irishness because it was the moment at which the Irish nation became dispossessed via dispersion. Historical records and literature that narrowly define the Irish as provincial, isolated agrarians fail to recognize the worth of an ambiguous national identity. Robinson maintains that the Famine provides historians a useful backdrop for examining national complexity:

> After all, emigration is not just a chronicle of sorrow and regret. It is also a powerful story of contribution and adaptation. In fact, *I have become more convinced each year that this great narrative of dispossession and belonging, which so often had its origins in sorrow and leave-taking, has become – with a certain amount of historic irony – one of the treasures of our society.* If that is so then our relation with the diaspora beyond our shores is one which can instruct our society in the values of diversity, tolerance and fair-mindedness.[24]

Her 1995 address on Famine commemoration and Irish humanitarian efforts against world hunger has more clearly influenced a contemporary literary trend in which recent Irish writers offer complexity in place of ideological certainty and embrace dispossession as empowering, rather than traumatic.

The historical novels that follow in the wake of Robinson's speech prove to be a useful medium for developing the themes of dispossession Robinson emphasized in her speech to the legislature about international humanitarian efforts. This is because they blend historical realism and imaginative reinterpretation by introducing intricate, variegated narratives that capture the ambiguities of Irish historical reality via spectrality.

We must keep in mind the differences between historical writing and historical fiction. Historical writing, on one hand, relies upon assumed factual accuracy; it implies 'the prestige of it happened.'[25] And despite Hayden White's observation that historical texts are best understood not as accurate and objective representations of the past, but as creative texts (*The Fiction of Narrative*), the term *history* still signifies factual representation to its audience. Historical *fiction*, on the other hand, does not require such strict adherence to fact: it is based upon a feel for the space and time it represents. Literary historian Steven Ungar maintains that, for some, this means, 'Fiction is considered defective because it lacks a function of reference to which, presumably, history can make a viable claim. For proponents of history as science, fiction defines exactly what history is not; it fulfills the function of "other" discourse in a proleptic gesture that diverts and forestalls judgment by casting it elsewhere.'[26] Fiction, however, is not history's opposite: it does not simply imply that which did not happen. Often it implies that which could or may have happened. Thomas Conley offers a differentiation: 'Where the historian reveals the ineffable dimensions of social order that the past could not control, the modern artist invests them in conscious designs that are not a product of change – in webbings of contradiction, ambivalence, and equivocation of language.'[27] Historical fiction, written at a temporal distance, provides a fit medium for complicating assumed historical fact through the complex estheticization of established historical narrative. O'Faolain and O'Connor take this complication a step further by actually narrating the process of estheticization.

My understanding of these two novels' spectral architecture, and their reliance upon the reemergence of the Famine narrative, draws upon Jacques Derrida's logic of the specter, which he observes as 'what one imagines, what one thinks one sees and which one projects – on an imaginary screen where there is nothing to see.'[28] The specter of the Famine, the ever-present memory of the Famine's traumatic dislocating consequences in the Irish collective consciousness, always informs Irish cultural and political identity construction. And when the specter is visible (a literal ghost haunts), for instance in Maud Gonne's play or during the sesquicentenary commemorations in 1995, what is seen is a projection of whatever one wants to see. The Famine, in other words, can mean whatever one makes it mean. For instance, a number of Irish historians and political commentators, such as Eoghan Harris and Conor Cruise O'Brien, claimed that Famine commemorations in 1995 would instigate a return to nationalist fervor for violence against Britain.[29] Of course their claims are also projections of their fears over the reemergence of sectarian violence in Northern Ireland.[30] It is important to keep in mind, however, that spectrality is never simply mimetic. The past does not return exactly as it was; it returns in a different guise. One of the differences gleaned from reading *My Dream of You* and *Star of the Sea* against one another is a broadening of the Famine narrative so that it does not fit neatly into a political allegory, even as such allegories are evoked in the course of dispossessing them.

Reading Irish history through the lens of spectrality allows readers to see revision in these novels not as corrective measure, but as a challenge to the possibility of presenting an accurate historical record. In both novels, ostensibly following in the wake of Mary Robinson's call to 'take [Famine victims'] dispossession into the present with us, to help others who now suffer in a similar way,'[31] revision is not about factual accuracy, but about breaking down the distinction between accuracy and inaccuracy. I use the terms 'accuracy' and 'complexity' to differentiate between two types of precision that historical and fiction writers attempt to achieve in their work. I understand 'accuracy' as the process of trying to create a definitive, precise account of an event – a report of what happened. The inherent difficulty with such reports is that while they can be factually true, they tend to be one-dimensional. Therefore, another term is necessary to describe historical documentation that aims at multi-dimensional reportage: complexity. Such accounts are more ambiguous and resist definitive conclusions.

Reading for complexity rather than accuracy is valuable because *not* drawing any definitive broad-scope conclusions allows us to actually use the smaller, more nuanced, personal lessons of history to greater advantage. Literary theorist Linda Hutcheon, for instance, draws upon Jean-François Lyotard's *The Postmodern Condition* (1979) to posit that historical fiction promotes a skepticism of factual truth by calling into question the 'facticity' of history's grand-narratives through an 'interrogati[on] of the nature of representation in historiography.'[32] Her observations lead her to suggest that readers be suspicious of the pose of broad historical accuracy and the assumed authenticity of fact.[33] As the following close readings will illustrate, *My Dream of You* and *Star of the Sea* unveil the process of producing a historical study and thereby undermine the pose of implied historical accuracy, while retaining history's worth as a fictional narrative that can shape individual and national identities.

Nuala O'Faolain (1940–2008) spent much of her literary career – as a columnist for the *Irish Times*, as memoirist, and as novelist – negotiating the problematic intersections between collective and individual Irishness.[34] Dividing her time between London, New York City, and Dublin, O'Faolain was a migrant Irishwoman, much like her ostensibly homeless protagonist in *My Dream of You* – a constantly on-the-move travel writer named Kathleen de Burca (Caitlín de Búrca). However, the sense of homelessness shared by writer and character is more a state of mind than a lack of actual physical space. In her search for what it means to be Irish, O'Faolain often threads together disparate spaces, texts, and times to challenge narrow definitions that have traditionally defined 'true' Irishness as provincial and homogeneous. *My Dream of You* is constructed as a frame around actual historical documents and Kathleen's embedded historical fiction, *The Talbot Book*. By amalgamating Irish and English settings, multiple historical genres, and past and present events, the novel resists narrative clarity and thereby challenges normative categorizations or definitions of Irishness.[35]

My Dream of You follows Kathleen's present-day quest to uncover the truth about an alleged affair that took place during the Famine between Marianne Talbot, the malnourished and abused English wife of Anglo-Irish landlord Richard Talbot, and one of their Catholic domestic servants, William Mullan. Kathleen's project simultaneously serves as a way for her to reengage with her own dislocated Irish identity. We learn that before returning to Ireland in order to research the Talbot case, Kathleen had been living in self-exile in England for more than a quarter century. She claims her emigration was solely due to Ireland's suffocating parochialism, which she sees as a lingering consequence of the Famine.

While literary scholar Miriam O'Kane Mara helpfully observes that the mirrored troubles of Kathleen de Burca and Marianne Talbot draw useful parallels between women's political roles in the Famine era and mid-twentieth century, I believe that Kathleen's interest in Marianne Talbot stems not simply from a sense of similarity, but from her recognition of hunger and silence as traumatic forms of dispossession in Ireland. Furthermore, I contend that it was the Famine that invited and allowed Richard to both systematically starve and silence his wife, dispossessing her of class and respectability. This act, played out on a local level, has become a dominant theme in national definitions of Irishness. Kathleen maintains,

> I put the two things together, home and the Famine, and I used to wonder whether something that had happened more than a hundred years ago, and that was almost forgotten, could have been so terrible that it knocked all the happiness out of people.[36]

She goes so far as to identify her present-day depression as an extension of her miserable Irish childhood, which forced her to leave the island. Furthermore, Kathleen identifies her Father's melancholy and rage as reactions to colonial oppression: 'The only feeling he showed about the Famine was rage against England. There was no pity in him.'[37] Her personal memories are conflated with spectral stereotypes as she explains that Ireland's violent nationalism and fervent Catholicism drove her to London. She recalls,

> My family has been the same size and shape in my head since I ran out of Ireland. Mother? Victim. Nora and me and Danny and poor little Sean? Neglected victims of her victimhood. Villain? Father. Old-Style Irish Catholic patriarch; unkind to wife, unloving to children, harsh to young Kathleen when she tried to talk to him.[38]

While her father's stereotypical abuse drove Kathleen out of Ireland, an academic interest in a similarly abusive nineteenth-century Anglo-Irish patriarch brought her back.

Though it is true that Kathleen was initially drawn to the Talbot case, as Mary Fitzgerald-Hoyt argues, not because it occurred during the Famine, 'but because its suggestion of grand passion in the most improbable circumstances attracts her,'[39] I will now map how both Kathleen's *The Talbot Book* and O'Faolain's *My Dream of You* turn on a keen historiographical awareness. To be sure, I am indebted to Fitzgerald-Hoyt's convincing argument that *My Dream of You* is primarily concerned with Irish history's 'multiple players, multiple narratives,' which serves as a strong point of origin for broader studies into contemporary historical novels about the Famine. My reading extends Fitzgerald-Hoyt's observations by focusing on Kathleen's writing process to illuminate how *My Dream of You* imbues its readers with this sense of historiographical awareness. Further, by pairing the novel with O'Connor's *Star of the Sea*, we can begin to see a wider historiographical movement in contemporary, postcolonial Irish literature of which *My Dream of You* is an essential part.

Kathleen originally conceives of her project as a comprehensive history of the Talbot affair and the resulting divorce case. She plans to construct her historical narrative using, as a starting point, fragments from the actual court proceedings heard in the House of Lords in 1856: *A Judgment of Talbot v. Talbot*. This document, however, only provides her with Richard Talbot's accusation against his wife and the details of her conviction. Marianne has no voice in this document. Kathleen's hope is to record the facts of the actual affair between Marianne Talbot and William Mullan, including its origin, development, and discovery. In order to unearth this information, Kathleen engages in traditional research methodologies: she looks in British and Irish archives for letters; works with Miss Leech, a research librarian in Ireland, to locate Estate reports; and does field research in Roscommon, where she talks with locals who have knowledge about local lore concerning the Talbot estate.

Each of these more traditional research methods yields very little information, and the little evidence that Kathleen does uncover offers her multiple and contradictory versions of the event. She is unable to locate accurate records from which to construct a definitive history of the affair, of the Famine, and of Irishness in the nineteenth century. Her aggravation with being unable to draw a definitive conclusion about the alleged affair leads her to abandon her fact-based historical project for a fictional one. Kathleen writes: 'Imagination of others doesn't go very far even when you're trying ... Yet here I was, trying to imagine a whole nation in the time of an unimaginable catastrophe!' (72). She convokes the traumatic memory of Famine, but finds that she cannot call up a clear image: 'The trauma must be deep in the genetic material of which I was made. I cannot forget it, I thought, yet I have no memory of it. It is not mine; but who else can own it?' (72–73). In order to gain a more complex understanding of the event, she turns to a less traditional mode of historical research – she invites the ghosts of Marianne Talbot and William Mullan to haunt her: 'It wasn't people I was thinking of. It was a shape, a blurred image – me outside somewhere, calling, and tragic ghosts listening to me and waiting for me to free them – that settled inside me' (22). Kathleen's request to be haunted calls attention to her hope of productively borrowing memories from the past to inform her research, and to recalibrate her own sense of contemporary Irishness, which she identifies as the lingering specter of early twentieth-century nationalism: parochial, patriarchal, abusive.

Kathleen's fruitless search for historical documents or convincing oral narratives illustrates how limiting a search for definition can be for a historian. She comes to the conclusion that her project will have to rely less on discoverable facts and more on imaginative reinvention. Ultimately, her inability to uncover a definitive account of the Talbot affair calls into question other Famine narratives that claim to be based upon factual evidence. O'Faolain highlights the incomplete historical records and the biases of local folklore that both nationalist and loyalist arguments employ as evidence for their claims concerning union with Britain. *My Dream of You* suggests that Irish history and the characters that populate it are significantly more complex than the ideologically influenced histories that both groups of writers produce. It reminds us that crooked landlords, Gombeen men, and lazy peasants are stereotypes that have been stripped of their contextual nuance in order to make political arguments. There were certainly generous landlords, honest tradesmen, and diligent peasants in Ireland in the 1840s, but not until the twenty-first century do they begin to populate nonsectarian Famine narratives.

My Dream of You complicates the historical record of the Famine by showing how a lack of historical accuracy affects the ways in which both individual and collective identities are constructed. Tracing Kathleen's interpolations of past into present, the novel illustrates how citing history says as much about the moment of citation as it does about the cited moment. As another contemporary Irish novelist and 2005 Man Booker Prize winner, John Banville, observed in a 1979 interview:

> Since I've started writing novels based in historical fact I've realized that the past does not exist in terms of fact. It only exists in terms of the way we look at it, in the way that historians have looked at it.[40]

My Dream of You incorporates a historiographical understanding similar to Banville's observation concerning critical perspective. By drawing on an actual historical document from the House of Lords (*The Talbot Judgment*), Kathleen's fiction intimates the significance of reimagining the past, borrowing from it, in order to reconstruct the present. For Kathleen, ghosts are imagined not as things to be exorcized, but rather to be convoked and borrowed from in a productive manner.

The novel enacts a dialectical relationship between past and present in which we see Kathleen using her traumatic personal history to understand Marianne's story even as Marianne's story influences Kathleen's identity reconstruction. Kathleen imagines Marianne as a distortion of herself and therefore reads Marianne's story through her own futile attempt to define herself as other-than-Irish. In *My Dream of You*, historical moments are layered, producing a spectral effect in which readers can see how past and present amalgamate to complicate one another. In '(Re)producing Identity and Creating Famine in Nuala O'Faolain's *My Dream of You*' (2007), Miriam O'Kane Mara highlights the connections that O'Faolain draws between the Famine and more recent oppression of women in Ireland.[41] Though her main focus is on women's bodies and their fertility as symbols for the health of Ireland, Miriam O'Kane Mara briefly observes the ways in which O'Faolain's novel lays bare the methods of (re)constructing history:

> O'Faolain's text allows the narrative of the past to change direction in retellings. As new information about Marianne's divorce case comes to light during Kathleen's research, she revises her developing novel. Such rewriting suggests an unreliable narrative, a shifting story without prevarication or misleading intent from its creator ... O'Faolain's entangling of past and present indicates the constructed nature of history and the importance of the present day to the representation of the past. Her protagonist's continuous revision and reconstruction of the embedded story represents the difficulty of looking to the mid-nineteenth century for authority. In focusing on the ways that history is constructed and refashioned, the text hints at the difficulties of knowing history and of identifying authentic Irish identity.[42]

And thus, I contend, by extension, *My Dream of You* challenges the use of a simplified history as a means of defining a true Irish identity via an accurate Irish historical narrative. What Mary Robinson, Nuala O'Faolain, and Joseph O'Connor seem to suggest is that the authenticity of Irishness is predicated upon its inauthenticity, its dispossession of any concrete, universal characteristics. In other words, Irish identity is a spectral identity. Like Derrida's specter, Irishness is 'an unnameable or almost unnameable thing: something, between something and someone, anyone or anything.'[43]

Through its demonstration of the ways in which writers interpret, invent, and falsify the past, the novel undermines the claimed accuracy of historical reportage. By slowly unveiling Kathleen's writing process – which includes an imaginative reconstruction of fragments from the Famine narrative – O'Faolain's novel breaks down the nationalist/loyalist belief in the possibility of accurate historical representation. And though Kathleen approaches revision as a way of updating her fact-based novel to be more historically accurate, her inability to arrive at a satisfactory conclusion concerning Marianne Talbot's guilt or innocence highlights the unreliability of both her fictional narrative and the Irish historical record. A closer look at the ideological valences in the three historical documents that Kathleen's research uncovers (the court proceedings, a pamphlet, and a tabloid), and her negative response to those subjective documents, illustrates O'Faolain's resistance to similar ideologically influenced presentations of Irish history and identity.

Drawing upon the 1856 Talbot v. Talbot divorce case, *My Dream of You* narrates Kathleen de Burca's research trip to Roscommon, Ireland, where she hopes to uncover a fuller and more accurate depiction of an alleged affair between Marianne Talbot, the wife of an Anglo-Irish landlord, and William Mullan, their Catholic servant. The document upon which Kathleen begins her inquest into the Talbot divorce is *A Judgment of Talbot v. Talbot*, which only outlines Richard Talbot's accusation and the details of Marianne's ultimate conviction. In the comparatively depoliticized environment of postcolonial Ireland in 2001, O'Faolain and her protagonist offer a text that illustrates historical uncertainty and therefore reinforces the impossibility of definitive accounts of what actually happened during the Famine. Kathleen's research, and by extension O'Faolain's novel, is predicated upon silence and inaccuracy – both intentional and unintentional.

To manifest this silence, the lack of communication between those who experienced Famine and those who write about it, Kathleen juxtaposes the dual traumas of nutritional and sexual starvation. We can better understand her technique by reading her narrative against Walter Benjamin's observation of historical narrative structures in 'On the Concept of History' (1940):

> Articulating the past historically does not mean recognizing it 'the way it really was.' It means appropriating a memory as it flashes up in a moment of danger ... The historian who proceeds from this consideration ceases to tell the sequence of events like the beads of a rosary. He grasps the constellation into which his own era has entered, along with a very specific earlier one.[44]

Kathleen's tortuous research mirrors the difficulty she experiences as she attempts to narrate her own involvement in an adulterous relationship. Kathleen is drawn to Marianne because her story is similar: both women are silenced by the accusation of adultery. While Marianne may be falsely accused, Kathleen is guilty (we'll get to this). The other event in this traumatic constellation is, of course, the Famine. O'Faolain's use of the Famine as a backdrop intensifies the mystery shrouding the Talbot case while simultaneously exposing contemporary silences in Ireland that promulgate continued gender and sexual inequality. Miriam O'Kane Mara has observed that, '[Kathleen's] failure to produce a novel from the fragments of history reflects the difficulty of assigning meaning to the time in which Marianne lived. That failure also highlights the irony that *My Dream of You* is itself a novel built from those fragments.'[45] Mara's statement illustrates her sense of the novel's overt constructedness and her use of the word 'irony' implies that the novel is itself a failed attempt to give voice to Irish victims, past and present. Even as Kathleen estheticizes the Famine, O'Faolain establishes her protagonist, Kathleen, as a naive outsider unable to piece together the fragments of this traumatic event without fictionalizing it. Fiction, for Kathleen (and, to be sure, for O'Faolain), offers a distancing mechanism similar to geographical and temporal distance.

Turning, for a moment, to Cathy Caruth's notion of trauma in *Unclaimed Experience* will shed some light on this need for 'distance.' Caruth maintains, 'The wound of the mind – the breach in the mind's experience of time, self, and the world – is not, like the wound of the body, a simple and healable event, but rather an event that ... imposes itself again, repeatedly, in the nightmares and repetitive actions of the survivor.'[46] O'Faolain's narrative frame illustrates how fiction can give voice via repetition where historical writing has induced silence. For instance, Miss Leech, the local Roscommon librarian charged with aiding Kathleen in her search for the definitive truth about the Talbot affair, declares early on that the House of Lords *Judgment* (an actual court document) is 'history without the economics, history without the politics, history without the mess.'[47] Miss Leech admits that she reads the document as a biased record of the alleged affair that wrongly implicates the Catholic peasant, Mullan. She approaches it from her own romanticized vision of the Irish past; however, the historical constellation by which Kathleen and Miss Leech uncover a number of inconsistencies and gaps in the sequential narrative finally complicates both women's certainty about the document's truth concerning Marianne's guilt. The novel, then, not only calls attention to the narrative structure of fragments, as Mara points out, but to the narrative structure of *historical* fragments in particular, thereby responding to critical questions in Postcolonial Studies about the political uses for which history is enlisted. Because of the sequential nature of *My Dream of You* – as new evidence is uncovered Kathleen reconstructs the Talbot case – my analysis necessarily relies upon some plot description in order to show the process by which fact becomes fiction.

Not long after arriving in Ireland (Kathleen had been living in self-exile in London) and discovering that the only evidence local libraries have concerning the Talbot case is a copy of the *Judgment* she already possesses, Kathleen admits her frustration: 'I'd copied out the story of Marianne and Mullan more or less as far as the *Judgment* knew it. There was nowhere to move to from there. I didn't have one piece of new material.'[48] Even at this early obstacle, an absence of evidence, Kathleen abandons her attempt at a historical reconstruction of the scandal and begins work on a piece of historical fiction – 'one based on a *feel* for the place and the people.'[49] Kathleen does her best to sort out inconsistencies and to fill in the gaps of the Talbot *Judgment* so that her historical novel, *The Talbot Book*, retains a semblance of fact, but it is here that *My Dream of You* begins to most forcefully expose the limits of historical objectivity. By detailing Kathleen's research and writing processes, O'Faolain highlights the authorial bias of even the most sincerely objective writer's work.

O'Faolain's novel is not simply a critique of audiences who receive Irish historical narratives as Truth, but an implication of Famine history as particularly perverted. Her text, set in the wake of the Famine years, calls our attention to the stereotypical crooked landlords, Gombeen men, and lazy peasants that historians have stripped of their contextual nuance in order to make one of two political arguments: Irish difficulty was the product of mistreatment by the English, or it was the result of an inherent inability to self-govern. Kathleen encounters a cast of generous landlords, honest tradesmen, and diligent peasants who complicate this established binary through aid to Marianne as she attempts to survive her husband's abuse. Furthermore, over a century and a half later, a kindhearted landlord assists Kathleen in her research efforts. It is only after independence (1922), and more recently the Good Friday Agreement (1998), that these characters begin to populate nonsectarian historical *novels* about the Famine.

As Kathleen begins writing the first chapter of her new project, a historical novel about the alleged Talbot affair, she draws not only on historical record, but also on her own lived-experience – the beginning of an affair with Shay Murphy, an Irish-born businessman who lives in London with his wife and who travels to Roscommon, alone, for monthly business – to imagine the romantic origin of Marianne and Mullan's relationship. Kathleen's romance with Shay informs her fictional story of Marianne's love for Mullan, which in turn helps her work through her own justifications for conducting an illicit affair with Shay. We can therefore read *My Dream of You* as a historiographical study of Famine scholarship: it argues that lived experience influences the historian's authorial decisions, and that only temporal distance has provided critics with a clearer perspective of initial biases.

Soon after Kathleen completes the first chapter of her novel, new evidence surfaces that contradicts her invented narrative, which she based wholly upon Richard Talbot's accusations against his wife as detailed in the *Judgment*. A pamphlet written by John Paget, Q.C. (a relation of Marianne Talbot) argues that she did not conduct an affair with her servant. Marianne, it appears, was the victim of a conspiracy: she and Richard were unable to conceive a son, and 'the Mount Talbot estate was bequeathed to Richard Talbot only on the condition that he had a son! [Richard] had to get rid of Marianne so that he could marry someone else.'[50] Richard, using the Famine as justification for food shortages even within his own house, began a program of underfeeding Marianne. Kathleen maintains, 'Since I came back to Ireland I've thought about the condition of hunger over and over again … Never, never did I think of a lady in a Big House being systematically underfed!'[51] And since malnourishment did not kill her, 'Richard Talbot thought to secure his wealth and his name by driving her insane.'[52] Paget's pamphlet explicitly challenges the apparently fictional narrative documented in the House of Lords *Judgment*. He claims that Richard enacted a plan to set Marianne up as an adulterer, thereby enabling him to take full custody of their daughter before incarcerating his wife in a Winsor asylum. Paget's pamphlet casts doubt upon the accepted 'truth' of the *Judgment* while also negating Kathleen's attempt at historical fiction based on details gleaned from the *Judgment*.

After reading the pamphlet, Kathleen admits that 'It had never even crossed my mind that Marianne and Mullan might not have been lovers.'[53] In part, this is because Kathleen has conducted two affairs of her own: one in London that instigated her research trip to Ireland, and the other seemingly influenced by her research. The result is our ability to detect the ways in which she has estheticized

Marianne's history to conform to her own. Kathleen has fallen into the trap of previous historians: accepting the *Judgment* as irrefutable because it is a legal document – a genre, like historical writing, that poses as factually accurate. The Paget pamphlet, however, forces her to recognize not only that her primary historical document (the *Talbot Judgment*) is both incomplete and biased, but that her perspective – even as a seemingly objective contemporary fiction writer – is imperfect:

> I had thought that the *Judgment* was a summary of all the evidence in both the Irish and the English proceedings. Now I saw that each of the three Lords had been reconstructing the argument that had led him to the conclusion he had reached, and each had naturally favored the evidence that had persuaded him towards that conclusion; therefore, they favored the evidence that made Marianne seem guilty, and gave short shrift to the evidence that did not.[54]

The discord between the *Judgment* and Paget's pamphlet raises doubt about any sort of claimed historical accuracy, especially accuracy bestowed upon narratives that are written to support or justify an agenda – be it an individual motive or an ideological program. Kathleen's research and subsequent revision self-consciously points her readers to sites of imaginative reinvention of Ireland's historical narratives and cultural myths, thereby highlighting the ways in which both history and fiction attempt to reconstruct Ireland's past not simply to overturn the validity of one historical mythology in favor of another, but to expose the process by which such mythologies are constructed.

Paget's pamphlet provides a necessary counterargument to the potentially false *Judgment*, yet it is impossible to know for certain if either document contains the truth about Marianne Talbot. It is not necessarily true that either Marianne had an affair with Mullan or that she was the victim of a conspiracy. The situation is more complex. Ultimately, these two discordant documents parallel the dissonance between nationalist and loyalist versions of the Famine as either the result of failing Irish social structures or British mismanagement. The actual event was more nuanced than either extremist position allows.

Yet Kathleen accepts the false dilemma: she believes that either the *Judgment* is true and therefore Paget's pamphlet is false, or vice versa. For the time being she chooses to believe Paget. For after reading Paget's argument, she dismisses the alleged affair between

Marianne and Mullan, and affirms Paget's conspiracy theory: 'Marianne Talbot would not have been degraded and driven insane if she had had a healthy womb and borne Richard a fine boy, and secured the inheritance of Mount Talbot.'[55] *My Dream of You*, through various framing devices, urges the reader to recognize this as a fallacy and to be critical of Kathleen's understanding of revision – historical and fictional – as a corrective measure, rather than as a challenge to the possibility of ever presenting an accurate historical record.

It isn't until a third and final document surfaces that Kathleen finally admits to the impossibility of definitively knowing what had transpired at Mount Talbot in 1848, and embraces ambiguity as a more accurate register of history. This, I believe, is the central argument of O'Faolain's historiographical novel. The final document, a deposition by the Reverend Mr. Sargent, assistant to Reverend McClelland (the same McClelland who had taken Marianne to the insane asylum in England after Richard Talbot informed him of his wife's affair), is arguably the least credible of the novel's three primary historical documents that mention the Talbot case. Miss Leech informs Kathleen, 'It is the front page of a short-lived London newspaper of the early 1850s. A tabloid, in today's parlance.'[56] Yet despite this source's publication in a less than reputable newspaper, Kathleen remains hopeful that it will offer her definitive proof of the affair, and excitedly questions Miss Leech, '*And? ... And?* Guilty or innocent?'[57] Even before she reads the article Kathleen believes that definitive evidence will surface. And, in fact, Mr. Sargent's eyewitness account does claim that Marianne was guilty of infidelity; however, he maintains that the man with whom she conducted the affair was not William Mullan. O'Faolain, therefore, provides a third option that contends with both the *Judgment* and Paget's pamphlet thus insinuating that further research may uncover additional accounts of the alleged affair and the period in which it may or may not have taken place.

O'Faolain's esthetic representation of a Famine-era sex scandal illustrates how, in Ireland, looking backwards often uncovers readily accepted oversimplified historical narratives. By transgressing geographical and temporal borders, uncovering little known documents, and unmasking the process of historical writing, *My Dream of You* offers a more complex rendering of the alleged Talbot affair than has been previously attempted, thereby arguing that similar questions be posed about the broader context of Famine. O'Faolain's historiographical novel begins the belated process of de-allegorizing Famine narratives, stripping them of familiar ideological frameworks in order to break imposed silences, which may in turn lead to a more creative, and therefore more inclusive, remembering of the past.

The Famine represents a turning point in Irish history, but rather than focusing only on what was lost or destroyed – and by whom – *My Dream of You* uses the Famine as a backdrop to illustrate the limits of historical 'facts.' As O'Kane Mara observes, '[b]y reacting to the Great Famine in particular, [Kathleen] provides another insight into why accessing the past is so difficult ... it depicts the site of loss, when old ways were destroyed.'[58] In this way, many Irish writers' requests to be haunted by the specters of historical moments in Irish history appear with greater intensity at the end of the twentieth century, after the Republic of Ireland entered into a peace process with Northern Ireland, which required an acceptance of Irish heterogeneity. Writers turn to the past in order to establish patterns of ambiguity in the traditionally ideological narratives that were in part responsible for many Irish conflicts. For instance, postcolonial cultural theorist Gayatri Chakravorty Spivak maintains:

> Now when a Jacques Derrida deconstructs the opposition between private and public, margin and center, he touches the texture of language and tells how the old words would not resemble themselves any more if a trick of rereading were learned. *The trick is to recognize that in every textual production, in the production of every explanation, there is the itinerary of a constantly thwarted desire to make the text explain ... [T]he will to explain [is] a symptom of the desire to have a self and a world.* In other words, on the general level, the possibility of explanation carries the presupposition of an explainable (even if not fully) universe and an explaining (even if imperfectly) subject. These presuppositions assure our being. Explaining, we exclude the possibility of the *radically* heterogeneous.[59]

The counter-hegemonic, postcolonial texts addressed in this Spivak essay are not innocent: they too harbor a 'desire to have a self and a world.' Their self and world, however, aim at radical heterogeneity. Despite ideology's aim at simplification through standardization, another postcolonial cultural theorist, Homi K. Bhabha, states quite clearly, 'Culture abhors simplification.'[60] Bhabha's observation stems from his understanding of colonialism as an agenda of obfuscation and postcolonialism as an embrace of uncertainty, ambiguity, and absurdity as ways of resisting ideological simplification.

By transgressing geographical and temporal borders, uncovering little-known documents, and unmasking the process of historical writing, *My Dream of You* offers a more complex rendering of the alleged Talbot affair than has been previously attempted, thereby arguing that similar questions be posed about the broader context of Famine. As Robinson points out, de-essentializing Famine narratives, calling forth narrative ghosts to dispossess them of familiar ideological frameworks, challenges the perceived accuracy of historical writing, which can in turn lead to a more creative remembering of the past.

In his novel *Star of the Sea*, Joseph O'Connor also presents a clear division between accepted historical representations of the Famine and more ambiguously imagined alternatives that have begun to appear in contemporary works of fiction. In a 2004 interview, O'Connor argues that fiction is capable of a more nuanced representation of wide-ranging Irish responses to the Famine than historical writing in Ireland has allowed. He suggests that moving beyond politically motivated attempts to assign definitive blame for mismanagement of the potato blight can give new meaning to the event. Echoing Mary Robinson's 1995 congressional address, O'Connor maintains,

> *Star of the Sea* is a novel and not at all a textbook about the Famine; but one thing I do hope it reveals is that the mythologies about the disaster on both extremes of the historical debate are reductive, disrespectful, and wrong, both morally and factually … The lesson to be drawn for modern Ireland, I believe, is not that we should hate the English (or anyone else), but that we should do more to help those many millions of the world's poor people who are suffering and dying from famine today. If our history means anything, it must mean that.[61]

O'Connor's use of fiction as an argument for Irish humanitarianism moves beyond the nationalist/loyalist divide in Ireland. He echoes postcolonial theorist Frantz Fanon's critique of the rhetoric of nationalism as simply the binary opposite of the rhetoric of imperialism in that it revises history to suit political ideology.[62] O'Connor and Robinson both conclude that Irish history demands Irish identity be grounded in dispossession. To this end, *Star of the*

Sea reconsiders definitive nationalist and loyalist claims about the Famine that tend to underscore Irish insularity. In short, it is a novel about reevaluation.

In '"Everything is in the Way the Material is Composed": Joseph O'Connor's *Star of the Sea* as Historiographic Metafiction,' Maeve Tynan argues that *Star of the Sea* draws attention to the various ways in which fiction 'mediates and constructs history.'[63] Tynan interprets O'Connor's borrowing from Victorian generic conventions as a semi-parodic postmodern pastiche aimed at recuperating the past, and concludes – by quoting Linda Hutcheon's *A Poetics of Postmodernism: History, Theory, Fiction* – that the novel 'both inscribe[s] and undermine[s] the authority and objectivity of historical sources and explanations.'[64] While I offer a parallel reading of *Star of the Sea*, my contextualization of the novel and the examples I draw upon for elucidation gesture beyond Tynan's textual observation that 'craftiness [is] involved in all forms of composition.'[65] Spectrality, as a theoretical lens, heightens our awareness of reemergent cultural factors (colonial trauma, gender and sexual discrimination, and political insularity) that originally led to the Irish artist's dual esthetic and political identity during the late nineteenth and early twentieth centuries. Such perspectives gives us a glimpse into how contemporary Irish writers use fiction to respond to the long-standing identification of the Irish artist as politically vested.

The titular ship of *Star of the Sea*, en route to deliver five thousand pounds of mercury to an American manufacturing company, also carries a cargo of Irish émigrés seeking refuge from the Famine. O'Connor's text argues, however, that escaping the Famine's consequences is impossible, even in the interstitial waters of the Atlantic. Famine is aboard the ship, and its presence exposes the various ways in which different classes of Irish emigrants were effected by and dealt with its wide-ranging and far-reaching consequences: displacement, starvation, and death. In fact, '[o]ne pictured the *Star* as a colossal beast of burden, its rib-timbers straining as though they might burst; flailed by an overlord into one last persecution, the hulk half dead already and we passengers its parasites.'[66] The more precise metaphor, the one O'Connor alludes to throughout the text, is the ship as Ireland's famished landscape, pockmarked with failing estates.

As on many estates, there exists on the ship a clear division between aristocracy and peasantry, between upper- and lower-class passengers, though here the difference between bankrupt lords and their servants is in title only, a fact that is highlighted because of the close quarters aboard the Star. The stench of poverty aboard the ship plagues both the evicted landlords and their displaced tenants. There is no escape from 'rotten food, rotten flesh, rotten fruit of rotting bowels ... tobacco smoke, vomit, stale perspiration, mildewed clothes, filthy blankets and rotgut whiskey.'[67] This observation both overlaps with and diverges from Sinéad Moynihan's recent study of the intersections between Irishness and Blackness in *Star of the Sea*. For Moynihan, 'O'Connor establishes a fundamental connection between the Great Famine and American Slavery'[68] to highlight 'the transatlantic transition undergone by countless Irish of the period: from oppressed race in the Old Country to oppressing race in the New World.'[69] When we look through the lens of spectrality, however, we are provided with a palimpsestic intersectionality of social and cultural categories that complicate Moynihan's reading of the novel. For at least one passenger aboard the ship undergoes the opposite transition: he is expelled from his role as oppressor in Ireland and is fated to a life of oppression in America.

O'Connor's juxtaposition of lord and servant illuminates the ubiquity of suffering caused by the Famine. His description of the fall of 'The Right Honourable Thomas David Nelson Merridith, the noble Lord Kingscourt, the Viscount of Roundstone, the ninth Earl of Cashel, Kilkerrin and Carna'[70] lays bare the often omitted effect that Famine had on the aristocracy. From O'Connor's perspective, Merridith was as powerless as his tenants to combat the horrors of Famine, and it is on the *Star* that this fact became most apparent. Yet *Star of the Sea* does not simply equate landlords with their tenants, it actively transitions them from oppressors to oppressed:

'You'll remain at New York for some time, Lord Kingscourt?'
   It took a moment for Merridith to realize whom the Captain was addressing.
   'Indeed,' he said. 'I mean to go into business, Lockwood.'
   Inevitably Dixon gave him a look. 'Since when did the gentry stoop to working for a living?'
   'There's a famine in progress in Ireland, Dixon. I assume you stumbled across it on your visit there, did you?'
   The Captain gave an apprehensive laugh. 'I'm sure our American friend meant no offence, Lord Kingscourt. He only thought – '
   'I'm quite aware of what he thought. How can an Earl be fallen low as a tradesman? ... Yes. So you see my predicament, Dixon. Not

a man on my estate has paid rent for four years. My father's death leaves me with half of all the bogland in southern Connemara, a great deal of stones and bad turf, a greater deal of overdue accounts and unpaid wages. Not to mention the considerable duties owing to the government'[71]

This is our introduction to Merridith, but as the novel progresses, and more of his back story is filled in, we learn that he was evicted from his estate twice: once by his father for choosing to marry Laura Markham rather than fulfilling his duty as Viscount by marrying a neighboring countess (Amelia Blake), and once by the Liability Collection Office for not paying his mortgage.

O'Connor's depiction of Merridith therefore complicates simpler nationalist and revisionist interpretations of the famine era in which either Irish peasants suffer and the English are to blame for their difficulties (nationalist), or Irish peasants suffer and the mismanagement of the natural disaster by the Irish government is responsible for their hardship (revisionist). O'Connor brings into focus others who are effected by the blight, each of whom is simultaneously sympathetic and damnable, thus exposing the problems with traditional historical writing and proving the need for historical fiction to ensure, at the very least, that one-dimensional conceptions of these events and the characters who populate them are replaced with more complex representations.

As I have already pointed out above (see pp. 25–27), constructing a more politically, culturally, and geographically diverse Irish population is contingent upon breaking silences which reinforce the oversimplified nationalist/revisionist perspectives that guide the majority of Famine representation. Both *My Dream of You* and *Star of the Sea* participate in the recent trend of calling attention to the ways in which Famine victims have been used to manipulate sociopolitical thought concerning the union between Ireland and England. *Star of the Sea* highlights the disparity between what actually happened in Ireland during the Famine and what is reported to have happened. It employs a narrative frame that exposes the ideological underpinning of competing Famine stories collected within that frame. *Star of the Sea* therefore rejects the pose of historical accuracy by illustrating the ways in which the genre can be manipulated.

Like *My Dream of You*, O'Connor's novel serves as a frame for his author-protagonist's historical writing. In an embedded narrative – *An American Abroad: Notes of London and Ireland in 1847*

– O'Connor's fictional author G. Grantley Dixon attempts to document the Famine's effect on a broad spectrum of individuals aboard the titular ship transporting emigrants from Dublin to New York. For the duration of the novel, the Star of the Sea is suspended between Ireland and America, dislocated from either place. Its dislocation parallels the displacement of individual passengers as well as collective conceptions of Irishness at that time. The broad range of dispossessed characters brought together on this transatlantic voyage – including landlords, servants, politicians, businessmen, and women – demonstrates how particular difficulties arising from the Famine forced individuals from all economic backgrounds to leave Ireland, illustrating that the overarching Famine narrative is significantly more complex than previously acknowledged. In the same interview cited previously, O'Connor observes:

> Ireland is a country where events which happened a long time ago are narrated as though they took place last week. The local people would point things out to us: deserted villages, Famine graves, ruined cottages. It was as though the landscape was a text. Some read it through a prism of nationalism or Anglophobia, others through a narrative of local tragedy. And, of course, others simply refused to read it at all ... And I find the silence around the disaster quite fascinating ... It's notable when you look at contemporaneous, eyewitness accounts of the Famine how very often the language of wordlessness features. ('I can't describe what I saw,' 'language fails me,' et cetera.) And subsequent writers have felt similarly dumbfounded by the sheer biblical scale of the disaster.[72]

Whereas *My Dream of You* succumbs to this 'language of wordlessness,' *Star of the Sea* explicitly challenges silences that fail to question politicized uses of the Famine. O'Connor juxtaposes the wordlessness of Famine victims with the sheer verbiage of politicized historical writing of his protagonists. The novel's framed structure complicates each individual character's interpretation of their Famine experience, thereby illustrating the subjectivity of politicized historical records that pose objectivity.

Star of the Sea subverts such oversimplified binaries by collecting a number of diverse yet interrelated documents that combine to create a narrative pastiche: the captain's register, newspaper articles, a number of letters (written before, during, and after the voyage), traditional and reimagined ballads, a fragment from Dixon's own abandoned novel (*The Blight*), and a commemorative epilogue written by Dixon in New York City on Easter Saturday, 1916, to be included in the 100th edition of *An American Abroad*. This is similar to the layering technique employed by O'Faolain in *My Dream of You*. However, whereas the slowly emerging documents uncovered by Miss Leech and Kathleen de Burca continually overturn historical 'facts' established by previously disclosed records, *Star of the Sea* juxtaposes these contentious narratives to show how authors adapt their texts to support a specific argument.

Both O'Faolain and O'Connor foreground the historian's subjective use of the past that haunts them. Each protagonist-historian borrows ideological myths from the Famine narrative to illustrate the divergent ways in which that narrative has been (re)imagined. In *Star of the Sea* in particular, two of the passengers aboard the ship, Pius Mulvey (a balladeer) and G.G. Dixon (a journalist), meditate on the constructedness of historical writing: its agendas, posed accuracy, and malleability. Mulvey at one point admits: 'He had discovered the alchemy that turns fact into fiction, poverty into plenty, history into art.'[73] Paying special attention to each of these characters' narrative theories and writing processes illustrates the fictional elements of historical representation. And like O'Faolain's novel, *Star of the Sea* challenges ideologically produced historical writing and conceptions of Irishness on the basis that they are politically and socially motivated. For as Dixon observes of his own writing, 'I would like to think I am objective in what I have put down, but of course that is not so and could never have been. I was there. I was involved.'[74] Both the ballad-maker and the storyteller admit to the subjectivity of historical 'fact' by highlighting the convoluted, incomplete, and falsified nature of their own Famine narratives – they act as historiographers.

I mentioned at the outset of this chapter that arguments concerned with assigning blame for the mismanagement of the potato blight in Ireland have bifurcated along ideological lines: Nationalist, which claims the British mismanaged the blight to the point that they actually created the Famine; and Loyalist, which blames the catastrophe on Ireland's underdeveloped social and economic structures. Joseph O'Connor claims that such oversimplifications of Irish history, and indeed the overwhelming interest in accurately assigning blame for Irish trauma, is the result of Irish artists' attraction to the ballad form. He maintains that the ballad does not allow for historical complexity:

> I have a theory that a society's predominant narrative forms say a lot about it. Much of what we know of the black experience in America comes from the blues, for example. This is a received form, like the sonnet, with tightly defined rules. And in Ireland, the ballad has always been the most popular form of all. This is an excellently economical form for storytelling, but it allows few gray areas or moral ambiguities. What has happened in Ireland is that we've had history as ballad, with good guys, bad guys, heroes, and villains.[75]

In short, O'Connor maintains that Irish history has been employed as a politically persuasive or morally didactic tool. His exposure of Irish historical writing as ballad – that is to say, with oversimplified divisions between 'good guys, bad guys, heroes, and villains' – addresses a larger concern about reading colonial and postcolonial literatures as allegory.

In 1986, postmodern literary critic Fredric Jameson proposed that all third-world literature be read as 'national allegories.'[76] Jameson's attempt to outline 'some general theory of what is often called third-world literature'[77] has been heavily criticized precisely for its generality. As Imre Szeman points out, 'The presumption that it is possible to produce a theory that would explain African, Asian, and Latin American literary production, the literature of China and Senegal, has been (inevitably) read as nothing more than a patronizing, theoretical orientalism, or as yet another example of a troubling appropriation of Otherness.'[78] Though not a third-world nation, Ireland's literature is also consistently read with an eye toward the relationship of literary production to national politics. A typical approach to reading Irish literature is to see it as necessarily about the nation – its constructions, its definitions, its blind spots. Recent historiographical novels such as *My Dream of You* and *Star of the Sea*, work to expose allegorical uses of the Famine, and do so by offering contemporary readers a reflexive self-gaze that exoticizes the narrative while (paradoxically) moving beyond allegorical objectification.

In *Star of the Sea*, Pius Mulvey and G.G. Dixon – both historians (one a balladeer, the other an ethnographic journalist) – offer up similar theories concerning the simple binary structure of Irish historical representation. O'Connor dispossesses Irish history of its balladic structure, that is, of its allegorical heroes and villains, by illustrating how easily his balladeer Pius Mulvey revises traditional folk songs by simply reversing the roles of hero and villain without consequence. These revisions suggest that histories are often composed of fixed parts – 'good guys, bad guys, heroes, villains'[79] – that are essentially interchangeable and reproducible in multiple historical contexts for various political ends. There is also another layer of argument in O'Connor's text, one that becomes clear when we consider that Dixon is an American journalist on assignment in Ireland charged with the task of writing a dishonest (read: exoticized) ethnography, and that Mulvey is an exiled fugitive. Not only are both men geographically displaced, they are also interstitial: they tell their stories while aboard a Famine ship sailing across the Atlantic from Ireland to Canada. O'Connor, therefore, makes the case that the malleability of historical fact becomes more clearly recognizable at geographical distance. And to be sure, Dixon's *An American Abroad*, which makes up one of the layers of O'Connor's narrative pastiche – which also includes the captain's register, newspaper articles, a number of letters (written before, during, and after the voyage), traditional and reimagined ballads, and a fragment from Dixon's own abandoned novel (*The Blight*) – is in its 100th edition! Therefore Dixon's commemorative Epilogue written in New York City on Easter Saturday 1916 enjoys temporal distance as well. Protagonists who suffer authorial displacement, near identical subject matter and setting, as well as curiously similar narrative structures found in *Star of the Sea* and *My Dream of You* (published only a year earlier), suggests the origins of a historiographical project in postcolonial Irish fiction, which continues in more recent works by Sebastian Barry – *The Secret Scripture* (2008); *On Canaan's Side* (2011) – and Colm Tóibín – *The Master* (2004).

Mulvey and Dixon both confess their own biases and agendas as chroniclers of history, which unsettles the reader's expectations that historical writing is at least objective if not accurate. Neither Mulvey nor Dixon is ever certain of what is true, false, or an amalgamation of the two. We watch, for instance, as Mulvey falsifies the events he reports in order to create a more enchanting tale that will help earn him a meal. Readers similarly witness Dixon taking liberty with facts in order to produce creative journalism in which he appears to be altruistic in his illumination of Irish suffering.

Pius Mulvey was born to 'dirt-poor smallholders' on an Irish estate in Co. Donegal. When he was sixteen years old (c. 1830), his father died from a horse kick; his mother passed a year later of grief. Shortly thereafter, for want of food, Pius Mulvey began to travel as a balladeer, reciting traditional songs in return for room and board in Irish and English public houses. His physical hunger quickly developed into a mental hunger – an obsession with preserving historical events:

> Mulvey began to ponder something that would come to obsess him. Singers were admired by almost everyone; they were annalists, chroniclers, custodians, biographers. In a place where reading was almost unknown they carried the local memory like walking books. Many of them claimed to know five hundred songs; a smaller number knew upwards of a thousand. Without them, Mulvey sometimes felt, nobody would remember anything, and if it wasn't remembered it hadn't truly happened.[80]

Mulvey's act of archiving the ancestral voice primarily functions as transgenerational memory. He attempts, through song, to communicate with the ghosts of ancient Ireland by calling them into his contemporary moment. He gives voice to misrepresented victims, arguably the task of O'Faolain and O'Connor as well. Initially, Mulvey's description of singers likens them to historians rather than artists; however, he quickly begins to craft counterfeit ballads that narrate fictional events, and he claims these as authentic traditional songs passed down for generations. Mulvey understands historical writing not in terms of accuracy, but rather as imaginative reinterpretation. His theory of the 'ballad as history' calls attention to O'Connor's concern that in Ireland 'we've had history as ballad' – an obfuscation of the complex motivations of individuals who are all too neatly designated as heroes and villains in the national story.

Pius Mulvey's theory of ballad construction does a couple of things: it allows readers to observe the ballad's composition, thereby illuminating the creative aspects of historical writing; it questions the usefulness of 'factual' representation; and it lays bare Mulvey's own authorial bias. In short, Mulvey is not a historian, but a historiographer. On one particular occasion, Mulvey demonstrates the ease with which the ballad-maker can create and re-create 'facts,' which, because of the novel's setting during the 1840s, forms obvious parallels with the Famine historians' similar ability. He manipulates the ostensibly fact-based ballad about a spurned recruiting sergeant in Connemara, Ireland, so that it will appeal to a different audience in Whitechapel, England.

The original ballad is based on Mulvey's cordial encounter with a British Sergeant while tilling 'the stony patch of [his] father's tenancy.'⁸¹ The Sergeant offers him a place in the King's army, claiming, 'No crown soldier would ever know starvation.'⁸² Mulvey declines the Sergeant's offer, telling him, 'Ye understand nothing of this place. Ye never will.'⁸³ The Sergeant 'shrugged and walked back down the way he had come.'⁸⁴ In his ballad, Mulvey elevates this unexceptional encounter into a verbal assault upon the British recruitment of Irish peasants:

> Myself and my brother were scratching the land,
> When up came a captain with gold in his hand
> And stories of soldiers all fearless and grand;
> Oh, the day being cheerful and charming.
>
> And says he, my fine farmers, if you will sign up,
> It's a handful of sovereigns I'll give you to sup.
> Away with you, Captain, you redbacked auld pup.
> For your words are most deeply alarming.
> ...
> And if ever we take up the musket or sword,
> It won't be for England, we swear to the Lord.
> For the freedom of Erin, we'll rise up our blade,
> And cut off your head in the morning!⁸⁵

Though his nationalist song served him well in Ireland, the people of London did not fill his busker's coffer. Mulvey, therefore, spends a few nights 'affixing ribbons of street names and crests of London slang; unpicking anything too disquieting or too noticeably Irish. Not a jot did it bother him to alter the ensemble.'⁸⁶ The revised Connemara ballad now describes a throng of Piccadilly street urchins for his London audience:

> Me and my chum dodgin' down in the Strand
> When up marches Major wiv sword in one 'and,
> And yarns of his soldierboys fearless and grand;
> Oh, the day bein' cheerful and charming.
>
> And says 'e, my gay cockerels, now sign up wiv me,
> And it's ten sparkling sovereigns you'll suddenly see,
> Wiv a crown in the bargain I'll toss in for free,
> For to drink the king's elf in the morning.
>
> Cut along with you, Major, we boldly did say,
> For we loves Piccadilly and 'ere we shall stay;
> To dodge all the night and to dally all day
> Is to live life most cheerful and charming.⁸⁷

In both instances, Mulvey argues that the narrated events actually occurred the way in which he relates them. In neither situation is his true. For 'He had discovered the alchemy that turns fact into fiction, poverty into plenty, history into art.'[88] However, Mulvey's 'alchemy' never really turns fact into fiction or history into art. Rather, the palimpsestic form in which the updated ballad is written over the original exposes the illusion that 'fact and fiction,' 'history and art' aren't already the same thing.

Star of the Sea (and indeed, *My Dream of You*) offers readers a historiographical theory as much as it does a fictional narrative. In postcolonial Ireland, in the wake of the Famine sesquicentennial (1995), the Good Friday ceasefire agreement (1998), and the Celtic Tiger economic boom of the 2000s, the environment for reassessing the past had finally arrived. And it is in the sphere of contemporary fiction in which we find some of the most attentive studies of how narrative (historical, political, fictional) is produced. Take, for instance, Mulvey's contemplation of the elasticity of historical facts:

> The facts of what had happened on that wintry day were hard to meld into the lines of the ballad; if you could even say clearly what the facts actually were. So he changed them a little to fit the rhyme scheme. It didn't really matter. Nobody would ever know the facts anyway; if they somehow found them out, they wouldn't find them worth singing. The main thing in balladry was to make a singable song. The facts did not matter: *that was the secret*. He wrote and scratched out; rewrote, refined.[89]

In historical writing, though, the 'facts' do matter to the audience, and Mulvey's alterations show how easily historical facts can be recalibrated to serve an author's agenda, thereby challenging the notion that any representation of an event is ever true – including traditional Famine narratives that serve as the backdrop for *Star of the Sea*. Furthermore, Mulvey's ballad-writing reminds readers that all texts have intended audiences. Whereas historical writing often harbors obfuscated political or social agendas, we are shown how Mulvey's ballad is constructed with a particular agenda in mind: to offer the audience an entertaining vision of itself. He conjures alternative realities that may or may not be historically accurate in order to establish a more enchanting historical narrative. His composition process employs a logic by which history (with all of its complexities and uncertainties) is a necessary falsification of the past.

In *Theatres of Memory* (1996), Raphael Samuel identifies this practice of translation as ancestor worship:

> Ancestor worship ... [offers] us a retrospective sense of belonging – what use to be called 'lineage' and today is known as 'roots' – to compensate for the insecurities of the here and now. It gratifies our needs for household gods, offering us a source of symbolic gratification and a transcendence of, or escape from, ourselves. Ancestor worship usually involves a double misrecognition, both of our own qualities and those of our predecessors; each, by a process of osmosis, is apt to take on the idealized character of the other. Ancestor worship is premised on a necessary falsification of the past.[90]

Star of the Sea, along with *My Dream of You*, suggests, in an Irish context, that the necessary 'sense of belonging' that Ernest Renan argues defines a nation depends upon this necessary falsification, which was established as part of the Irish historical narrative during the Famine years. Whereas O'Faolain interprets falseness via silence and omission, O'Connor represents this falsification literally. Pius Mulvey – O'Connor's historiographical raconteur – distorts the facts of his Famine experiences for personal gain.

Likewise, the fictional G. Grantley Dixon writes an epilogue to *Star of the Sea*'s embedded manuscript, *An American Abroad: Notes of London and Ireland in 1847*, in which he calls attention to his dishonest reporting of the Irish Famine, again underscoring misrepresentations of the Famine for personal gain. At the behest of his publisher, Mr. Thomas Newby, Dixon is sent on what we might read as a parodic ethnographic journey to Ireland in 1847 to observe and record idyllic Irish life. His assignment was to write a 'collection of impressions of the Emerald Isle. Mist on the lakes. Jolly swineherds with queer wisdom. Pepper[ed] up with a few pretty colleens.'[91] However, Dixon's observations do not reflect an exotic culture isolated on a serene pastoral island. Rather, he writes about a cast of starving characters that reflects the traumatic cultural and political upheaval in England, Ireland, and the Americas in the mid-nineteenth century.

O'Connor points out in an interview that he hopes his novel highlights the Irish Famine's importance to all three nations: 'The Famine [is] a centrally important event in the development of three countries – not just Ireland, but also Great Britain and the United States.'[92] In other words, it is an event dispossessed of allegorical specificity. By moving beyond socially and politically reductive binaries that divide Ireland and England (to say nothing of America), *Star of the Sea* participates in a broad historiographical program among contemporary Irish novelists to establish postcolonial dispossession as a defining characteristic of Irishness.

In his 1916 epilogue, appropriately titled 'The Haunted Man,' Dixon reflects on the international significance of the Irish Famine by juxtaposing references to it against those of the Great War (1914–1918):

> What happened took place in 1847, an important anniversary in the history of fictions; when stories appeared in which people were starving, in which wives were jailed in attics and masters married servants ... A time when things were done – and other things not done – as a result of which more than a million would die; the slow, painful, unrecorded deaths of those who meant nothing to their lords. What happened is one of the reasons they still die today. *For the dead do not die in that tormented country, that heartbroken island of incestuous hatreds; so abused down the centuries by the powerful of the neighbouring island, as much by the powerful of its native own.* And the poor of both islands died in their multitudes while the Yahweh of retributions omitted down his hymns. The flags flutter and the pulpits resound. At Ypres. In Dublin. At Gallipoli. In Belfast. The trumpets spew and the poor die. *Yet they walk, the dead, and will always walk; not as ghosts, but as press-ganged soldiers, conscripted into a battle that is not of their making; their sufferings metaphorised, their very existence translated, their bones stewed into the sludge of propaganda. They do not even have names. They are simply: The Dead. You can make them mean anything you want them to mean.*[93]

Dixon's enjambment of these two great tragedies is itself an example of propaganda. He conflates the victims of Famine with the casualties of war (in the battles of Ypres and Gallipoli, 1915). 'The Haunted Man' disarticulates the Irish/British divide that was intensified during the Famine years via palimpsestic layering: 'the poor of *both* countries' 'who died unrecorded deaths' in *both* tragic events have been 'metaphorised ... into the sludge of propaganda.' At the exact moment in Irish history when revolutionary rhetoric was at its most intense (during and after the 1916 Easter Rebellion against British rule in Ireland), Dixon, horrified that the specters of Famine victims have been called upon to justify blood sacrifice, attempts to marry the dispossessed poor of Ireland and Britain to prevent further bloodshed. He argues, 'That sometimes there must be struggle is not to be doubted. With which weapons it is fought remains the question.'⁹⁴ As the authors of war employ the dead to justify armed rebellion, Dixon conjures their ghosts to argue against it.

Though Dixon writes in the moment of Irish revolution, he is granted a historiographical perspective of that moment through O'Connor's temporal distance. Dixon's epilogue can therefore work to expose the political use of Famine victims to justify paramilitary rebellion against British rule in Ireland. His argument, as well as O'Connor's, is that any writer can make nameless victims mean anything s/he wants them to mean. Readers of Irish history can be sure of only a few very basic truths about the Famine: in the wake of natural disaster (a potato blight), bitter racism, and poor economic policies, many died horrific deaths both in Ireland and abroad, and the memory of that period provoked a series of Irish rebellions against the British Empire that culminated in the 1919–1921 War of Independence. For Dixon, rewriting history for personal or political gain 'is no fitting memorial for the landless of the past.'⁹⁵

One of the consequences of the Famine's ubiquity is the ease with which its dispossessed victims across the globe are relegated to the status of political allegories. Dixon identifies the disastrous silence that paradoxically speaks in support of the marginalization of Famine victims both domestically and internationally:

> Nothing had prepared him for it: the fact of famine ... Dixon had no words for it. Nobody did. And yet could there be silence? What did silence mean? Could you allow yourself to say nothing at all to such things? To remain silent, in fact, was to say something powerful: that it never happened: that these people did not matter ... They deserved no place in printed pages, in finely wrought novels intended for the civilized. They were simply not worth saying anything about.⁹⁶

O'Connor's narration of historical silence is slightly different from that of O'Faolain. Kathleen encounters silence while trying to acquire information about the Famine and the Talbot affair. Dixon is 'traumatized into muteness' by the events he witnesses first hand. Yet looking back upon 1847 from 1916, Dixon is able give voice to these underrepresented Famine victims.

Using his newspaper column at the *New York Times* as a platform for cultivating a humanitarian effort in Ireland, Dixon sought to provide a definitive and stirring account of Irish suffering at the hands of wealthy landlords. He reports minimal success: 'I was told that the book brought to the attention of some of the reading public the sufferings being endured in Ireland at the time of the Great

Famine; but if so, it did little to end those sufferings.'[97] In a self-reflexive critique Dixon acknowledges that his work was socially ineffective and that to gain widespread attention, he would have to romanticize his subject.

Again, Dixon maintains that adhering to historical objectivity is dubious at best: 'I would like to think I am objective in what I have put down, but of course that is not so and could never have been. I was there. I was involved.'[98] In other words, he had stake in how his readers interpreted his Famine narrative. Dixon's falsified historicism wins him the admiration of a woman, his publisher, and a general readership (his historical narrative is, after all, in its 100th edition). Yet he concludes his most recent epilogue by admitting that he imagined various aspects of his text – a text that is O'Connor's fiction to begin with – and readers are left wondering what, if anything is certain, accurate, or true:

> The above events all happened. They belong to fact. As for the rest – the details, the emphases, certain devices of narration and structure, whole events which may never have occurred, or may have happened quite differently to how they are described – those belong to the imagination. For that no apology whatsoever is offered, though some will insist that one is needed. Perhaps they are correct, by their own lights anyway. To take the events of reality and meld them into something else is a task not to be undertaken coldly or carelessly. On the question of whether such an endeavour is worthwhile or even moral, readers may wish to pronounce for themselves. Such questions must hover over any account of the past: whether the story may be understood without asking who is telling it; to which intended audience and to what precise end.[99]

Dixon offers these parting words both as a disclaimer concerning the accuracy of his report, and as a historiographical theory. His admission that most events were imagined echoes Kathleen de Burca's uncertainty concerning the truth of the Talbot affair. Kathleen does not finish the historical novel she set out to write, and Dixon admits that his was almost wholly imagined. Yet these writers' narration of their creative processes reminds readers how the Famine has been manipulated over time for socio-political gain.

My Dream of You and *Star of the Sea* resist oversimplification of the Famine by releasing it from its mythology and presenting it as the founding moment of dispossessed Irishness – another version of the myth, to be sure, but one that is decidedly more nuanced than previously offered. Both novels, invested in actively dismantling homogenous versions of Irish history, define Irishness via dispossession. Spectrality offers a way of understanding the textual mechanism by which both texts attempt to re-present Irish history as a narrative of dispossession:

> The legend of the specter, the story, the fable (*Märchen*) would be abolished in the [act of writing it down], as if the specter itself, after having embodied a spectrality in legend and without becoming a reality, came out of itself, called for an exit from the legend without entering into the reality of which it is the specter.[100]

The legend of a definitive, anti-colonial Irishness, which emerged from consequences of the Famine, is challenged in these two novels that depict Irishness – both during and after the Famine – as something other than definitive or even locatable.

The specter of the Famine is exorcised not because O'Faolain and O'Connor have successfully liberated the Irish from it, but rather because they have allowed their contemporary audiences to confront it as an oversimplified legend that has come to mean whatever propagandists want it to mean. O'Faolain and O'Connor resist traditional nationalist/loyalist divisions, which they see from a postcolonial perspective as being the result of an outdated, politically motivated falsification of the past. In doing so, their novels take up Mary Robinson's call to complicate historical oversimplifications. In these novels, history becomes more useful as a medium to search for possible answers to modern problems than as a weapon in a dichotomous debate over the 'true' nature of Irishness. In the end they show us that Irish identity can only be understood in terms of dispossession: ambiguous, protean, spectral.

Notes

1 Kevin Whelan. 'The Revisionist Debate in Ireland,' *boundary 2* 31.1 (2004): 196.
2 John O'Rourke. *The History of the Great Irish Famine of 1847* (Charleston: BiblioLife, 2008), p. 33.
3 Whelan, 'Revisionist Debate in Ireland,' 198.
4 Cecil Woodham Smith's father claimed descent from Lord Edward FitzGerald, one of the leaders of the United Irishmen Rebellion in 1798 against British rule in the Kingdom of Ireland: see Elizabeth Malcolm. '"On Fire." The Great Hunger: Ireland 1845–1849,' *New Hibernia Review* 12.4 (2008): 143–149.

5 Lord K.P. Dufferin. *Irish Emigration and the Tenure of Land in Ireland*. 2nd edn (London: Willis, Sotheran, and Co., 1867), p. 309.
6 R.F. Foster. *Modern Ireland: 1600–1972* (London: Penguin, 1988), p. 326.
7 Foster, *Modern Ireland*, p. 322.
8 Terry Eagleton. *Heathcliff and the Great Hunger: Studies in Irish Culture* (London: Verso, 1995), p. 13.
9 José Manuel Estévez-Saá. 'An Interview with Joseph O'Connor.' *Contemporary Literature* 46.2 (2005): 163.
10 Eagleton, *Heathcliff and the Great Hunger*, p. 13.
11 Christine Kinealy. 'The Great Irish Famine: A Dangerous Memory.' *The Great Famine and the Irish Diaspora in America*. Ed. Arthur Gribben. Amherst, MA: University of Massachusetts Press, 1999, pp. 250–251.
12 In *Nation and Narration*, postcolonial cultural theorist Timothy Brennan argues that unadulterated language, homogeneous race, and geographical borders do not define a nation or a people. Rather, Renan claims, nation is a sense of belonging. And Brennan maintains that all nations are discursive constructs: 'The nation ... is an abstraction, an allegory, a myth that does not correspond to a reality that can be scientifically defined. Race, geography, tradition, language, size, or some combination of these seem finally insufficient for determining national essence, and yet people die for nations, fight wars for them, and write fictions on their behalf': Brennan, 'The National Longing for Form,' *Nation and Narration*. Ed. Homi K. Bhabha (London: Routledge, 1990), p. 49.
13 For the actual historical documents from which O'Faolain quotes, see *The Talbot Judgment: House of Commons Sitting*, 28 February 1856, series 3, Vol. 140, cc1544–63; and Talbot v. Talbot: A Report of the Speech of Wm. Keogh, Esq., M.P., Solicitor General for Ireland, on Behalf of the Appellant, Before The High Court of Delegates. London: Thomas Blenkarn, 1855.
14 The Houses of the Oireachtas is known in English as the Legislature of Ireland, and includes both the Dáil Éireann (Representatives) and Seanad Éireann (Senate).
15 Mary Robinson. 'Cherishing the Irish Diaspora: An Address.' *Irish Diaspora*. 29 October 1995, 1.
16 Robinson, 'Cherishing the Irish Diaspora,' 13.
17 Eagleton, *Heathcliff and the Great Hunger*, p. 5.
18 Angela Bourke, ed. *The Field Day Anthology of Irish Writing: Irish Women's Writing and Traditions* (New York: New York University Press, 2002), p. 913.
19 Maud Gonne. 'The Famine Queen.' *Irish Writing: An Anthology of Irish Literature in English 1789–1939*. Ed. Stephen Regan (Oxford: Oxford University Press, 2004), p. 184.

20 Jacques Derrida. *Specters of Marx: The State of the Debt, the Work of Mourning, and the New International*. 1993. Trans. Peggy Kamuf. (New York: Routledge Classics, 2006), p. 78.
21 Robinson, 'Cherishing the Irish Diaspora,' 14.
22 Christine Kinealy. *The Great Irish Famine: Impact, Ideology and Rebellion* (New York: Palgrave, 2002), p. 4. Emphasis original.
23 The ceasefire lasted 17 months: it officially ended with the bombing of the London docklands on 9 February 1996.
24 Robinson, 'Cherishing the Irish Diaspora,' 5. Emphasis added.
25 Michael de Certeau. *The Writing of History*. Trans. Thomas Conley (New York: Columbia University Press, 1975), p. 42.
26 Stephen Ungar. 'Against Forgetting: Notes on Revision and the Writing of History.' *Diacritics* 22.2 (1992): 67.
27 Thomas Conley. 'Translator's Introduction: For a Literary Historiography.' Introduction. *The Writing of History*. By Michel de Certeau. Trans. Thomas Conley (New York: Columbia University Press, 1975), p. xi.
28 Derrida, *Specters of Marx*, p. 125.
29 Kinealy, 'A Dangerous Memory,' pp. 251–253.
30 On 31 August 1994, antagonistic political parties, the British military, and the Provisional Irish Republican Army (IRA) announced a ceasefire in Northern Ireland. The ceasefire inaugurated the peace process, and was followed by the Good Friday Agreement on 10 April 1998, which established a commitment by all parties to rely exclusively on peaceful and democratic means for reconciliation. In this atmosphere, it seemed as if liberation from the colonial burden was a possibility.
31 Robinson, 'Cherishing the Irish Diaspora,' 14.
32 Linda Hutcheon. *The Politics of Postmodernism* (New York: Routledge, 1989), p. 50.
33 Hutcheon, *The Politics of Postmodernism*, p. 67.
34 In an interview that coincided with the publication of her memoir *Are You Somebody?* (1996), she insists, 'You don't get to be an Irish woman of my age and say "I, I, I" with any confidence, because "I" has been frightened out of you': quoted in Maura J. Casey, 'Appreciations: Nuala O'Faolain,' *New York Times*, 13 May 2008.
35 Her understanding of the tensions between individual and national identity is similar to Hamid Naficy's observations of home: 'Home is anyplace; it is temporary and it is moveable; it can be built, rebuilt, and carried in memory and by acts of imagination,' in Naficy, 'Framing Exile: From Homeland to Homepage.' Introduction. *Home, Exile, Homeland: Film, Media and the Politics of Place*. Ed. Naficy (London: Routledge, 1999), p. 5.
36 Nuala O'Faolain. *My Dream of You* (New York: Riverhead Books, 2001), p. 5.

37 O'Faolain, *My Dream of You*, 71.
38 O'Faolain, *My Dream of You*, 21.
39 Mary Fitzgerald-Hoyt. 'Writing the Famine, Healing the Future: Nuala O'Faolain's My Dream of You.' *Ireland's Great Hunger: Relief, Representation, and Remembrance*, Vol. 2. Ed. David A. Valone (Lanham, MD: University Press of America, 2010), p. 91.
40 Ronan Sheehan. 'Novelists on the Novel: Ronan Sheehan Talks to John Banville and Francis Stuart.' *The Crane Bag* 3.1 (1979): 84.
41 See James M. Smith. *Ireland's Magdalene Laundries and the Nation's Architecture of Containment*. (South Bend, IN: University of Notre Dame Press, 2007); Catherine O'Connor. '"The Smell of Her Apron": Issues of Gender and Religious Identity in the Oral Testimonies of Church of Ireland Women in Ferns, 1945–1965.' *Anáil an Bhéil Bheo: Orality and Modern Irish Culture*. Eds. Nessa Cronin et al. (Newcastle upon Tyne: Cambridge Scholars, 2009), pp. 127–136.
42 Miriam O'Kane Mara. '(Re)producing Identity and Creating Famine in Nuala O'Faolain's *My Dream of You*.' *Critique* 48.2 (2007): 199.
43 Derrida, *Specters of Marx*, p. 5.
44 Walter Benjamin. 'On the Concept of History.' *Walter Benjamin: Selected Writings (1938–1940)*. Vol. 4. Ed. Howard Eiland and Michael W. Jennings (Cambridge, MA: Belknap, 2003), pp. 391, 397.
45 Mara, '(Re)producing Identity,' 213.
46 Cathy Caruth. *Unclaimed Experience* (Baltimore, MD: Johns Hopkins University Press, 1996), pp. 3–4.
47 O'Faolain, *My Dream of You*, 109.
48 O'Faolain, *My Dream of You*, 153.
49 O'Faolain, *My Dream of You*, 77. Italics, ellipses original.
50 O'Faolain, *My Dream of You*, 323–324.
51 O'Faolain, *My Dream of You*, 322.
52 O'Faolain, *My Dream of You*, 337.
53 O'Faolain, *My Dream of You*, 318.
54 O'Faolain, *My Dream of You*, 324.
55 O'Faolain, *My Dream of You*, 353.
56 O'Faolain, *My Dream of You*, 412.
57 O'Faolain, *My Dream of You*, 412. Italics original.
58 Mara, '(Re)producing Identity,' 212.
59 Gayatri Chakravorty Spivak. *In Other Worlds: Essays in Cultural Politics* (New York: Methuen, 1987), p. 105.
60 Homi K. Bhabha. 'DissemiNation: Time, Narrative, and the Margins of the Modern Nation.' *Nation and Narration*. Ed. Homi K. Bhabha (London: Routledge, 1990), p. 303.
61 Estévez-Saá. 'An Interview with Joseph O'Connor,' 165–166.
62 See for instance Frantz Fanon, 'On National Culture,' *The Wretched of the Earth*, Trans. Richard Wilcox (New York: Grove Press, 2005),

pp. 145–180, especially his examination of tradition on page 160. See also Salman Rushdie's 'Imaginary Homelands' in which he argues that 'redescribing a world is the necessary first step towards changing it. And particularly at times when the State takes reality into its own hands, and sets about distorting it, altering the past to fit its present needs, then the making of the alternative realities of art, including the novel of memory, becomes politicized,' in Rushdie, *Imaginary Homelands* (New York: Penguin, 1992), p. 14 (emphasis added).

63 Maeve Tynan. '"Everything is in the Way the Material is Composed": Joseph O'Connor's Star of the Sea as Historiographic Metafiction.' Eds. Maria Belville, Marita Ryan, and M. Tynan. *Passages: Movements and Moments in Text and Theory* (Newcastle upon Tyne: Cambridge Scholars, 2009), p. 80.
64 Hutcheon qtd in Tynan, 'Everything is in the Way the Material is Composed,' p. 89.
65 Tynan, 'Everything is in the Way the Material is Composed,' p. 94.
66 Joseph O'Connor. *Star of the Sea* (New York: Harcourt Inc., 2002), xiv.
67 O'Connor, *Star of the Sea*, xvii.
68 Sinéad Moynihan. '"Ships in Motion": Crossing the Black and Green Atlantics in Joseph O'Connor's *Star of the Sea*.' *Symbiosis: A Journal of Anglo-American Literary Relations* 12.1 (2008): 48.
69 Moynihan, 'Ships in Motion,' 55.
70 O'Connor, *Star of the Sea*, 4.
71 O'Connor, *Star of the Sea*, 7–8.
72 Estévez-Saá, 'An Interview with Joseph O'Connor,' 163–164.
73 O'Connor, *Star of the Sea*, 101.
74 O'Connor, *Star of the Sea*, 373.
75 Estévez-Saá, 'An Interview with Joseph O'Connor,' 166.
76 Fredric Jameson. 'Third-World Literature in the Era of Multinational Capitalism.' *Social Text* 15 (1986): 69.
77 Jameson, 'Third-World Literature,' 68.
78 Imre Szeman. 'Who's Afraid of National Allegory? Jameson, Literary Criticism, Globalization.' *South Atlantic Quarterly* 100.3 (2001): 803.
79 Estévez-Saá, 'An Interview with Joseph O'Connor,' 166.
80 O'Connor, *Star of the Sea*, 92.
81 O'Connor, *Star of the Sea*, 86.
82 O'Connor, *Star of the Sea*, 89.
83 O'Connor, *Star of the Sea*, 90.
84 O'Connor, *Star of the Sea*, 90.
85 O'Connor, *Star of the Sea*, 95–97.
86 O'Connor, *Star of the Sea*, 177.
87 O'Connor, *Star of the Sea*, 178.
88 O'Connor, *Star of the Sea*, 101.

89 O'Connor, *Star of the Sea*, 96. Italics original.
90 Raphael Samuel. 'Ancestor Worship.' *Island Stories: Unraveling Britain: Theatres of Memory*. Vol. 2. Ed. Alison Light, Sally Alexander, and Gareth Stedman Jones (London: Verso, 1999), p. 272.
91 O'Connor, *Star of the Sea*, 116.
92 Estévez-Saá, 'An Interview with Joseph O'Connor,' 165.
93 O'Connor, *Star of the Sea*, 364. Emphasis added.
94 O'Connor, *Star of the Sea*, 364.
95 O'Connor, *Star of the Sea*, 364.
96 O'Connor, *Star of the Sea*, 122–124.
97 O'Connor, *Star of the Sea*, 367.
98 O'Connor, *Star of the Sea*, 373.
99 O'Connor, *Star of the Sea*, 380–381.
100 Derrida, *Specters of Marx*, 130.

2

The specter of Famine during World War II

In his 1967 documentary film, *Rocky Road to Dublin*, Irish filmmaker Peter Lennon took an intimate look at postcolonial Irish life. The opening voice-over narration indicated that mid-century Ireland was in a state of arrested development:

> In the 40s, while Europe was tearing itself to pieces, Ireland, neutral, drifted even further from the reality of the outside world. We weren't even allowed to call it a war; officially it was The Emergency – For us a tranquil and serene emergency. The 50s brought a deepening depression: unemployment, emigration, and oppressive sense of frustration. We weren't encouraged to look too closely into what had gone wrong.[1]

Lennon's narration implies that Ireland's declaration of neutrality on 2 September 1939 established a false sense of security among the Irish people during World War II by isolating them from the global conflict. Éamon de Valera, then Prime Minister of Dáil Éireann (Irish House of Representatives),[2] convinced Irish President Douglas Hyde and his Republican Fianna Fáil government to adopt a policy of non-engagement. For many, past colonial abuses – including England's mismanagement of the potato blight, which according to nationalist ideologues caused the Great Famine (c. 1845–1852)[3] – necessitated Ireland's removal from the war; therefore, the Irish government declared neutrality, in part, to increase political distance between the Irish Republic and the British Commonwealth.

Sebastian Barry's novel, *The Whereabouts of Eneas McNulty* (1998), reverses Fianna Fáil's implicit enlistment of the Irish Famine as rationale for non-engagement in World War II. Famine imagery operates within the novel's carefully crafted subtext as a means of critiquing Irish neutrality during the war. Barry references particular historical images from WWII, such as the MS *St. Louis* cargo ship that transported Jewish emigrants to America, and conflates them in the mind of his protagonist with particular historical images from the Irish Famine, such as nineteenth-century coffin ships transporting Irish emigrants to Canada. It is extremely important to understand from the outset that neither Barry nor I compares or suggests any sort of similarity between the Irish Famine and the Jewish Holocaust.[4] Rather, by juxtaposing imagery from each event, I argue that Barry's placement of these tragedies in conversation with one another defines them as very different, yet similarly avoidable, transnational traumas. Contemporary readers can then interpret Barry's Famine subtext as a critique of Irish non-engagement.

Though critics have noted Barry's use of the Famine in his novel, and others the use of WWII imagery, none has yet consolidated these two observations in order to locate a critique of Irish neutrality in the novel's spectral register – the site where presence and non-presence, generality and specificity overlap; the site where 'interpretation ... transforms the very thing it interprets.'[5] *The Whereabouts of Eneas McNulty*'s carefully crafted ambiguity invites readers to bring various contexts and subtexts into contention with one another in an arena bereft of specificity. In this way, the novel illustrates Jacques Derrida's notion of spectrality as that theoretical lens aids our reinterpretation of the novel.

When read in a specifically Irish context, it is possible to see the novel as rejecting the longstanding nationalist use of the Famine narrative as an argument for separation from England and therefore the wider European community.[6] Indeed, the social and cultural observations of these contemporary novels become even more important as cultural critics continue to wrestle with the implications of postcoloniality in Ireland. Joseph Cleary rightly maintains that '[t]oo often reduced on all sides to a drama between nationalism and its critics, the real novelty of [postcolonial Irish studies] may well lie elsewhere ... From its inception, the colonial process was never simply a matter of the subjugation of this or that territory.'[7] When we uncover Barry's subtextual logic, we can begin to see a wider argument about the intersectionality of political and cultural history emerging in his works. A perfect example comes from the imagery employed by Barry in *The Whereabouts of Eneas McNulty*, which creates a palimpsest upon which the colonial Irish trauma of Famine suffering and emigration is overlaid with the twentieth-century trauma of Jewish displacement and persecution. Barry later provides a theoretical commentary on this spectral imagery in his

2008 novel, *The Secret Scripture*, which I discuss at length later in this chapter.[8]

The Famine subtext in Barry's novel asks readers to imagine an alternative narrative for Ireland that is rooted in trauma, emigration, and dispossession. *Eneas McNulty*, through a juxtaposition of the cultural topographies of World War II and the Great Famine, seek to alter dominant conceptions of Irishness during The Emergency. The traditional understanding of Ireland as provincial, isolated, and disinterested during the mid-twentieth century is undermined in these texts, which illustrate that though Ireland was neutral during the war, Irish individuals were not.[9] By reading the trope of the past-haunted-present in ways that are reminiscent of, yet ideologically divergent from, the way politicians like de Valera have used the specters of Irish history to make arguments for non-engagement, contemporary readers can perceive the presence of Famine (imagery, ideological meaning, political mandate) undergirding these authors' representations of World War II.

Although Ireland had recently won Free-State status within the British Empire (1922), it was still, to borrow a term from critics Derek Attridge and Marjorie Howes, a semi-colonial nation.[10] The Free-State government, therefore, used wartime policy to assert Ireland's sovereignty. Historian Patrick Keating points out, 'A policy of neutrality embeds nationalism and self-determination, that is, the desire of the nation to assert its separate cultural identity, independent statehood, and sovereignty against a hostile international environment.'[11] Intensified by a sense of isolation from the rest of Europe, Ireland's lingering civil-war divisions between pro-treaty and anti-treaty factions reignited – this was one of the conflicts Fianna Fáil hoped to avoid by removing Ireland from the political battlefield.[12] Terrence Brown succinctly explains how non-belligerence during the war years ironically deepened the divide in Irish culture as effectively as joining the Allied Forces might have done:

> The period 1939–1945 ... for most Irish men and women, was not experienced simply as a time when Ireland opted out of history but when her own history and the maintenance of her recently won independence were of primary concern. The cultural isolation of the preceding twenty years was perhaps deepened, but the healing effects on Civil War division in Irish society of a genuine external threat might be set against that in any overall evaluation. For many, the years of the war were simply a continuation of prewar experience, in economically straitened circumstances, with the language, national

sovereignty, religion, and protection of Irish distinctiveness as the dominant topics of intellectual and cultural concern in a society still moulded by its essential conservatism.[13]

Brown maintains that neutrality was a consequence of independence. For de Valera's government, past colonial violence necessitated Ireland's removal from the war so that domestic divisions could begin to heal. Meaning, Ireland would develop into a more ethnically, politically, and religiously homogenous nation – or what the political theorist Benedict Anderson has called the imagined community of the nation. This utopian vision, however, did not materialize. Divisions further deepened due to continuing disputes concerning what a homogenized Ireland should look like.

Éamon de Valera confirmed Ireland's precarious state in a 1939 radio address in which he attempted to justify non-engagement: 'In a sense, the Government of a nation that proposes to be neutral in a war of this sort, has problems much more delicate and much more difficult of solution even than the problems that arise for a belligerent.'[14] In addition to quelling domestic tensions, de Valera saw Irish neutrality during World War II as a way to establish political distance between Ireland and Britain. Elizabeth Bowen called the declaration 'Éire's first *free* self-assertion.'[15] For many of the Irish people, however, neutrality led to a sense of dislocation from the European community. Those seeking to homogenize Irishness tended to view isolation from the war as a productive way to protect and maintain their unique (and now independent) identity; those who resisted homogenization often felt that the policy of neutrality delayed Ireland's economic and social development by removing it from the crucible that solidified a modern, transnational European community.

Surprisingly few mid-century Irish writers published literature about World War II, mainly because of strict censorship laws; however, historical and political writing abounds and is often devoted to contemplating the moral disparity between Irish exceptionalism and Irish cosmopolitanism, exploring what such divisions meant in terms of identity construction in the postwar, globalized landscape. My conception of *exceptionalism* is that of a tendency to remain politically and culturally separate from other nations in order to protect distinctiveness. In mid-century Ireland, exceptionalist ideology implied Republican nationalist reluctance to participate in global affairs as a way of agitating for sovereignty. Conversely, I use the term *cosmopolitanism*, like many scholars of modernism, to delineate an inclusionist doctrine that aims at international affiliation and integration into the global community.[16] In 'The Aesthetics of Irish Neutrality,' Clair Wills points out the heightened awareness of the ethical problem with exceptionalist agendas during times of global crisis. She is particularly critical of de Valera's advocacy for neutrality: 'One of the most striking aspects of [The Emergency], and the most damaging in the long run, was de Valera's refusal to acknowledge – publicly, at any rate – the moral dimensions of the war.'[17] Because of Ireland's difficulties as a colony within the British Empire, which include the Great Irish Famine (c. 1845–1852) and violent military conflicts throughout the early twentieth century, de Valera promoted neutrality as a way of liberating Ireland from the memory of these colonial abuses. Wills maintains, 'He never appeared to see the war in broad terms of European morality but concentrated on Ireland's destiny within a domestic framework far removed from the struggle against Nazi Germany.'[18] De Valera's myopic political vision would continue to haunt Irish writers well after the war had ended.

World War II provided many Irish individuals haunting images from their colonial past. Sebastian Barry, for instance, seems to have opposed de Valerean neutrality based upon their subscription to a different moral logic emerging from the memory of nineteenth-century colonial abuses. We might gain a clearer understanding of Barry's critique of neutrality if we read his texts through the lens of Derridean spectrality – especially Derrida's theory of repetition, which, according to Christopher Prendergast, 'rests, fundamentally, on a critique of entrenched versions of Marxism that locate Justice historically in some material embodiment or other.'[19] That is to say, Derrida reads moments of historical repetition as sites of clarity in which the symbolic status of an event becomes recognizable in a different context. One does not, according to Derrida, discover the meaning of the past; one constructs it from the recognition of the past self as a specter of some present Other.

In *The Whereabouts of Eneas McNulty*, the most profound realizations about the moral problem of Irish neutrality come after a recognition of the similarity between imagery of displaced Jewish Holocaust victims and dispossessed victims of the Irish Famine. For 'What exactly is the difference from one century to the next?' Derrida asks in *Specters of Marx*,

> Is it the difference between a past world – for which the specter represented a coming threat – and a present world, today, where the specter would represent a threat that some would like to believe is past and whose return it would be necessary again, once again in the future, to conjure away?[20]

The crucial point here is that when the past erupts into the present, it is experienced as a *continued* trauma, which highlights the symbolic necessity of the old-in-the-new. For Barry, images of the Holocaust are reminiscent of images from the Famine.

Hauntings – the conflation of temporalities, events, or peoples – are private, singular events. Derrida's specter, therefore, challenges the assumed boundary between self and other, and doing so, provides a way of understanding Barry's conflation of traumatic imagery not as a direct comparison between the Irish Famine and the Jewish Holocaust, but rather as an opportunity to identify the self-as-other. Derrida maintains,

> Before knowing whether one can differentiate between the specter of the past and the specter of the future, of the past present and the future present, one must perhaps ask oneself whether the *spectrality effect* does not consist in undoing this opposition, or even this dialectic, between actual, effective presence and its other.[21]

Here, Derrida's theory of spectrality adds to Sigmund Freud's concept of the Uncanny. Freud argues that the uncanny evokes fear from individuals who are confronted by a repressed belief or memory. His essay contains an explication of the German words *heimlich* and *unheimlich* (known/familiar; unknown/unfamiliar). These terms enjoy a dialectic relationship to the end that Freud can suggest 'the uncanny is that species of the frightening that goes back to what was once well known and had long been familiar,'[22] but has become (through repression) unfamiliarly horrifying. In other words, the uncanny is an unwilled revelation of what has been concealed from both others and the Self. Fear is evoked when the hidden is exposed due to a recognition of the familiar Self in a wholly and unfamiliar Other, or vice versa. Thus, Derrida's specter moves beyond Freud's Gothic uncanny. Consider, for instance, Derek Hand's description of time in the Irish Gothic novel *par excellence*, Charles Maturin's *Melmoth the Wanderer* (1820): 'Here the Gothic has full reign: the supposed progression from past to present collapses into *the nightmarish ever-present* of the eternal wanderer' (emphasis added).²³ In the Gothic mode, hauntings are a thing to be avoided; conversely, in what I'm calling the spectral mode, hauntings are invited.

Derrida's notion of historical spectrality implies active conjuration – whether the conjurer recognizes s/he is calling forth the past, or not. For contemporary Irish writers, active conjuration appears to be a self-conscious narrative technique for representing two historical events simultaneously. What this offers readers of Sebastian Barry's fiction is a way to recognize how *Eneas McNulty* imagines an ethics of Irish engagement based upon a productive haunting of the World War II moment by the Famine past.

Historians and cultural critics have routinely pointed to the nineteenth-century Famine as the origin of Ireland's isolationist policies. 'Pervading all,' Declan Kiberd observes, 'was a sense that [the Famine] was the final betrayal by England.'²⁴ And Roy Foster maintains, 'Post-Famine Ireland, then, entered upon a complex process of social readjustment.'²⁵ The Irish began taking steps towards self-sufficiency that were fueled, writes Foster, by 'an abiding resentment of "England"':²⁶ urbanization, industrialization, and agricultural modernization. In *The Whereabouts of Eneas McNulty*, readers can interpret World War II as the moment at which the specter of Irish isolationism, inaugurated by the Famine, *comes back* in order to be established as an official foreign policy via Fianna Fáil's declaration of neutrality.

When read in an Irish context, the novel can be understood as critiques of the way in which the Republican government employed specters of the past to constitute an isolationist foreign policy during World War II. For politicians, such as de Valera, England's disregard of Ireland's pleas for help during the Famine necessitated a reversal of roles when asked to join the Allied Forces in the fight against Nazi Germany. Barry's text overlaps images of Irish suffering during the Famine years with images of Jewish persecution during World War II. While this overlap of the Famine and World War II serves as a catalyst for humanitarian engagement, and does seem to validate a nationalist reading of the Famine (e.g., these are parallel genocides), both texts transform the very bedrock of nationalist arguments for neutrality into an equally powerful argument against it.

Sebastian Barry was born in 1955 into a Catholic, loyalist family living in postwar Dublin – a city, Peter Lennon observed, in the midst of a deepening depression. Though Ireland had recently been declared a republic in 1949, lingering partition with the North maintained civil-war-era divisions between nationalist and loyalist factions. Barry's own family lineage defies those divisions, which generally assumed Catholics as nationalist sympathizers and Protestants as loyalist, or Unionist, supporters.[27] It is of little wonder, therefore, that his fiction explores the intersections between individual Irishness and constructions of collective identity.

Barry grew up in the 1960s and 1970s when, according to him, 'the wounds of [the civil war] still informed everything about modern Ireland.'[28] The frequency with which Ireland's past troubles manifested in some present European other established for Barry a sense of international camaraderie that serves as a foundation for his fiction. For instance, he recalls that during the 1990s, when he was working on *The Whereabouts of Eneas McNulty*, 'Any news story you might have read about Bosnia is well-echoed in the history of the Irish civil war, things done to each other by people who a year before had been fighting side by side for freedom.'[29] He developed this sense of the-past-haunted-present in his novel, in which mid-century Jewish persecution echoes the history of the Irish Famine. Barry's fiction, therefore, does not simply recapitulate Ireland's domestic disputes; rather it argues for Ireland's participation in the broader European community by juxtaposing international trauma.

In an interview conducted on the occasion of the Man Booker Prize, Sebastian Barry discusses his 2008 shortlisted novel *The Secret Scripture*. At the conclusion of that interview, as an extension of the themes considered in the novel itself, Barry resists narrow nationalist definitions of Irish identity that aimed at exceptionalizing and isolating Ireland:

> I'd say it is important to be defined as an Irish writer. I mean, in a way I long for it, because the sort of Irish I felt myself to be as a child was not, perhaps, considered to be truly Irish. This is a difficulty almost every Irish person has, though, I've found. No one feels they quite fit the adjectives ascribed. So you have to, in a way my work has been an effort to include myself among the adjectives that define Irishness. I don't know after thirty years if I've even got near. But I would be very proud, if this isn't too complicated a thought, to be an Irish writer, if the sort of Irish I am is Irish.[30]

Barry admits that his childhood understanding of Irishness as unproblematically Catholic *and* Loyalist was out of joint with dominant mid-century conceptions of what it meant to be Irish.

This incongruity accounts for his hope 'to include [him]self among the adjectives that define Irishness.' Yet, the final sentence of his response appears contrary to his stated desire of including himself among the traditionally accepted adjectives that define Irishness. He states, 'I would be very proud ... to be an Irish writer, *if the sort of Irish I am is Irish.*'[31] Barry does not seem willing to conform to some fundamental model of Irishness; rather, his work reconceptualizes the model to be more inclusive. His fiction opens up the narrow definitions of Irishness so that Barry's 'sort' might be included. To this end, *The Whereabouts of Eneas McNulty* refuses to conform to Fianna Fáil exceptionalism, instead reversing de Valera's use of Ireland's founding myths to define the nation and its people as exceptional, self-sufficient, and disinterested in European troubles.

In another interview, published along with *The Whereabouts of Eneas McNulty*, Barry calls attention to his novel's international scope. The novel moves beyond the contentious debate surrounding Ireland's foundational mythology in order to embed Irish history within the larger European narrative:

> All our founding myths in Ireland have been based on revolutions and new beginnings and I suppose I wanted to write a book that had as its shadow the reverse of that, a kind of unfounding myth, if there is such a word. An anti-epic with an ambiguous hero. Because we have had in Ireland in recent years to try to accommodate the two traditions, Nationalism and Unionism, in order to create a new ground for a new beginning. Because when we have concentrated on either one or the other, terrible exclusions and murders have taken place, and unendingly.[32]

The Whereabouts of Eneas McNulty employs the Famine as both a founding and unfounding myth all at once – unfounding because it is the record of the unraveling and dismantling of agrarian Gaelic culture, and founding because that trauma formed a touchstone in the creation of a modern Irish nationalist identity. Barry, however, offers a different reading of the Famine as a founding narrative: he wrests it out of the hands of those Republican nationalists who have claimed it for a separatist epic, and uses it to form a relationship between Irish and European victims of hegemonic violence. When read in this way, the novel argues for Ireland's necessary engagement in the global fight against ethnic and religious persecution. Barry imagines an Irish *inter*national identity that is more cosmopolitan than his diametrically opposed ancestors could have ever brought themselves to acknowledge. His archetypal wanderer, Eneas McNulty, is the manifestation of this cosmopolitan Irishness by which Barry criticizes the immorality of non-engagement during World War II.

The Whereabouts of Eneas McNulty is governed by historical repetition, and Barry cues his readers to transnational patterns of recurrence early on in the novel when he juxtaposes two displaced characters – his own Eneas McNulty and Virgil's Æneas: 'The name Eneas ... was taken from the Roman story about a long-suffering and wandering sea-captain.'[33] Barry establishes Eneas McNulty as the specter of Æneas, which prepares readers to recognize other specters and spectral moments within the text.

The name Eneas resonates with two separate yet similar historical moments, and creates a palimpsestic (spectral) relationship between the two heroic figures. Elizabeth Cullingford observes that

> Although his frustrated desire to return home to Sligo aligns him more closely with the Greek Odysseus than with the Roman Aeneas, the protagonist's name ... comes to symbolize his alignment with the British Empire. Aeneas, the Trojan founder of the Roman Empire, was the grandfather of Brutus, the legendary founder of Britain.[34]

Eneas McNulty's name, which aligns him with the British Empire, identifies him as an agent of that Empire to those rebelling against British oppression. Furthermore, his decisions to voluntarily enlist in the British Merchant Navy as a protector of France during World War I, and to take a job in the British-run Royal Irish Constabulary police force (RIC) in Sligo after the war, branded him as a traitor to Republican Ireland.[35] At a time when violent nationalism was on the rise, Eneas's decisions – based on his own ethical drive to protect those who are oppressed – earned him exile under the threat of death.

Like Æneas – who was forced to flee his native Troy after it was sacked by the Spartan army and embark on a prolonged sea-voyage, which ultimately ended with a fortuitous landing in Italy – Eneas McNulty fled Sligo to become a transnational wanderer. Much of the novel charts Eneas's wanderings during the years of World War II. Barry filters images of this war through Eneas's understanding of Irish history to craft a layered articulation of twentieth-century European and nineteenth-century Irish atrocity. Moreover, he presents Eneas as the model Irishman who breaks the rank and file of nationalist politics in order to act ethically. Barry crafts a text that layers images from the Irish Famine over images of the World War II to illustrate the immorality of using politics to justify non-engagement in humanitarian relief efforts.

In her article 'Colonial Policing,' Elizabeth Cullingford argues that resonances of the Famine in *The Whereabouts of Eneas McNulty* are tenuous at best. Questioning Barry's use of the Famine to describe war-torn France, Cullingford observes, 'The analogy with the famine ... which is not mentioned elsewhere in the book except to suggest that those who behaved most cruelly to the starving poor were often the Irish themselves, is in the French context somewhat forced.'[36] Cullingford, however, may have overlooked an important, if slightly obfuscated, reference to the Famine that allows us to read the novel as a scathing attack on Irish non-engagement.

The first instance in which the Famine haunts the landscape of World War II occurs twelve years after Eneas was exiled from Ireland and began coursing herring in the North Atlantic. Eneas's recognition of this historical echo takes place while he is working on 'a broken-lunged one-masted fishing boat,' captained by Simon Cousins and operating out of Grimsby, England.[37] The men sight a ship traveling east towards Europe, returning a cargo of 'dark-clothed and infinitely sober' people to the continent.[38] Though left unnamed in the novel, Cullingford identifies the ship as the MS *St. Louis*, which sailed from Hamburg to Cuba in 1939 under the command of Captain Gustav Schröder, a non-Jewish German and a member of the anti-Nazi Resistance, seeking asylum for over 900 Jewish refugees.[39]

The Jewish exodus from Germany and Austria began in 1933. By 1940, nearly half had escaped to other countries in Western Europe and the Americas, though many ports denied them entry. Captain Schröder of the *St. Louis*, however, refused to return his ship to Germany until all the passengers had been accepted into a free country.[40] In *The Whereabouts of Eneas McNulty*, Eneas observes the *St. Louis* returning from the Americas after being denied port in Cuba, the United States, and Canada. Cullingford maintains, 'The asylum-seekers were eventually accepted by Britain, France, Belgium, and the Netherlands, but except for Britain these countries were swiftly occupied by the Nazis, and 250 of the original 937 passengers died in the Holocaust.'[41] Eneas spots the vessel on its way to England:

> And one time, as they are returning from the distant grounds, bearded and tired, Eneas sees a great ship passing to the south, whose name he

can almost make out, it goes by so close. And it's not a regular ship taking its known course along the allotted lanes, and as such might be classed a danger to a small fishing vessel, if Simon Cousins and Eneas were so inclined to view it. And indeed Simon Cousins looks very black in the face at the sight of it, and Eneas can sympathize with his anger and distress, but is also more simply amazed by the ship.[42]

The ship's irregular course betrays it as a rogue passenger ship, not a fishing vessel or freightliner that would have customarily navigated those waters along strictly plotted lanes. And though Eneas initially misattributes his captain's anger to the ship's disregard for those shipping lanes, readers can understand Cousins's look of distress as his recognition of the people lining the rails as displaced Jews seeking safe-haven from Nazi prison camps.

The passengers' inevitable fate is reflected by their sober expressions:

> [Eneas] can make out clearly lining the rails of the great ship hundreds, maybe thousands of people, looking out silently on every side, port and starboard. And they seem to him dark-clothed and infinitely sober, like prisoners beyond reprieve, like children being ferried far from hearth and happiness.[43]

A closer reading suggests Barry may have employed more Famine imagery than scholars have so far noted. His description of the passengers as 'prisoners beyond reprieve' works on two levels: For Simon Cousins, they are damned by their Jewish ethnicity and forced to flee Europe for the safety of America. On the other hand, Eneas McNulty recognizes their resemblance to Famine victims who were ferried away from their homes by bankrupt landlords that saw the Irish as children for whom Britain could not sufficiently provide. Though Cullingford points out Barry's allusion to the Jewish Diaspora aboard the ship, she dismisses the spectral echo of Irish emigrants that were forced to make a similar journey from Ireland to the Americas aboard nineteenth-century Famine ships. Barry describes the passengers as disinterested, 'as if some other picture is fastened over their eyes, bigger and perhaps terrible.'[44] His use of the word *other* to describe the 'terrible picture' fastened over the eyes of the ship's passengers can oscillate readers between seeing that picture as the Jewish Diaspora and Irish emigrants. Simultaneously viewing this ghost-ship through the lens of both Derridean spectrality and Irish history, we can see an analogous image from both historical moments contaminate this single scene of attempted escape.

When Simon Cousins and Eneas McNulty returned to port, Eneas began questioning his fellow sailors about the vessel. Haunted by the memory of Famine, Eneas asks if it was a ghost ship that they saw. In sea-lore, sighting a phantom ship is a portent of doom. The *St. Louis*, however, might be a ghost ship of a different kind. It does not signal Eneas's doom, for he has already been damned by exile. This ghost ship – not a phantom at all, but a real craft with real passengers – can be read as a *revenant* of nineteenth-century Famine ships.

> [Eneas] is told nothing about it, and has recourse to giving up a sixpence for a decent newspaper, to see if there might be a clue there. And indeed the *Grimsby Echo* can tell him in its dark print and chaste paper that the ship he has seen holds a strange cargo of Jews being returned to Germany, certain there to be imprisoned as enemies of Christ and country. That no port on God's earth would take them, and that they had lain outside Dublin port and been refused and Southampton, and what affects him strongly, not only had crossed the Atlantic to be refused by the President of America himself, but had anchored not far from Galveston in the Gulf of Mexico, the very heartland of emigrants and lonesomeness.[45]

Again, Barry's word choice and imagery asks readers to see a double vision. On the surface, the *St. Louis* literally transports a 'cargo of Jews being returned to Germany' because it has been denied port in Dublin and America. Though Éamon de Valera had closed the ports to the Royal British Navy in 1939, there is no factual evidence that the captain of the *St. Louis* requested asylum for his passengers in Dublin, nor that such a request would have been denied. In fact, Cullingford writes, 'The US Holocaust Memorial Museum (which has recently traced all but two of the passengers), maps the ship's direct return to Antwerp: there was no detour to Dublin.'[46] Barry's fictional depiction of the ship 'lain outside Dublin port' and 'refused entry' can be read, then, as a direct attack on de Valera and Irish neutrality.

On another level, Barry's text recalls two situations that speak directly to the memory of Irish emigration during the Famine years. First, his claim that the Gulf of Mexico is 'the very heartland of emigrants and lonesomeness' references nineteenth-century Famine emigration to New Orleans, as well as post-civil war communities established by displaced Irish laborers on Galveston Island in Texas.[47] He expresses disdain that European Jews fleeing certain death were turned away at the same ports that provided safe-harbor to Irish emigrants a century earlier.

Secondly, the *St. Louis*, having 'crossed the Atlantic to be refused' entry, calls to mind the Famine ships that had lain in quarantine outside Grosse Île in the St. Lawrence River in Canada. During the Famine, mass evictions of penniless tenants from equally destitute estates resulted in mass emigration from Ireland to Grosse Île. Often, landlords paid for their tenants' passage to Britain and North America because sending them overseas on poorly built, and under-provisioned cargo ships (which became known as coffin ships because of the high death rates due to cholera, typhus, dysentery, and malnourishment) was cheaper than providing them with a livable wage in Ireland. Because passage to Canada was far cheaper than to the United States, the majority of Famine ships embarked on the three thousand mile journey to Quebec.

Thirty miles up the St. Lawrence from Quebec was the small quarantine station on Grosse Île. As part of the Cork Multitext Project on Modern Irish History, Donnchadh Ó Corráin contributed an article on migrants and economic refugees from the Famine. He reports specifically on the number of ships refused entry into Canada at Grosse Île:

> On 26 May 1847 there were 30 vessels with 1000 emigrants waiting at Grosse Île; on 31 May 1847 there were 40 vessels waiting, stretched in a line two miles long down the St Lawrence river; there were 1100 cases of fever in the sheds and tents of Grosse Île, short of bedding, sanitation and careers, and just as many ill in ships waiting to disembark; and another 45,000 emigrants were believed to be on the way.[48]

In his recent historical novel, *Star of the Sea* (2002), examined in Chapter 1, Joseph O'Connor depicts Famine ships lying in wait off the North American coast, echoing Ó Corráin's statistics, and reinforcing Barry's employment of the Famine ships as a reminder of the calamity that followed Ireland's disregarded plea for help:

> Forty or more ships are reported to be waiting to go into Canada, lined several miles down the river, with upwards of fifteen thousand emigrants on board, almost all from Ireland; many of these with cholera and typhus and entirely without means to be treated or even quarantined. It is accounted that on some vessels not a single man, woman or child is without affliction, neither passengers nor crew. On two vessels, it is said, all have died: every last human soul on board. Nothing less than an undiminished calamity may be expected now, with enormous loss of life.[49]

Eneas's spectral vision, the overlapping and amalgamation in his mind of ships carrying human cargo of displaced Irish and Jewish emigrants, allows Barry to simultaneously present the Jewish Diaspora and Irish emigration during the Famine – what Edward Brennan and Terry Eagleton have called the Irish holocaust.

In 1989, Brennan, Ireland's ambassador to Canada, remarked, 'The Great Famine was Ireland's holocaust, and the slow-sailing vessels ... became coffin ships in which many would-be emigrants died a lingering and painful death.'[50] Later, in 1995, Terry Eagleton contends, 'The [Famine] strains at the limits of the articulable, and is truly in this sense the Irish Auschwitz.'[51] Brennan's and Eagleton's equation of the Famine with the Holocaust risks gross inaccuracy and insensitivity. It is useful, however, to point out that such politically charged analogies have been used to indict the British for Irish suffering during the nineteenth century. It is equally important to note that Barry does not equate the two. Rather, via a spectral framework, his novel draws upon two historical moments at once. That is, Barry brings the Famine and the Holocaust into the same historical space to illustrate the dangers of inaction and to argue that any human suffering is unacceptable. His attack on Irish non-engagement in World War II becomes explicit following Eneas's identification of the Jewish passengers aboard the *St. Louis* as a 'cargo of hated people,' much like the Famine victims of the nineteenth century – and like Eneas himself:

> As a hated man Eneas feels the force of their useless journey. And he thinks of that fella De Valera, now king of Ireland, piously refusing the ship entry, and it makes a racket in his noggin. Oh why exactly he could not say, but surely, he hopes surely, there is a host of other men and women who feel the same storm of disquiet and anger he does, in the mottled lean-to by the Captain's house. And he thinks the sighting of the ship has been a thing of terror lent to him, and he would have taken them all in the Captain's ship like shining herring if he had known, impossible though it would have been. For what is the world without rescue, but a wasteland and a worthless peril?[52]

For Barry, de Valera's refusal to admit the *St. Louis* entry into Dublin illustrates the inhumanity of Ireland's isolation from Europe during the war. Cullingford observes, 'De Valera's asylum policy, under which fewer than seventy Jews were admitted to Ireland during the Emergency, certainly could not be construed as generous ..., and in the novel his refusal to rescue these homeless souls weighs heavily against him.'[53] This spectral conjuring of Famine ships from Ireland's colonial past allows Barry to explore what it meant to be Irish during The Emergency; and through this unequivocal critique of World War II neutrality, he argues for a new use of the Famine as a catalyst for Irish humanitarian efforts in similar contemporary crisis.

Barry presents Eneas McNulty as the new global citizen – after Eneas sees the *St. Louis* and learns the fate of its passengers, he is motivated to reenlist in the British Army despite Ireland's neutrality and his own exile for enlisting with the British during World War I. Barry's novel depends upon resonances of the Famine in the Irish collective consciousness to argue against the immorality of non-engagement. In fact, the Famine continues to pervade Barry's narration of Eneas's entire experience in war-torn France to highlight the ethical justification for his reenlistment.

The second textual revisitation of the Famine upon the landscape of World War II occurs after Eneas's landing at Dunkirk, France. As a member of the British Army 'C' Company, he 'is sent with his new comrades to rescue France from the threat of Hitler.'[54] Barry's description of France, and its displaced citizens, is again filtered through Eneas's Irish perspective of the war as an echo of the Famine:

> [Eneas and his company] pass through districts livid with fear and death, and through columns of lost people they pass, men and women without homes and deep in rags and, he supposes, an echo and a remembering icon of those perished souls along the Irish seaboards a hundred years before, when the hag of Famine showed her dark face and dripping bones.[55]

These displaced French citizens call to mind evicted Irish tenants during the Famine, much like the Jewish exiles aboard the *St. Louis* called to mind Irish emigrants: they are starving, dislocated, suffering from fever, and without possessions.

Neutrality, though designed to heal and console the Irish nation, did neither of these things for Ireland. Nor did that policy aid Ireland's standing within the European community. Barry sees a continuum between the suffering of Irish Famine victims and victims of Occupied France, and refuses de Valera's version of history that cites Irish trauma endured during the Famine as reason for isolation. He recognizes, in France, traces of the Irish troubles that originated from mismanagement of the potato blight, and therefore

Barry separates Eneas from his company during a bombardment at the beach and enlists him to help recover a failing French vineyard as a way of illustrating that violent military action was not the only option for engagement in the war.

The Whereabouts of Eneas McNulty draws upon the past as a call to action justified by the necessity of aiding those in need of help despite perceived political consequences. To illustrate this necessity, Barry introduces Jean, a French winemaker, who pleads with Eneas to help him mend his broken vineyard.[56] Haunted by the specter of Famine in Ireland, Eneas delays returning to his company in order to aid Jean:

> He is willing to fight the fight of clay and seed as long as he is allowed. To be the strange champion of the sorrow-beleaguered farmer ... And Eneas feels his own father's hunger for the health of flowers and plants in the old garden in Finisklin in his own blood now, giving a strength to his arms that is both tireless and tender.[57]

Barry's language ('the sorrow-beleaguered farmer') and his reference to generational hunger stretching back to his father, lays the image of the potato blight in Ireland over the image of Jean's barren vineyard. Eneas's 'tireless and tender' strength seems to stem from the memory of long-lasting consequences of the Famine. Because the Irish did not receive sufficient aid to survive the potato blight, Eneas aids Jean so that he does not experience similar tragedy.

Ultimately, Eneas's involvement in World War II complicates the assumption that participation in the war meant engaging in combat alongside the British (though Eneas did enlist with combat in mind), and that neutrality meant refraining from even acknowledging that there was a conflict. Looking back on Eneas's service in the British army, the novel's narrator observes, 'He begins to feel a certain pride for all he has done as a soldier. What better thing than to spruce a French farm, better than maiming and killing he hopes.'[58] Barry argues for a non-violent engagement in humanitarian crises by showing readers Eneas's effectiveness in Jean's fields during the war.

Barry's novel is the product of a haunting in which he allows Ireland's colonial past to inform and influence his sense of personal responsibility during transnational conflict. Recognizing Sebastian Barry's use of this spectral effect as a critique of Irish neutrality, one can uncover a political mandate urging for humanitarian efforts if not military action – 'The world without rescue [is] but a wasteland and a worthless peril.'[59]

Architects of national identity – historians, politicians, and artists alike – have always criticized, via reinvention, their predecessors, using revised national myths to expose their predecessors' particular manipulations of history as falsified. Historians and artists often reshape the past to escape the present, but they can also evoke the past (in its various and varied articulations) to better understand the present from which they hope to escape. At the turn of the twenty-first century, Sebastian Barry's fiction reinterprets and transforms the Irish historical narrative to help shape contemporary Ireland's dramatically changing political, economic, and social circumstances. In *The Secret Scripture*, which we can read as a sequel to and commentary on *The Whereabouts of Eneas McNulty*, Barry more directly engages with the ways in which Irish history has been falsified, inviting readers to see Irish historical revisionism not as a corrective measure but as a challenge to the possibility of ever presenting an accurate historical record.

The Secret Scripture is the product of overlapping two invented personal records: Roseanne McNulty/Clear's 'Testimony of Herself,' written in her one hundredth year and hidden beneath the floorboards of her room in the Roscommon Regional Mental Hospital; and Dr. Grene's 'Commonplace Book,' in which he records his psychiatric evaluations of Roseanne as well as his analysis of the collected papers of a local parish priest that contradict Roseanne's testimony. The overlap and interplay between these embedded texts lays the foundation for a single narrative (the novel) that exposes the common pitfalls of historical representation: misremembering, misperceiving, and the 'necessary falsification' of the past.

Near the novel's close, Roseanne contemplates the nature of the autobiographical document she has constructed, and its relationship to Ireland's historical narrative:

> I am beginning to wonder strongly what is the nature of history. Is it only memory in decent sentences, and if so, how reliable is it? I would suggest, not very. And that therefore most truth and fact offered by these syntactical means is treacherous and unreliable. And yet I recognize that we live our lives, and even keep our sanity, by the lights of this treachery and this unreliability, just as we build our love of country on these paper worlds of misapprehension and untruth. Perhaps this is our nature, and perhaps unaccountably it is part of our glory as a creature, that we can build our best and most permanent buildings on foundations of utter dust.[60]

Roseanne's conclusion that history (individual and national) is useful precisely because it is 'treacherous and unreliable' proposes the transformation of Ireland's conservative mythology for a more ambiguous national identity in the present. At stake in such transformation is a more egalitarian, post-national identity compatible with an increasingly globalized economy and culture.

The Secret Scripture, therefore, is entirely about reinvention. For, as Roseanne writes in her secret scripture, 'History as far as I can see is not the arrangement of what happens, in sequence and in truth, but a fabulous arrangement of surmises and guesses held up as a banner against the assault of withering truth.'[61] Roseanne's recognition of historical narrative as a fiction ('misapprehension and untruth') constructed of dust makes historical instability explicit. Her use of the word dust recalls the earlier observation of John Kane, Roscommon's orderly, concerning the permanence of dust in Roseanne's room: 'I sweep it every day and there is always dust, by God there is, ancient dust. Not new dust, never new dust.'[62] Taking the two comments together illustrates Barry's understanding of historical repetition: history, like dust, is something that is always to come or comes back, via the phenomena of spectral recurrence. In *Dust: The Archive and Cultural History* (2002), Carolyn Steedman also characterizes the phenomena of recurrence in terms of dust – a substance which, in her reading, is more than just a physical remnant; it is also the intentional act of attempting to remove from, or add to, the always already present:

> 'Dust' is one of those curious words that in its verb form, bifurcates in meaning, performs an action of perfect circularity, and arrives to denote its very opposite. If you 'dust,' you can remove something, or you can put something there. Viz.: you cleanse a place – usually a room in a house – *of* dust, in a meaning that seems to have been established at the same time as that of its opposite action, which is to sprinkle something with a small portion of powdery matter, as in 'to make dusty' (1530), or later, 'to strew as dust' (1790).[63]

Dust is always already present. It returns, but in actuality, it never went away – which is what makes the specter (and dust) a useful metaphor for Irish cultural myths that can never be discarded, only transformed. Steedman explains, 'This is what Dust is about; this is what Dust *is*: what it means and what it is … It is about circularity, the impossibility of things disappearing, or going away, or being gone. Nothing *can be* destroyed.'[64] So, if one dusts (that is, cleans) one space, that dust (noun) is transferred to a new space, which is dusted (that is, made dusty). *The Secret Scripture* asks us to rethink the cultural significance of historical narration so susceptible to transformation, particularly histories that may have been deliberately falsified.

In this way, Barry has taken on the dual role of novelist and historiographer: he explores, by means of one invented life, the overt constructedness of Ireland's variegated and undead past. Barry invites his readers to interpret his most recent novel not merely as an esthetic object, but also as a theory concerning the esthetics of historical representation and identity construction. His characters write in neat aphorisms about the (re)constructedness of historical narratives, prompting readers to question, as does Dr. Grene, 'the written word [which] assumes authority but...may not have it.'[65] Barry establishes his novel's political significance via the intersection between Roseanne's personal history and an Ireland beleaguered by the perpetually open wounds of colonial trauma and revolution. *The Secret Scripture* focuses on the unchecked authority by which the Irish Catholic Church rules over the haunted conscience of Irish individuals for much of the twentieth century. Roseanne recalls,

> I seemed to be 'haunted' by a figure that sometimes appeared, seemed to appear, at the far edges of where I was, in what might have been a black suit, and what might have been a brown hat, but even when I gathered my courage and walked towards him, the few times I thought I saw him, he instantly disappeared. But such matters were the nature of those days.[66]

This haunting figure turns out to be the appropriately named Father Gaunt, a corrupt Catholic priest, who launches a campaign of discrimination against Roseanne and her Presbyterian father. Fr. Gaunt personifies the specter haunting much of Ireland during the twentieth century. It was the idea behind Catholic essentialism – that to be Irish meant *to be* Catholic and *not to be* Presbyterian, or even Protestant – which lead to Fr. Gaunt's false accusation that Roseanne was conducting an extramarital affair – much like the accusation Richard Talbot levels at his wife Marianne in *My Dream of You*. Fr. Gaunt's sort of Catholic superiority also led (in part and on a larger scale) to Irish insularity and therefore economic stagnation during the World Wars and after.[67]

Fr. Gaunt encounters Roseanne one day while she is speaking to an old acquaintance, John Lavelle, alone in a remote area, and he incorrectly assumes they are having an affair. Without allowing Roseanne to explain how they had innocently happened upon each other, Fr. Gaunt charges her with nymphomania and annuls her marriage to Tom McNulty (brother of Eneas McNulty). The McNultys subsequently exile her to a small shack out on Strandhill where she is to live in solitude.

Early on in the novel, Roseanne writes of her father (and by extension of herself), 'As a Presbyterian he might be thought to have no place in the Irish story.'[68] Yet, as Dr. Grene later attests, Roseanne's story *is* Ireland's story: 'Of course Roseanne's life spans everything, she is as much as we can know of our world, the last hundred years of it. She should be a place of pilgrimage and a national icon. But she lives nowhere and is nothing. She has no family and almost no nation.'[69] This passage is illustrative of *The Secret Scripture*'s engagement with Irish identity construction in the post-Catholic era. The novel does not simply recount a typical narrative of dispossession, it also works to transform Irishness into an identity of dispossession – one built upon 'foundations of utter dust.' Dr. Grene describes Roseanne as simultaneously 'nowhere,' 'nothing' *and* 'everything,' 'a national icon.' In other words she is spectral, both absent and present. By presenting Roseanne's uncertain history as reflective of Irish history, *The Secret Scripture* refocuses the way we look at Ireland's historical narrative (its intentional and unintentional omissions and misrepresentations) and the writers who produce it.

The Secret Scripture makes clear not only that national history and identity are malleable, but also highlights the manner in which Irish artists play an active role in shaping the national narrative and collective identity in fiction. We see this shaping take place in the narratives of Roseanne and Fr. Gaunt; both operate as metatextual fictions that engage with historical representation. Barry's novel illustrates the way in which these individuals can transform Roseanne's personal history through imaginative reinventions of the past: As Roseanne ruminates on her own past she becomes a specter of herself, dispossessed of both individual and national identity. She wonders if she could somehow warn herself against going on the walk that led to her John Lavelle: 'It is all so long ago and I am still afraid ... Roseanne, Roseanne, if I called to you now, my own self calling to my own self, would you hear me? And if you could hear me, would you heed me?'[70] We encounter, then, a character that haunts herself, or at least hopes for the possibility of transforming her own past via haunting.

Roseanne's desire to haunt, or to be haunted (even by her own self), promotes 'haunting' as potentially productive. She cannot actually go back in time to warn herself about the fateful meeting with Lavelle, but she can rewrite the events in her autobiography as she pleases: her version becomes truth, in a way, through her act of writing paired with Dr. Grene's act of interpretation. In the end, Dr. Grene gets the final word – Fr. Gaunt and Roseanne both having died. But one might also hear Barry's own voice in Dr. Grene's assessment of these two authors: 'I believe [Fr. Gaunt and Roseanne] have written not so much wrongful histories, or even competing histories, but both in their human way quite truthful, and that from both of them can be implied useful truths above and beyond the actual verity of the "facts."'[71] Sebastian Barry has made a similar declaration about the usefulness of uncertainty in the act of (re)crafting history. When asked, in an interview about the nature of memory and storytelling, if truth is achievable, Barry answered definitively, 'No, hardly, but what might be achievable is a preference for one sort of misapprehension over another, for gentleness over cruelty, no matter how backed up with fact, for mercy over torture, etc.'[72] Barry is clearly aware of the social significance of his fiction. Neither *The Whereabouts of Eneas McNulty* nor *The Secret Scripture* trades one misapprehension of history for another. Rather, each illustrates how competing histories might be used in collaboration to reinscribe the intricacies and contradictions and tragedies of revolutionary Ireland that have been necessarily falsified. For Barry, reinventing historical discourse, which always exists as necessary falsifications of the past, is an explicitly political act.

Notes

1. Peter Lennon, *Rocky Road to Dublin*. 1967 (London: BBC, 2006) DVD.
2. De Valera also acted as his own minister for external affairs.
3. A popular peasant adage maintains, 'God sent the potato-blight, but the English caused the Famine' (quoted in Declan Kiberd, *Inventing Ireland: The Literature of the Modern Nation*. [Cambridge, MA: Harvard University Press, 1997], p. 21).
4. The Nazis actively destroyed a group of people and made it their national mission to commit genocide. The Famine, it can be argued, arose from incompetence, malaise, and unresponsiveness. The Nazis

were interested in the active destruction and annihilation of an entire people; the British were simply shrugging their shoulders. One nation set up death camps to murder people by the trainload, the other let a natural disaster run its course.
5 Jacques Derrida, *Specters of Marx*. 1993. Trans. Peggy Kamuf (New York: Routledge Classics, 2006), p. 63.
6 For instance, Lieutenant Colonel John P. Dugan recalls, 'We were anti-British rather than pro-German.' To which Commandant Owen Quinn adds, 'We must emphasize this to you, though; certainly we knew nothing about the concentration camps in Germany' (Qtd. in Benjamin Grob-Fitzgibbon, *The Irish Experience During the Second World War: An Oral History* [Dublin: Irish Academic Press, 2004], p. 201).
7 Joe Cleary, *Outrageous Fortune: Capital and Culture in Modern Ireland*. Field Day Files I. Eds. Seamus Deane and Brendán Mac Suibhne (Dublin: Field Day Publications, 2007), pp. 44–45.
8 *The Secret Scripture* can be read as a supplement to *The Whereabouts of Eneas McNulty*, as the novel's protagonist Roseanne Clear-McNulty was a minor character in the earlier novel. In addition to being short-listed for the Booker Prize, *The Secret Scripture* won the 2008 Costa Book of the Year and the James Tait Black Prize for fiction (2009).
9 In his article 'Unneutral Neutral Éire' (1946), R.M. Smyllie observed, 'Éire was nonbelligerent – that is to say, she was not officially concerned in the war, although so many of her children served the Allied cause', 324.
10 See Derek Attridge and Marjorie Howes. *Semicolonial Joyce* (Cambridge: Cambridge University Press, 2000). Print.
11 Patrick Keating, *A Singular Stance: Irish Neutrality in the 1980s* (Dublin: Institute of Public Administration, 1984), p. 7.
12 Following the War of Independence (1919–1921), Michael Collins, Arthur Griffith and others met with Representatives of the British government, led by David Lloyd George, to negotiate the Anglo-Irish Treaty (or The Articles of Agreement for a Treaty Between Great Britain and Ireland). Under the treaty, Ireland was to become a self-governed dominion of the British Empire. The failure to establish Ireland as a sovereign republic caused a split in The Dáil, which resulted in civil-war (1922–1923) fought between two opposing groups of Irish nationalists: Free-State Pro-Treaty faction and the Republican Anti-Treaty opposition.
13 Terrence Brown, *Ireland: A Social and Cultural history 1922–2002* (London: Harper Perennial, 2004), p. 168.
14 Eamon de Valera, *Ireland's Stand: Being a Selection of the Speeches of Eamon De Valera During the War (1939–1945)*. 2nd edn (Dublin: M.H. Gill and Son, LTD., 1946), p. 8.

15 Elizabeth Bowen, qtd. in Claire Wills, 'The Aesthetics of Irish Neutrality During the Second World War.' *boundary 2: An International Journal of Literature and Culture* 31.1 (2004): 121.
16 Bruce Robbins, *Secular Vocations: Intellectuals, Professionalism, Culture* (London: Verso, 1983); and Amanda Anderson, *The Power of Distance: Cosmopolitanism and the Cultivation of Detachment* (Princeton, NJ: Princeton University Press, 2001).
17 Wills, 'The Aesthetics of Irish Neutrality During the Second World War,' 123.
18 Wills, 'The Aesthetics of Irish Neutrality During the Second World War,' 123.
19 Christopher Prendergast, 'Derrida's Hamlet.' *SubStance* 34.1 (2005): 46.
20 Derrida, *Spectres of Marx*, p. 48.
21 Derrida, *Spectres of Marx*, p. 48. Derrida's theory of spectral repetition builds upon his earlier advocation of the tout autre in *The Gift of Death* (1991). His assertion that 'every other is completely or wholly other' because every 'other' is private, or secret, is actually the basis for human similarity. Every individual is similarly singular. See Peter Goldman's 'Christian Mystery and Responsibility: Gnosticism in Derrida's *The Gift of Death.*' *Anthropoetics* 4.1 (1998) in which he explains, 'Humans are singular in that each has a private and "secret" interior scene of representation (the memory or imagination), but humans are also similar for exactly the same reason' (10).
22 Sigmund Freud, *The Uncanny*. Trans. David McLintock (New York: Penguin Classics, 2003), p. 124.
23 Derek Hand, *A History of the Irish Novel* (Cambridge: Cambridge University Press, 2011), p. 82.
24 Declan Kiberd, *Inventing Ireland: The Literature of the Modern Nation* (Cambridge, MA: Harvard University Press, 1997), p. 21.
25 R.F. Foster, *Modern Ireland: 1600–1972* (London: Penguin, 1988), p. 341.
26 Foster, *Modern Ireland*, p. 342.
27 Barry's maternal great-grandfather belonged to the British-run Dublin Metropolitan Police force (and served as the inspiration for Thomas Dunne in Barry's play, *The Steward of Christendom*), and his maternal grandfather belonged to the British Army Corps of Royal Engineers. Also, family legend surrounding his great-uncle Charlie was the inspiration for Eneas McNulty: see Sebastian Barry, 'A Conversation with Sebastian Barry,' 'Afterword.' *The Whereabouts of Eneas McNulty*. Sebastian Barry. (New York: Penguin, 1998), p. 7.
28 Barry, 'A Conversation,' p. 8.
29 Barry, 'A Conversation,' pp. 8–9.
30 Sebastian Barry, 'Man Booker Interview.' *The Man Booker Prize for Fiction YouTube Channel*. 15 October 2008. www.youtube.com/user/

TheManBookerPrize. 8 December 2010.
31 Barry, 'Man Booker Interview.'
32 Barry, 'A Conversation,' p. 6.
33 Barry, *The Whereabouts of Eneas McNulty*, 27.
34 Elizabeth Cullingford, 'Colonial Policing: The Steward of Christendom and The Whereabouts of Eneas McNulty.' *Éire-Ireland: A Journal of Irish Studies* 39.3–4 (2004): 32.
35 Barry comments, 'The actual story of Eneas, as it unfolded, consistently surprised me. It interested me greatly that he was on the "wrong" side of official history and yet might be an innocent man, enduring the punishments and exclusions of the guilty … It was an act of foolishness and shortsightedness on Eneas's part to join the police when he did, but at the same time the police had provided a refuge and a living for many an Irish family. All such have been demonized by official history' ('A Conversation,' p. 9).
36 Cullingford, 'Colonial Policing,' pp. 31–32.
37 Barry, *The Whereabouts of Eneas McNulty*, 128.
38 Barry, *The Whereabouts of Eneas McNulty*, 131.
39 For further reading see Irwin F. Gellman, 'The *St. Louis* Tragedy,' *American Jewish Historical Quarterly* 61.2 (1971): 144–157. Print; Barry J. Konovitch, 'The Fiftieth Anniversary of the *St. Louis*: What Really Happened,' *American Jewish History* 79.2 (1989–1990): 203–210. Print; Sarah A. Ogilvie and Scott Miller. *Refuge Denied: The St. Louis Passengers and the Holocaust*. (Madison, WI: University of Wisconsin Press), 2006. Print; *The Double Crossing: The Voyage of the St. Louis* (Holocaust Memorial Foundation of Illinois and Loyola University of Chicago. Distributed by Ergo Media, Inc., Teaneck, NJ, 1992). DVD; *Sea Tales: The Doomed Voyage of the St. Louis* (Distributed by A & E Home Video, New York, NY, 1996). DVD; *The Voyage of the St. Louis* (Distributed by Galafilm, Inc., Montreal, Canada, 1995). DVD; *Voyage of the Damned* (Distributed by Avid Home Entertainment, Van Nuys, CA, 1992). DVD.
40 *Voyage of the St. Louis*. United States Holocaust Memorial Museum. n.d. www.ushmm.org. 8 October 2009.
41 Cullingford, 'Colonial Policing,' p. 30. Additionally, Sarah Ogilvie and Scott Miller report, 'Of the 620 St. Louis passengers who returned to continental Europe, we determined that eighty-seven were able to emigrate before Germany invaded Western Europe on May 10, 1940. Two hundred and fifty-four passengers in Belgium, France and the Netherlands after that date died during the Holocaust. Most of these people were murdered in the killing centers of Auschwitz and Sobibór; the rest died in internment camps, in hiding or attempting to evade the Nazis. Three hundred sixty-five of the 620 passengers who returned to continental Europe survived the war' (*Refuge Denied*, pp. 174–175).

42 Barry, *The Whereabouts of Eneas McNulty*, 131.
43 Barry, *The Whereabouts of Eneas McNulty*, 131.
44 Barry, *The Whereabouts of Eneas McNulty*, 131.
45 Barry, *The Whereabouts of Eneas McNulty*, 132.
46 Cullingford, 'Colonial Policing,' p. 31.
47 A number of reports about the Irish in New Orleans maintain that 'As New Orleans was a thriving port city, the itineraries of many boats ended [t]here and the passengers simply stayed. In addition, Irish immigrants often found cheap passage to New Orleans because after cotton ships unloaded their cargo in Liverpool, captains needed to load their holds up with human ballast for the return trip' (Niehaus, *Irish in New Orleans*). Additionally, 'New Orleans has always held an appeal to the Irish due to its Catholic traditions and because French and Spanish residents also harbored anti-British sentiments' (Niehaus, *Irish in New Orleans*). The Irish presence in Galveston is also well documented. Susan Hardwick claims, 'The Irish came into Galveston on trains from the north in the years after the Civil War ... [And] in 1874, the first Ancient Order of the Hibernians division was organized in Galveston, no doubt because "the city's populace included Hibernians who had moved from Boston and Philadelphia areas, and most of the dock workers were of Irish birth"' (74–75). For additional information on the Irish in New Orleans and Galveston, see: Joseph Beine, 'Ships Arriving at the Port of New Orleans from Belfast, Liverpool and Londonderry.' (NARA Microfilm. May 2000). Web. 16 December 2009; John Finn. *New Orleans Irish: Famine Exiles*. (Front Royal, VA: Holy Family Church Press, 1997); John Brendan Flannery. *The Irish Texans* (San Antonio, TX: Institute for Texan Cultures, 1995); Susan Wiley Hardwick. *Mythic Galveston* (Baltimore, MD: Johns Hopkins University Press, 2002); Deirdre M. Mageean. 'Emigration from Irish Ports.' *Journal of American Ethnic History* 13.1 (1993): 6–30; Earl F. Niehaus. *The Irish in New Orleans, 1800–1860* (Baton Rouge, LA: Louisiana State University Press, 1965); Cath Madden Trindle. *Irish Emigration*. 2008. Web. 16 December 2009.
48 Donnchadh Ó Corráin. 'Emancipation, Famine & Religion: Ireland Under the Union, 1815–1870.' *Multi-text Project in Irish History*. 23 January 2006. multitext.ucc.ie/d/Emancipation. 10 October 2009. p. 14.
49 O'Connor, *Star of the Sea*, 254–255.
50 Michael Quigley, 'Grosse Île: Canada's Famine Memorial.' *The Great Famine and the Irish Diaspora in America*. Ed. Arthur Gribben (Amherst: University of Massachusetts Press, 1999), p. 151.
51 Terry Eagleton, *Heathcliff and the Great Hunger* (London: Verso, 1995), p. 13.
52 Barry, *The Whereabouts of Eneas McNulty*, 132–133.

53 Cullingford, 'Colonial Policing,' p. 132.
54 Barry, *The Whereabouts of Eneas McNulty*, 135.
55 Barry, *The Whereabouts of Eneas McNulty*, 135.
56 Jean claims, 'I need friend, *brother*, son, father' (emphasis added 146). His request for Eneas to act as his brother calls to mind an illustration from the 17 October 1846 issue of *Punch* magazine titled 'Union is Strength.' The caption to Richard Doyle's illustration reads, 'John Bull: "Here are a few things to go on with, *Brother*, and I'll soon put you in a way to earn your own living"' (*Punch Cartoons*, emphasis added). While this illustration argues that the English government did offer aid to Ireland (John Bull offers the family of four a small basket of bread), Doyle's illustration depicts the sorrow-beleaguered farmer with his hands covering his face in shame. Eneas's refusal to allow Jean to suffer a similar fate is directly related to his recognition of 1840s Ireland in 1940s France.
57 Barry, *The Whereabouts of Eneas McNulty*, 150–151.
58 Barry, *The Whereabouts of Eneas McNulty*, 157.
59 Barry, *The Whereabouts of Eneas McNulty*, 133.
60 Sebastian Barry, *The Secret Scripture* (New York: Viking, 2008), p. 293.
61 Barry, *The Secret Scripture*, 55.
62 Barry, *The Secret Scripture*, 32.
63 Carolyn Steedman. *Dust: The Archive and Cultural History* (New Brunswick, NJ: Rutgers University Press, 2001), p. 160.
64 Steedman, *Dust*, p. 164.
65 Barry, *The Secret Scripture*, 135.
66 Barry, *The Secret Scripture*, 233.
67 Brown, *Ireland: A Social and Cultural History*, pp.109–184.
68 Barry, *The Secret Scripture*, 36.
69 Barry, *The Secret Scripture*, 183.
70 Barry, *The Secret Scripture*, 187.
71 Barry, *The Secret Scripture*, 280.
72 Barry, 'A Conversation.'

Part II
Revolution

3

Ancient warriors, modern sexualities: Easter 1916 and the advent of post-Catholic Ireland

It is not surprising that the political implications of the 1916 Easter uprising against British rule in Ireland heavily overshadow the rebellion's pressing social elements.[1] Overwhelmingly, both nationalist and loyalist histories focus primarily on the struggle for independence, deemphasizing the concurrent social pursuits of class equality, gender equality and sexual freedom. At the end of the twentieth century, in the wake of the peace process in Northern Ireland and economic stability across the island, contemporary Irish fiction writers began re-mythologizing the Republican narrative of the Easter Rising. In this chapter, I explore contemporary fictional reconstructions of the Rising that convoke the intersections between numerous, and often overshadowed, social discourses central to the rebellion.

As a by-product of independence, certain aspects of the rebellion have been buried; namely, the revolutionary sexual politics which co-championed the Rising. This is largely because Catholicism does not approve of revolutionary sexual politics. Ironically, however, in the 1970s, the public became aware that Catholic priests had been using their office to sexually abuse women and children, thereby opening up room for a less censored view of the intersecting social agendas that comprised the Rising. A central part of the revolution registered at the time was a revolution of sexual and gender politics. This chapter will look at two novels that offer an alternative Rising narrative to replace the prominent Catholic nationalist rendering of that event: Roddy Doyle's *A Star Called Henry* (1999) and Jamie O'Neill's *At Swim, Two Boys* (2001).

Both novels excavate feminist and queer discourses that have been hidden behind the façade of Ireland's conservative national narrative by imagining such narratives at the time of the Easter Rising. Reading both novels through the lens of spectrality – a narrative mode that conflates temporalities, events, or peoples – and in the context of Ireland's waning conservatism at the end of the twentieth century, offers us a clearer notion of how both texts reconsider the founding mythology of modern Irish culture. *At Swim, Two Boys* places gay lovers and ideals of homosexuality at the absolute core of the Rising, thereby implying the revolutionary notion that Ireland was in fact founded by and upon the principles of queer politics. *A Star Called Henry*, while certainly invested in acknowledging class divisions in early twentieth-century Dublin, also imagines feminist characters as crucial participants in the rebellion.

I aim to highlight the ways in which Doyle and O'Neill reintegrate and intersect these previously suppressed social discourses into representations of the Easter Rising. They do so at a time when Irish historians and cultural critics were also beginning to look back at the immediate post-Rising environment that produced sterilized histories of the event. For instance, Margot Gayle Backus maintains, 'This purging of social issues ... was enabled through the promotion of spectacularly martyred males ... as screen figures obscuring the discourses of socialism, feminism and sexual liberation within post-Rising Irish nationalism.'[2] Fervent nationalists had obscured or altogether erased the intersectionality of nationalism, feminism, socialism, and sexual liberation from Ireland's historical narrative.[3] Irish historian Brian Lewis observes,

> The Irish nationalism associated with the Easter Rising had elements of a genuine human emancipatory rhetoric, especially with the involvement of the socialist leader, James Connolly, but overwhelmingly its ethos was that of De Valera and Patrick Pearse (notwithstanding the latter's own sublimated homosexuality), informed by a heavily conservative, family-based, agrarian Catholicism. The new Ireland did not have room for sexual deviants.[4]

As Lewis's parenthetical aside suggests, Pádraig Pearse's latent pedophilia has often been overshadowed by his nationalist politics and martyrdom, which established him as a hero of Catholic Ireland.[5] This is not an isolated issue. For instance, Eoin Duffy's (1892–1944) homosexuality is similarly overlooked because of his position as a figurehead of the Republican nationalist movement – he was chief of staff of the Irish Republican Army (IRA) in 1922 and later elected the first president of Fine Gael.

Furthermore, the importance of Kathleen Lynn (1874–1955), a lesbian captain in the Irish Citizen Army during the Easter Rising, is almost completely written out of the 1916 narrative despite her crucial role in the rebellion: 'Lynn was active at City Hall, and when the leader there – Sean Connolly – was killed, she and the bisexual Helena Moloney (an Abbey Theater actress) took over as the senior officers.'[6] Margot Backus points out that these and other 'inconvenient' female rebels were marginalized and erased from the archives because they did not fit neatly into the patriarchal Catholic-nationalist hegemony:

> Constance Markievicz, lieutenant in Connolly's socialist Irish Citizen Army and dedicated suffragist, famously observed that 'three great movements' – nationalism, feminism, and socialist trade unionism – were complexly intersecting in Ireland during the time of the Rising. As [David] Lloyd concedes, 'only one of [them] could be subsumed in the declaration of independence of 1916 and the struggle for autonomous state institutions'; nonetheless, all these struggles were unquestionably represented among those who rose on Easter Monday.[7]

As Backus makes clear, the Irish Catholic Church had held firm authority over Irish life and politics from the time of the religious renaissance that followed Catholic emancipation in 1829.[8] For most Irish republican nationalists, therefore, the quest for sovereignty was a decidedly Catholic pursuit.

According to Irish historical novelist John Banville,

> The rising was a Catholic affair, from top to bottom, and as such was unique in the annals of Irish revolutionism ... With certain exceptions, [James] Connolly among them, the 1916 leaders evinced an almost sickly level of Catholic piety, which after the Rising helped to consolidate their reputations among the previously sceptical [sic] Catholic population.[9]

Following Ireland's bloody but successful campaign for independence at the start of the twentieth century, political leaders pledged to govern in accordance with Catholic dogma and therefore privileged the Church and its clergy as the guiding structure of Irish society. It followed that in postcolonial, independent Ireland, Catholic bishops held considerable authority over national legislation – including regulations concerning sexuality, which limited the sale of contraceptives, banned divorce, censured (and censored) women, and criminalized homosexuality and abortion.

Catholicism's fall from grace in Ireland began in the 1970s and accelerated throughout the 1990s, when a number of sexual abuse cases against its clergy became highly publicized in the media.[10] In 1998, Thomas Inglis maintained, 'Suddenly, the Church [had] lost its sacredness and [had] become another interest group in civil society which [was] open to the same inspection as any other.'¹¹ In the wake of these publicized abuses, two full-scale investigations were undertaken to uncover the breadth of the Church scandal. In 2009, both investigations concluded and their reports were released to the public.[12] Public response to both the Ryan Report and the Murphy Report serves to reinforce the obvious loss of Church authority in Ireland. For instance, a retired public official, Liam McGlynn, commented, 'I think they have lost a generation. I haven't been to church for quite some time. My faith has been seriously damaged.'[13]

These reports confirm Mary Kenny's 2000 observation that the 'veritable avalanche of clerical scandals,' finally acknowledged by the Irish government, ensured that 'the very concept of "Catholic Ireland" was by the end of the century, gone.'[14] With the collapse of Catholicism as Ireland's moral compass, the conservative social construction of Irishness also began to collapse. Specifically, as noted by Terrence Brown, 'the moral policing in sexual matters the church had enforced in the early decades of independence had almost completely broken down.'[15]

The result of this collapse was the beginning of the secularization of Irish morality, which has become decidedly more tolerant of homosexuality and women's liberation since Catholic Law began to lose its prestige. This loss of authority over Irish life finally opened the doors for the decriminalization of homosexuality and for the sexual liberation of Irish women in the 1990s:

> In 1993 the Fianna Fáil Minister for Justice was able to put a bill through the house of the Oireachtas to decriminalize homosexual relations between consenting adults. It met with surprisingly little dissent, despite the fact that the age of consent was set at seventeen.[16]

This bill overturned Britain's Criminal Law Amendment Act of 1885, which the Supreme Court of Ireland had previously upheld, in 1980, as constitutional under article 50 of the 1937 Constitution.[17] The British Courts reversed the Act in 1967.[18]

Following the decriminalization of homosexuality in Ireland, the ultraconservative Catholic moral standard that required women to repress their sexuality – to the point that young girls who were considered overly flirtatious or too beautiful were incarcerated in punitive institutions such as the Magdalene laundries – also began to relax. Marguerite Corish points out, 'The fact that women [were] becoming more and more alienated from Catholic teaching on the family and on sexuality [was] bound to have huge consequences for the whole fabric of Irish society.'[19] One such outcome of a reestablished feminist voice in Ireland was that these Catholic-run Magdalene laundries, which were set up in the 1840s to 'rehabilitate' 'fallen women,' were officially closed on 25 September 1996 amidst controversy that the clergy regularly beat and raped the incarcerated women. Sexual abuse cases led to further investigations of the asylums that uncovered evidence of other physical, psychological, and emotional abuses that the women – some sought refuge in the laundries of their own accord, many were incarcerated against their wills – were forced to endure.

Although abortion remains illegal in Ireland, several other key changes to the Constitution signal the loosening grip of Catholicism on Irish public policy: the Fifteenth Amendment (approved in November 1995 and signed into law in June 1996), repealed the constitutional ban on divorce, thus further empowering women to govern their own lives. This movement towards equality was also reflected in the workforce. According to Ireland's central statistics office, between 1991 and 1996 the number of women in the workforce increased by 102,000 and a further 128,000 between 1996 and 2000 – surpassing the growth over the previous 20 years.[20] Furthermore, according to the Irish congress of Trade Unions, in 1997 the average earning of women workers was estimated at 70 percent of men's earnings, which is comparable to the 73 percent reported by U.S. economists in 1997.[21]

The fall of the Catholic vanguard in Ireland at the turn of the twenty-first century ripened the cultural moment for *At Swim, Two Boys* and *A Star Called Henry* to reestablish the 'unacceptable' facets of the Easter Rising as intrinsic elements of the event. Margot Backus points to the challenge faced by Irish authors seeking to depict the intersections of nationalism and socialism:

> [Works such as W.B. Yeats's] 'Easter, 1916' banished from bourgeois nationalism the socialism, feminism, and sexual liberation that were shameful reminders of specific slurs such as endemic poverty, filth, effeminacy and sexual incontinence with which the Irish as a group had been stigmatized over the course of the nineteenth century.[22]

O'Neill and Doyle work to overcome this division by establishing 'feminism and sexual liberation' as founding characteristics of modern Ireland. Both writers resist the widely accepted and wildly oversimplified hegemonic depictions of the Easter Rising by calling up repressed images and themes from the rebellion that run contrary to recently failing Catholic moral strictures. These fictions conjure the specters of previously subaltern discourses of the Rising to the present, thereby reweaving homosexuality and feminism into the history of Irish nationalism.

Jacques Derrida's examination of Karl Marx's *Eighteenth Brumaire of Louis Napoleon* (1852) in *Specters of Marx* (1994) offers a way for contemporary readers to reimagine the energies at work both at the time of the Easter Rising and in cultural memories of the event. His theory of spectrality provides us a way of understanding anew the intersectionality of revolutions in Ireland on Easter Monday, 1916, and aids contemporary reconceptions of why the reintegration of sexual and gender politics into critiques of empire in the work of Jamie O'Neill and Roddy Doyle is significant to the development of Irish national identity in the twenty-first century.

Early on in *Specters of Marx*, Derrida calls into question time's linear trajectory in words borrowed from Shakespeare's Prince Hamlet: 'The time is out of joint.'[23] Past, present, and future become – for Derrida – unreliable temporal markers, especially in times of social upheaval. He claims that revolutions can be understood as a convergence of disjointed times, thereby creating spectral moments. In short, no revolution is ever hermetic. As Marx observes about the French Revolution of 1848, they all borrow from the past. *At Swim, Two Boys* and *A Star Called Henry* borrow the revolutionary spirit of the Easter Rising (which itself borrowed from classical Greek and ancient Celtic mythology) to launch a sexual revolt against the conservative mores of the failing Catholic church. These novels can be read as declarations of twenty-first-century homosexual and feminist Irishness. Yet to grant historical weight to these previously suppressed elements of Irish identity, both novels situate homosexuality and feminism at the center of Ireland's defining moment of independence.

Derrida draws upon Marx's theory of revolution in the *Eighteenth Brumaire* to illustrate that the more one tries to create a new identity – in Ireland's case, an updated, post-Catholic national identity – the more one has to borrow from the past. He quotes Marx's observation of the 1848 French Revolution:

> Just when they seem engaged in revolutionizing themselves and things, in creating something that has never yet existed, precisely in such periods of revolutionary crisis they anxiously conjure up the

spirits of the past to their service and *borrow* from them *names*, battle-cries and costumes in order to present the new scene of world history in this time-honoured disguise and this *borrowed language*.[24]

Both Marx and Derrida suggest that this act of 'borrowing' reverses dominant conceptions of 'haunting' as a terrifying event to be escaped and forgotten. Marx observes the possession of 1848 rebels by the specters of 1789–1799, and the haunting of the 1789–1799 rebels by the specters of the Roman Republic and the Roman Empire.[25] Marx's understanding of revolution as a spectral event leads Derrida to conclude,

> It [was] indeed a matter of convoking or conjuring the spirits as specters *in a gesture of positive conjuration*, the one that swears in order to call up and not to drive away … The more the new erupts in the revolutionary crisis, the more the period is in crisis, the more it is 'out of joint,' then the more one has to convoke the old, 'borrow' from it.[26]

Self-invention, both individual and national, was similarly central to the spirit of 1916. Unhappy with their colonial history, a number of Irish writers and politicians set out to invent a national story that called for Irishmen to sacrifice themselves for national independence in the vein of the 1798 United Irishmen Rebellion.[27] Architects of the Easter Rising reached back to the rebels of the 1798 Rebellion and even earlier Celtic heroes, such as Cuchulainn and Finn MacCool, as a way of calling forth their pre-Norman, precolonial ancestry to construct an Irish identity not imposed upon them by Imperial Britain.

O'Neill and Doyle's conjuration of 1916 in service of contemporary Irish identity construction relies upon a myth-building technique similarly employed by architects of the Easter Rising (Pearse, Markievicz, Yeats). That is to say, both groups of artists – those writing during and immediately following the Rising and those writing about the Rising at the turn of the twenty-first century – use the same literary trope of the-past-haunting-the-present in order to inject their revolutions with an ancient heroic spirit. The significance of this similarity is that in both instances, ghosts are imagined not as things to be exorcized, but rather to be convoked and borrowed from in a productive manner. Both novels, therefore, call forth the 1916 Easter Rising and valorize (homo)sexual characters and themes that hegemonic nationalism previously demonized. Derrida's use of Marx to explain historical spectrality offers readers a way into O'Neill's and Doyle's criticism of prevailing twenty-first-century Irish social mores:

> The resurrection of the dead in those [previous] revolutions served the purpose of glorifying the new struggles, not of parodying the old; of magnifying the given task in imagination, not of fleeing from its solution in reality; of finding once more the spirit of revolution, not of making its ghost walk about again.[28]

Though national independence was later won as a result of a chain of events set in motion by the 1916 Rising, the revolution for sexual liberation and gender equality continues into the twenty-first century. In *Transformations in Irish Culture*, Luke Gibbons similarly observes 'that transformations induced by contact with the new may activate a transgressive potential already latent in the old, in the cast-offs and rejects of history.'[29] Spectrality gives us a vocabulary to discuss this 'transgressive potential.' And both novels by O'Neill and Doyle illustrate how borrowing the spirit of revolution from an early-twentieth-century 'successful' bid for independence can reanimate Ireland's unfinished sexual revolution at the century's end.

A number of critics, including Michael G. Cronin, Joseph Valente, and Jodie Medd, have observed that Jamie O'Neill's *At Swim, Two Boys*, an explicit homosexual romance, reimagines homosexuality and Irish nationalism as complementary, rather than contentious, elements of modern Irishness.[30] I build upon their observations to show *how* O'Neill links homosexuality and ethnicity via spectrality to make a contemporary political argument about queer rights in Ireland, and why it wasn't until the turn of the twenty-first century that such an argument was possible.

Cronin observes that the novel 'illustrates how gay male identity is being deployed to maintain notions of equality and pluralism that underpin [contemporary] liberal ideology.'[31] Similarly, Valente argues, '*At Swim Two Boys* thus sets forth a narrative parallelism that invites its readers to consider the historical, political, and ideological affinities between dissident sexual identity and ethnocolonial identity in an Irish context.'[32] And Jodie Medd synthesizes these arguments to conclude,

> O'Neill's novel catachrestically appropriates the related discourses of history, the nation, and its 'people' to (re)imagine a temporal and national space for gay Irish subjectivity ... O'Neill's novel so thoroughly intermeshes nationality and gay sexuality in a network of

metaphors and correspondences that it pressures and transforms the very terms of national belonging and citizenship.[33]

By offering his readers viable counter-hegemonic models of Irish heroism for the twenty-first century, O'Neill explicitly challenges the Catholic nationalist paradigm of conservative Irish polity, which produced legislation that continues to refuse the legitimacy of gender change, condemns same-sex marriage, and prevents gay couples from adopting.

O'Neill engineers a new mythology for the Easter Rising by overlaying it with the narrative of a queered Greek military legend. This layering exposes the Rising's homosexual subtext and therefore imagines Ireland as a Republic founded upon the Hellenistic ideal of homosexual love. Within the cultural climate of what is now being termed 'post-Catholic Ireland' (c. 1993 – present), one in which popular opinion of Catholicism and its leaders has degenerated to an all-time low, O'Neill's novel emerges from the rubble of a militant nationalism imbued with Church ideology to proclaim homosexuality a morally legitimate national identity because gay love was present at, and in many ways responsible for, the birth of the nation.

At Swim, Two Boys centers on a swimming expedition that ends up coinciding with the Easter Rising, and focuses on the gay-coming-of-age relationship between the two boys who participate in both events. In 1915, long-lost schoolmates Jim Mack and Doyler Doyle reunite and plan a swim for the following Easter that will take them from the Forty Foot – a popular men's bathing area just outside of Dublin – to the Muglins – a small island in Dublin Bay. Throughout the year, as Doyler teaches Jim how to effectively swim in open water, the boys' passion both for one another and for Irish independence intensifies. Not long after the swim is scheduled, Jim begins to imbue the event with heroic significance. He exclaims to Doyler, 'When we swim out there we'll bring with us a flag to raise. We'll raise the Green and claim the Muglins for Ireland.'[34] Jim's green flag suggests a dual purpose for the swim: it will declare the Muglins for Ireland, and simultaneously declare Ireland, in the words of Joseph Valente, as a 'queer nation.'[35] Valente explains that this dual purpose is evidenced by Jim's green flag in the text:

> Understood in the broader context of their relationship, this symbolic gesture serves to invoke the prospect of a queer nation, especially since during this period green is not only the national color of Ireland

but also, thanks to Oscar Wilde's notorious green carnation, the color most closely associated with a queer subculture.[36]

Furthermore, the temporal proximity of the swim and the Rising suggests that the rebellion is as much a sexual revolution as a political one. Therefore, O'Neill establishes early on the importance of viewing images in his text with a double vision.

By intersecting the boys' gay coming-of-age narrative with revolutionary nationalism, O'Neill sets the swim within the historical space of the Easter Rising and ultimately asks, 'What is Ireland that you should want to fight for it?'[37] Both Jim and Doyler are aware of what the swim signifies for them personally: it is the foundational moment of their sexual maturation. They require, however, the mentorship of another to explain what their personal commitment to each other, twinned with their revolutionary zeal, could mean in a broader context.

O'Neill introduces the self-consciously Wildean Anthony Mac-Murrough, who narrates the similarities between the boys' swim and the Easter Rising, as a way of reintegrating a homosexual discourse into Ireland's founding moment in 1916. The underlying leitmotif of *At Swim, Two Boys* is O'Neill's idea of an inclusive nation (one that recognizes the intersectionality of political ideologies, economic classes, sexual orientations, and gender identity), and one man's quest to cultivate the developing love between two boys in order to help them construct an Ireland in which their love is free to speak its name.

MacMurrough, the nephew of an influential Catholic nationalist who describes him as 'very Wildean,'[38] has recently returned to Ireland from England following a two-year prison sentence for gross indecency – Oscar Wilde's sentence for the same offense. And as Valente points out, 'It is precisely as a Wildean intellectual, compact of classical learning and a searching analytical wit, that MacMurrough mentors his charges':[39] under MacMurrough's tutelage, Jim Mack begins to understand the significance of his attraction to Doyler as well as their impending swim. Late in the winter of 1915, Jim recalls that 'he [had] heard Doyler mutter, "We will rise. We Will." And Jim had bit his lip to still the shiver in his spine. That day would come, sure as their Easter swim. And he too would rise with Doyler.'[40] The double entendre on the word *rise* is blatant. MacMurrough, haunted by the figure of Wilde to the point that he seems possessed by Wilde, is the lynchpin of O'Neill's meditation on twinned sexual and political desires in Ireland: it is through him that O'Neill argues for a Republic founded, in part, on homosexual love.

O'Neill's use of haunting – calling forth the specters of 1916 (both the *revenants* that inhabited the event, and those produced by it) to outfit contemporary struggles against inequality – borrows the spectral technique employed by the architects of heroic Irishness during 1916, but to different ends. During the Celtic Revival (the cultural arm of the revolution in Ireland), the warrior ideal was depicted as a male, willing to sacrifice himself in order to rescue a feminized Ireland from her oppressor. The most salient model is presented by W.B. Yeats and Lady Gregory in *Cathleen ni Houlihan* (1902). The ideal Irishman is depicted in two ways: as the avenger of a poor old woman whose 'four beautiful green fields' were taken from her,[41] and as the willing martyr, enchanted by a young woman's dominant beauty.[42] At the turn of the twenty-first century, however, O'Neill draws upon the Greek warrior ideal to re-present heroic queer Irish identity. His method of undermining exclusively heterosexual depictions of Irish heroism echoes the method used by late-Victorian esthetes in the 1890s to legitimate homosexuality in England.

In constructing this new vision of the 1916 Rising with homosexuality at its center, O'Neill reminds us that the social 'revolution' at the end of the nineteenth century was also, at least in part, enacted via sexual refashioning. In *Hellenism and Homosexuality in Victorian Oxford* (1994), Linda Dowling traces the emergence of coded homosexuality in nineteenth-century England. Dowling explains that the introduction of Hellenism as an antidote for the decline in English civic values coincided with Oxford reformers' implementation of Greek studies as 'an alternative source of transcendent value to replace the basis previously provided by Christianity.'[43] She maintains that because Greek civic philosophy and political theory had been introduced to the public by cultural theorists such as J.S. Mill and Matthew Arnold in order to pacify anxiety over cultural stagnation and decay, '[t]he language of male love could be triumphantly proclaimed the very fountain of civic health in an English polity imperatively in need ... of some authentic new source of ideas and intellectual power.'[44] These proclamations were made by Oxford-educated esthetes such as Walter Pater, J.A. Symonds, and Oscar Wilde who adopted Hellenism to validate existing structures of tutorial homosociality at Oxford, thereby constructing a homosexual code that insisted on queer cultural dominance as central to Western Civilization.⁴⁵

In a chapter titled 'Victorian Manhood and the Warrior Ideal' Dowling observes, 'The great irony' of mid-Victorian liberals' use of Hellenism to 'rescue Britain from stagnation and future decay,' is that it 'persuade[d] the late-Victorian homosexual apologists that in Hellenism they themselves would find a no less powerful ... legitimating counterdiscourse of social identity and erotic liberation.'⁴⁶ At the turn of the twenty-first century in Ireland, Jamie O'Neill adopts Hellenism to a similar end: he uses the revolutionary rhetorical structures of late-Victorian Hellenism to reinscribe a queer dimension in the foundational national myth of 1916. He does this through creating a character that fuses the two discourses of queer Hellenism and Irish nationalism (MacMurrough, the specter of Wilde), reconstructing an older man/younger man relationship in which MacMurrough 'educates' Jim and Doyler in Greek 'ethics' (much like Pater and Ruskin had educated Wilde and his cadre). O'Neill then dramatizes the queer nationalist coming-of-age of two characters whose very participation in this crucible event – 1916 – revises the national narrative and therefore redefines Irishness to include gay.⁴⁷ In short, O'Neill convokes the very vehicle of Irish heteronormativity – the Catholic, nationalist volunteer – and claims in it, via Jim Mack's homosexuality, 'a no less powerful ... legitimating counterdiscourse of social identity and erotic liberation.'⁴⁸

The central instance in which O'Neill borrows from Hellenistic culture occurs when he points out the dual layers of meaning in the traditional Irish-Republican anthem, 'A Nation Once Again.'⁴⁹ He illustrates how the song's image of three hundred Greek soldiers simultaneously promotes anticolonial resistance and homosexual devotion. The ballad's first verse conjures the specters of precolonial, Celtic Ireland, as well as the ancient Greek and Roman forces that opposed the Persian Empire, in order to rally the Young Ireland volunteers (1848) to rebel against England:

> When boyhood's fire was in my blood
> I read of ancient freemen,
> For Greece and Rome who bravely stood,
> Three hundred men and three men;
> And then I prayed I yet might see
> Our fetters rent in twain,
> And Ireland, long a province, be
> A Nation once again!⁵⁰

Via the relationship between Jim Mack and Doyler Doyle, O'Neill calls attention to Davis's nationalist rhetoric as one that blends precolonial 'ancient freemen' – who were unfettered by British occupation – with the ancient Greek legend of the Spartan 300, who during the Battle of Thermopylae in 480 B.C. held Xerxes's army and the Persian Empire at bay. O'Neill casts these Spartan warriors as a Hellenic sacred band of lovers, who celebrate homosexual love as the strength of their nation. MacMurrough maintains,

> You know those Greeks the song refers to? ... They were from Sparta. ... It was considered among the soldiers – and the soldiery was every citizen in Sparta – considered disreputable if a soldier among them did not have his lover.[51]

By calling attention to the way this anti-imperial band of gay lovers can be understood as specters of the 1916 rebels, O'Neill injects homosexuality into Ireland's founding mythology of 1916. And by bringing heroic Greek homosexuality into the historical space of the Easter Rising, O'Neill uses the song in his novel to queer Irish history, thereby calling for a rejection of lingering Catholic-nationalist demonization of homosexuality in contemporary Ireland.

At Swim, Two Boys re-presents Ireland's founding mythology following the fall of conservative Catholicism in Ireland, highlighting the homosexual subtext in the Spartan legend. As Dowling points out, this subtext was made clear by 'a [nineteenth century] German-inspired revolution in historiography ... [that] had made the crucial discovery that *paiderastia* or Greek love was itself martial in origin.'[52] O'Neill draws upon this reading of the Spartan legend in order to call attention to a similar subtext in Ireland's Rising narrative.

MacMurrough explains to Doyler that he has excavated these subtexts so that Doyler and Jim might have heroic models by which to govern their lives:

> 'The entire world grows up on those stories. Only difference is, I told him the truth, that they were lovers, humping physical fellows.' *Yes, and Jim had grasped instinctively that significance: that more than stories, they were patterns of the possible.* And I think, how happier my boyhood should have been, had somebody – Listen, boy, listen to my tale – thought to tell me the truth. Listen while I tell you, boy, these men loved and yet were noble. You too shall love, body and soul, as they; and there shall be a place for you, boy, noble and magnificent as any. Hold true to your love: these things shall be. (Emphasis added)[53]

Like the final stanza of W.B. Yeats's poem 'Easter, 1916,' which acknowledged the transformation of 'MacDonagh and MacBride / And Connolly and Pearse'[54] into martyrs for nationalist Ireland, O'Neill's novel constitutes contemporary gay identity by depicting Jim and Doyler as heroic Spartan warrior-lovers, and thereby offers contemporary readers a blueprint of how to articulate queer sexuality in the twenty-first century as both Irish and heroic.

At Swim, Two Boys participates in a long tradition of looking backwards for heroic models that might inspire contemporary revolution. O'Neill borrows identity construction techniques from Irish Revival writers who commonly summoned the images of precolonial Celtic heroes, such as Cuchulainn and Finn MacCool, in order to refute English caricatures of the Irish as buffoons unable to govern themselves. In other words, Revivalists worked to re-construct an Irish identity that had already been established, and strove to make precolonial Ireland present *once again*. O'Neill employs a similar technique to reinscribe a queer discourse into the Irish historical narrative so that Ireland might become a 'queer nation' once again. Rather than drawing upon Celtic folklore to recover a past Irishness, O'Neill instead conjures gay lovers from Greek mythology and notorious Irish homosexuals – such as Oscar Wilde, Padraig Pearse, and Roger Casement – in order to retrieve models upon which to *re*-construct a queer Irishness in the twenty-first century.

Another pivotal scene in the novel occurs when MacMurrough is literally haunted by the specter of an inmate he became acquainted with while serving his hard-labor sentence in London's Wandsworth prison. Scrotes, an obvious allusion to Socrates and Hellenism (and scrotum), is an Oxford academic convicted for his arguments concerning the legitimacy of gay identity. He died serving a hard-labor sentence, and returns to haunt MacMurrough as a benevolent, philosophizing ghost who encourages him to cultivate Jim and Doyler's juvenile curiosity for one another into a mature devotion. Scrotes argues,

> The struggle for Irish Ireland is not for truth against untruth. It is not for the good against the bad, for the beautiful against the unbeautiful. These things will take care of themselves. The struggle is for the heart, for its claim to stand in the light and cast a shadow its own in the sun.[55]

Scrotes calls attention to the continuation of the fight for sexual liberation in Ireland, which began as a component of the revolutionary spirit during the Easter Rising and persists into the secular revolution against Catholic cultural hegemony in the 1990s. At the time of the Rising, the heart's 'claim to stand in the light' referred to the participation of social reformers such as Kathleen Lynn, Helena Moloney, and Eoin Duffy in the Easter Rising – their intersecting agendas of national and sexual liberation underscored one particular intersection of Irish identity: Republicanism and homosexuality. For O'Neill, sexual freedom in the twenty-first century means re-mythologizing those heroic acts via a Greek model, and reinscribing them into the national narrative as a way of resisting the cultural and historical negation of Irish homosexuality.

Scrotes's vision of a 'queer nation'[56] is in direct response to MacMurrough's earlier question about the possibility of being openly gay in the Irish Free-State. Earlier, '[MacMurrough] thought of that phrase from Wilde: *What one has done in the secret chamber one has some day to cry on the housetop.* Wilde had meant in confession. Was it conceivable to cry out with pride?'[57] Scrotes's answer is yes, as long as the boys recognize their 'desire [as] praiseworthy and good.'[58] Therefore, he instructs MacMurrough to call forth a legend that is populated with queer heroes so that the boys might be motivated 'to cry out with pride':

> Help these boys build a nation their own. Ransack the histories for clues to their past. Plunder the literatures for words they can speak. And should you encounter an ancient tribe whose customs, however dimly, cast light on their hearts, tell them that tale; and you shall name the unspeakable names of your kind, and in that naming, in each such telling, they will falter a step to the light.[59]

This is the work of *At Swim, Two Boys*. O'Neill ransacks history for moments of paired queer/nationalist revolution and reconstructs them via spectrality. Three historical contexts erupt into and layer upon one another: ancient Greek pederasty, the late-Victorian homophile movement, and twentieth-century Irish revolution.

In a recasting of Victorian Oxford's homosocial tutor/pupil relationships (Pater, Symonds, Wilde), Anthony MacMurrough introduces Jim and Doyler to Greek legend because an Irish parallel does not exist. The boys become the Irish equivalent of the Spartan band of lovers. O'Neill appends a buried, and often deemed 'inconvenient,' homosexual voice to Ireland's founding mythology by reversing the dominant nationalist narrative that depicts young Irish males defending a feminine Ireland. Jim fights for Doyler, a *male* personification of the nation:

> 'We'll be asked to fight for Ireland, sure I know that,' [Jim said].
> 'But what is Ireland that you should want to fight for it?' [MacMurrough asked].
> 'Sure I know that too.' He raised a shoulder, his head inclined then turned: an attempt to shrug shake and nod, all the same time. When he was shy or self-conscious of something he would say, his body would often fail him. 'It's Doyler,' [Jim] said.
> 'Doyler is your country?'
> 'It's silly, I know. But that's how I feel. I know Doyler will be out, and where would I be but out beside him? I don't hate the English and I don't know do I love the Irish. But I love him. I'm sure of that now. And he's my country.'[60]

Though this passage seems to read like a rejection of nationalism altogether, replacing national allegiance with personal devotion, O'Neill ultimately conflates the national and domestic spheres through Jim's pronouncement that Doyler is his country.[61] In answering MacMurrough's question – 'What is Ireland that you should want to fight for it?' – Jim does not discount militant nationalism, but declares that his motivation for volunteering is to rise up in defense of his love for Doyler, and by extension to fight for the possibility of a queer Ireland.

At Swim, Two Boys is a layered narrative wherein the Greek past erupts into Irish revolution (via late-Victorian Hellenism) as a reference point, or 'pattern of the possible,'[62] a way to visualize how homosexual and nationalist identities intersected at the moment Ireland declared its independence. The greater significance of O'Neill's queering of the Easter Rising is that he establishes the very event that helped place the Catholic Church in a position of power as a site of heroic homosexuality. His novel participates in the immense cultural upheaval at the end of the twentieth century in Ireland – public outcry against hypocritical moral standards of the failing Catholic Church – by reintegrating themes of sexual liberation back into the Irish historical narrative. Like *At Swim, Two Boys*, Roddy Doyle's *A Star Called Henry* subverts assumptions about sexuality and gender during the revolutionary years in Ireland that have long gone unquestioned. Doyle's novel employs a similar textual logic, which challenges oversimplified accounts of the Rising that depict it as a unified declaration of independence rather than an intersection of social concerns.

Roddy Doyle's *A Star Called Henry*, the fictional memoir of Henry Smart, is a parodic portrait of Irish history during the revolutionary years of 1901–1919.⁶³ Doyle juxtaposes Henry's coming-of-age with Ireland's push for independence, and focuses on the suffrage movement in early twentieth-century Ireland. The novel, which unveils previously suppressed issues of gender discrimination, can be read in concert with cultural liberalization movements in Ireland at the turn of the twenty-first century. Doyle mines the oppressive patriarchal Rising narrative, originally constituted through the lens of Catholic hegemony, for heroic female warriors to haunt his text.

Doyle reestablishes the often-deemed 'inconvenient' characters and themes from the Easter Rising as intrinsic to the celebrated event. He conjures obscured feminist images from 1916 and presents them as essential elements of Ireland's revolution at the end of the twentieth century when, due to the fall of the Irish Catholic Church, issues of gender equality had intensified. Furthermore, Doyle's novel continues to resonate in our current cultural moment as social critics continue to highlight current manifestations of gender discrimination. Doyle spends a great deal of time and energy to summon the spirit of the 1916 rebels' fight for gender equality to present-day Ireland, thereby positing such discrimination as the defining issue of both the 1916 Rising and the present revolution against cultural conservatism in twenty-first-century Ireland.

The first sentence of Doyle's novel establishes the primacy of women in his text: 'My mother looked up at the stars.'⁶⁴ Henry's mother, Melody Nash, has been destroyed by marital and social expectations that required her to serve the nation primarily as childbearer and homemaker. Constant pregnancy and extreme poverty take their toll on Melody, who ultimately drinks herself to death after her husband, Henry Smart Sr., abandons her. Melody's situation depicts the importance of social reform movements in Ireland at the beginning of the twentieth century, and highlights the continued struggle against gender inequality at the turn of the twenty-first century. Many blamed this inequality on the Churches, even before Catholicism won constitutional recognition as something of a ruling power in 1937.⁶⁵ In 1915, for instance, Constance Markievicz identified the Churches of Ireland as the root of oppression against women: 'Women are everywhere today in a position of inferiority. And the Churches, both Catholic and Protestant, are to blame for this, for both foster the tradition of segregation of the sexes.'⁶⁶ Her assessment of bipartisan Church-led discrimination against women continues to hold true in the late twentieth century, and in this context we can read Doyle's novel as a direct critique of sexism in Ireland.

Doyle's choice of a male narrator is important to a feminist reading of the text. Henry Smart, a self-proclaimed superman, wanders about Dublin during the first half of the book announcing to the world, 'My name is Henry Smart! The one and only Henry Smart!'[67] As he matures, he claims authority over the other orphans of the Dublin street gangs,[68] boasts of his ability to impress women,[69] and proclaims his superiority over his fellow Citizen Army volunteers.[70] Doyle then positions a number of uncompromising women alongside Henry, the stereotypical alpha male, who exceed his charisma and heroism. The most notable of these women is Henry's schoolteacher and eventual wife, Miss O'Shea. She dominates Henry intellectually, physically, and sexually; and through his own narration, readers witness Henry's unabashed admiration and respect that construct the novel's argument for gender equality.

Arguably Doyle's main protagonist, Miss O'Shea (a mathematics teacher, member of Cumann na mBan, and gunner in the Easter Rising) is a hyperbolized embodiment of the heroic female rebels from the Easter Rising who had modeled themselves on the legends of ancient Celtic warrior queens. The novel suggests that Irish women hail from a noble lineage and should be regarded as such, not bound as prisoners of domesticity. In a 2003 interview, Doyle alluded to his motivation for creating Miss O'Shea in the likeness of the women of 1916:

> In the short term I think [The Easter Rising] was [a failure], because what it created was a pretty grim place really. I know that as I sit here now I wouldn't have been comfortable in it at all … The inequality is *still* quite striking and just unacceptable. (Emphasis added)[71]

A Star Called Henry reinterprets and updates the mythology of the Easter Rising in order to offer contemporary readers a viable myth for the modern world. Miss O'Shea serves as an example to women of the twenty-first century – who, Doyle seems to argue, should conjure the spirit of the women of 1916 in order to incite rebellion against present-day discrimination. Indeed, according to Fearghal McGarry, whose 2010 study of the seventeen hundred first-person accounts of the Rising that were recently released by the Bureau of Military History, 'The Rising can be seen as an inspiring example of the revolutionary nature of the struggle for independence: "Even before the Russian Army had women soldiers," Moloney proudly declared, "the Citizen Army had them." [BMH WS 391 (Helena Moloney)]'[72]

Doyle's novel echoes Constance Markievicz's call for the women of 1916 to conjure up, and fashion themselves after, ancient Celtic heroines – much like the men of that time who strove to live in the image of Cuchulainn.

In October 1915, Markievicz, an active participant in the Irish Citizen Army, declared:

> Ancient Ireland bred warrior women, and women played a heroic part in those days. Today we are in danger of being civilized by men out of existence. What distinguished Ireland chiefly of old was the number of fighting women who held their own against the world, who owed no allegiance to any men, who were the super-women – the Maeves, the Machas, the warrior-queens.[73]

A Star Called Henry suggests that at the turn of the twenty-first century women are still 'in danger of being civilized by men out of existence.'[74] Like Anthony MacMurrough in Jamie O'Neill's *At Swim, Two Boys*, whom Scrotes instructs, 'Help these boys build a nation their own. Ransack the histories for clues to their past. Plunder the literatures for words they can speak,'[75] Roddy Doyle ransacks Irish history to build a foundational myth free from gender inequality. He identifies a feminist discourse within the larger Rising narrative that has been submerged beneath Catholic nationalism, and creates a narrative that better reflects the realities of both women in 1916 and women in contemporary Ireland. Doyle looked to the women of Cumann na mBan – a Republican women's paramilitary organization – for a model upon which to base Miss O'Shea:

> I began to read about Cumann na mBan and these women, these extraordinary women – some of them quite eccentric women. They found their voice in Cumann na mBan, this organisation [sic] for women, and then it was stifled somewhat. So she'd be one of these people who'd be very, very disappointed by what was going on.[76]

As a result of his research, Doyle discovered the story of Margaret Skinnider, a sniper in the Citizen Army, and the only female wounded in action during the Easter Rising.

Margaret Skinnider (1893–1971) was born to Irish parents near Glasgow, Scotland, where she grew up and made her living as a mathematics teacher. She became involved in the women's suffrage movement in Glasgow, and according to her memoir, *Doing My Bit for Ireland* (1917), in 1915 joined a Glasgow division of Cumann na mBan.[77] Skinnider, who became acquainted with Markievicz during her frequent trips to Dublin, answered Markievicz's call for Irish women to embody the spirit of ancient Celtic heroines – such as the warrior queen Sgathaich, the matron of teachers and of female independence[78] – by taking up arms in the Easter Rising and later agitating for the introduction of common incremental salary [scales] for women and single men in 1949. Discussing the Celtic Revival in general, and Irish women in particular, Skinnider recalls, 'Our pride was growing tremendously – pride not in what we have, but in what we are.'[79]

During the Rising, Skinnider was stationed at the garrison in the College of Surgeons under the command of General Michael Mallin and Con Markievicz. She was shot three times while attempting to set fire to a number of houses in order to block the retreat of British soldiers:[80] 'I had been shot in three places, my right side under the arm, my right arm, and in the back on my right side.'[81] She survived, and after serving a short prison sentence in Kilmainham Gaol, fled to America in 1917 to write her memoir. At the end of that year she returned to Dublin, teaching, and agitating for women's rights. In 1949 she successfully lobbied for 'the introduction of common incremental salary [scales] for women and single men.'[82]

Margaret Skinnider's biography haunts Doyle's text, and the fictional Miss O'Shea is the manifestation of her specter. Like Skinnider, Miss O'Shea is a mathematics teacher,[83] a member of Cumann na mBan,[84] 'can fire a gun as well as any man,'[85] is thrice shot,[86] and serves a short prison sentence in Kilmainham Gaol[87] before eventually emigrating to America in the novel's sequel, *Oh Play That Thing* (2004). Doyle directly borrows the revolutionary spirit of Skinnider to institute Miss O'Shea as the champion of women's suffrage in Ireland. The example *par excellence* of Miss O'Shea's declaration of equality takes place in the G.P.O., and coincides with Ireland's declaration of independence.

Doyle's narration of the Rising highlights the complex intersections between nationalism, feminism, and socialist trade unionism – intersections that have, according to Margot Backus and David Lloyd, been drastically deemphasized to establish nationalism's precedence among the three. In *A Star Called Henry*, however, Doyle drowns out the voices of Patrick Pearse and James Connolly in order to resurrect and centralize the obscured discourses of the Rising. Whereas Pearse summoned Cuchulainn to his side, Doyle summons Sgathaich to stalk through the G.P.O.

Most Doyle scholars tend to read his novels as examinations of economically oppressed, urban working-class males.[88] These critics often refer to *A Star Called Henry* as primarily concerned with economic inequality in twentieth-century Ireland. To be sure, Henry admits that his motivation for joining the Citizens Army is solely economic: the army provided him with proper clothing and a place to sleep.[89] Moreover, as the bombardment begins on Easter Monday, Henry falls in line with the Socialist aim of emancipation for the working class:

> I shot and killed all that I had been denied, all the commerce and snobbery that had been mocking me and other hundreds of thousands behind glass and locks, all the injustice, unfairness and shoes – while the lads took chunks out of the military.[90]

Certainly this is retribution for his difficult childhood; and, in Doyle's novel, Henry's economic motivation clearly eclipses the nationalist narrative. In turn, however, Miss O'Shea's radical feminism subjugates Henry's socialist agenda. In this way, Doyle's novel continues the work of nationalist women's groups such as Inghinide na hÉireann, which 'sought to radicalize those previously excluded from political activism, including women, children, and the working class.'[91]

Doyle juxtaposes the climactic moment of the Easter Rising with Miss O'Shea's sexual climax in the basement of the G.P.O. Henry recalls,

> I was downstairs, in the basement, in a hot little room with much more dust than air. Did I hear the shell hitting the Loop Line? Did I hear the clang? I did, but I thought the noise was coming from me. I was falling onto my back when it happened. I'd been pushed on top of a high bed made of blocks of stamps, sheets and sheets of the things, columns of them, sticky side up. I was stuck there with my britches nuzzling my ankles as Miss O'Shea grabbed my knees and climbed on top of me. This skirt, she said. – Wait ... I'll say I tore it for Ireland, said Miss O'Shea. – And it's no lie.[92]

Miss O'Shea, whose Christian name Henry purposefully never learns (even after they are married she remains Miss O'Shea) in order that she retain authority over him, directs Henry to the basement and schools him in the art of love-making. In the above passage, she is clearly in control of Henry, whom Doyle has until now set up as the playboy of the Western world.[93] Throughout the first half of the novel, Henry exists as a representative of the patriarchal male, and is here reeducated by Miss O'Shea. He is confused by the sounds of attack above and is immobilized on a bed of stamps where she pins him down. Her authority over Henry leaves him 'feel[ing] like the king of the world and a complete and utter fuckin' eejit.'[94] Henry's emasculation seems to embody the sort of national transformation for which Doyle argues.

While the British dropped hot bombs and incendiary shells on the Post Office and sprayed machine-gun fire at what history assures us were fearless men, Henry Smart – the self-proclaimed most fearless of them all,[95] the Übermensch – is conquered by Miss O'Shea. In the same breath she orgasms and declares, 'I didn't come here to make stew, Henry ... I'm here for my freedom. Just like you and the men upstairs ... I want my freedom too ... To do what I want.'[96] Miss O'Shea qualifies her declaration of freedom. In addition to seeking freedom for Ireland, just like the men upstairs, she simultaneously fights for gender equality – the freedom to do what she wants. Her motivation reflects the Socialist Feminist agenda, which suggests that the end of women's oppression can only be achieved through intersectionality.

According to Rosemarie Tong, 'The way to end women's oppression, in Socialist Feminists' estimation, is to kill the two-headed beast of capitalist patriarchy or patriarchal capitalism.'[97] McGarry's study of oral histories of the Rising confirm that 'Separatists rarely drew distinctions between moral, cultural, and political values and considered themselves more virtuous than their constitutional rivals.'[98] In the Irish context, the Easter rebels resisted imperialism, capitalism, and sexism as a multi-faced beast. Readers can look back at Doyle's depiction of Miss O'Shea – who fights in 1916 both for the nation and for women of the nation – as an argument for contemporary gender equality. *A Star Called Henry* reverses past and present cultural misogyny by objectifying Henry. Doyle writes a strong male protagonist who is overwhelmed by an even stronger female protagonist.

Though Miss O'Shea's sexual domination of the playboy Henry Smart serves to reverse prevailing conceptions of gender roles, it isn't until after the Rising – when she stalks out of the G.P.O. shouting, 'I can fire a gun as well as any man!'[99] – that she becomes completely possessed by the ghosts of ancient warrior-queens. Doyle's heroic depiction of Miss O'Shea during the War of Independence responds to the popular canonization of the sixteen Easter week martyrs, all males. His novel suggests that the men had died, and those who didn't 'had to drink hard and quickly to be able to ignore [their ghosts].'[100] Meanwhile 'the women of the Gaelic League and Cumann na mBan were queuing up for their own three minutes of immortality – longer maybe ...'[101] Doyle provides a portrait of Irish women who take up the cause while the men 'were toasting [their] own deaths.'[102] After the Rising, *A Star Called Henry* makes plain, men were simultaneously drinking to the memory of the Easter martyrs, and to their own likely deaths in the War of Independence. For the men in Doyle's novel, the Rising was a success because it instigated the War of Independence, which they saw as the final step towards Irish sovereignty. The women of the Gaelic League and Cumann na mBan, however, were in the midst of fighting a multi-faceted war, and didn't yet have reason to toast anyone's death.

During the War of Independence, Miss O'Shea and Henry Smart come under the command of General Michael Collins, and rise through the ranks to become two of his most effective assassins. Miss O'Shea outshines even Henry, earning the moniker 'Our Lady of the Machine Gun'[103] and the respect of her fellow soldiers: 'She'll soon have us free of [the Black and Tans] and that'll be a day worth getting up for.'[104] The event that earned her that respect Doyle partially borrowed from the life of Margaret Skinnider, and hyperbolized in order to lend weight to his argument for gender equality.

On a bombing run designed to destroy a Black and Tan barracks, Miss O'Shea and Henry are ambushed. She is shot three times before Henry takes a single bullet, yet she manages to rescue *him* from capture or death:

> Another bullet entered Miss O'Shea; she dashed ahead of me, knocked forward by the shot ... As I swerved to catch her and lifted my arm to hoist her to my shoulder, the bullet slid in and I was falling hard and I couldn't see anything, didn't know anything, and when I was able to see again and think, when I looked and saw the ground jumping below me, she was carrying me.[105]

Doyle reverses the gender roles of the Skinnider story in which William Partridge carried Margaret Skinnider safely back to the College of Surgeons – according to Con Markievicz, 'Margaret's only regret was her bad luck in being disabled so early in the day...'[106] In *A Star Called Henry*, Doyle exaggerates Skinnider's pugnacious reaction to her wound when Miss O'Shea explains, 'I knew when the third bullet hit me that I could stand up to anything. I've nothing to fear. There's no stopping me now, Henry.'[107] The specters of Markievicz's ancient warrior-queens and the heroic fortitude of Margaret Skinnider haunt Doyle's text, inciting him to reverse chivalric tradition by sacrificing Miss O'Shea to rescue Henry.

His magnification of Skinnider's character additionally serves to evoke, in contemporary readers, aggressive enthusiasm for challenging constitutionally sanctioned sexism. Doyle maintains, 'I'm not a historian and I don't want to be.'[108] He therefore amplifies Skinnider's heroism and summons her revolutionary spirit to his turn of the twenty-first century text in order to argue against gender inequality in the present. For it is as the specter of Skinnider that Miss O'Shea both conquers and saves Henry Smart, thereby usurping his role to become Ireland's Über*frau*. Miss O'Shea reminds readers of 'the Maeves, the Machas, the warrior-queens,' the early twentieth-century roots for contemporary Irish feminism.[109]

Doyle's glorification of Margaret Skinnider – as Miss O'Shea – in *A Star Called Henry*, challenges the dominant depiction of Ireland and Irishness as exclusively Catholic, nationalist, and patriarchal. The novel offers contemporary readers a portrait of the heroic women from 1916 who proclaimed Irishness as also secular, feminist, and matriarchal. In 'Demythicizing/Remythicizing the Rising,' José Lanters maintains,

> Doyle demolishes many of the pious images associated with the received sacrificial myth of 1916, while at the same time writing into existence the myth of those who were never given a place in the official version: independent, sexually active women, slum dwellers, and those who were not of Gaelic, Catholic descent.[110]

A Star Called Henry juxtaposes emerging twenty-first-century post-Catholic Ireland against early twentieth-century revolutionary Ireland, arguing that Irish women were not then, nor are they now, inferior to their male counterparts.

In their respective novels, Jamie O'Neill and Roddy Doyle call upon the ghosts of the Easter Rising past to translate the language of an early twentieth-century political revolution into that of a twenty-first-century sexual one. Borrowing the words of Derrida and applying them to *At Swim, Two Boys* and *A Star Called Henry*, contemporary readers can recognize how both novels 'find again the *spirit* of the revolution without making its *specter* return.'[111] Both novels seek to inspire positive conjuration; both urge contemporary subaltern groups to reclaim their prominence in Irish culture at a time when broad cultural enthusiasm for both Catholicism and nationalism is waning.

Derrida's examination of Marx's *Eighteenth Brumaire of Louis Napoleon* has offered a convenient way to examine both novelists' involvement in the liberalization of Ireland. Drawing upon Derrida's theories of spectrality allows readers to recognize the 'difference-in-similarity' between conservative nationalist-inspired national origin myths constructed at the time of the Rising (which themselves summon the specters of earlier rebellions) and foundational queer and feminist mythologies constructed at the end of the twentieth century. These later sexualized and gendered narratives convoke the specters of 1916, classical Greece, and Celtic Ireland in order to subvert gender inequality and sexual bias that persists in our contemporary moment. In other words, the gender politics that guide depictions of the Easter Rising in *At Swim, Two Boys* and *A Star Called Henry* summon the spirit of nationalist revolution to present-day Ireland, only to undermine the specter of Catholic nationalism's oppressive reality.

Notes

1 In David Lloyd's, 'Regarding Ireland in a Postcolonial Frame,' in *Ireland After History*. Critical Conditions: Field Day Essays and Monographs 9. Ed. Seamus Deane. Notre Dame, IN: University of Notre Dame Press, 1999, p. 37, he observes 'That [Social] movements – agrarian movements, women's movements, labour movements, to name only a few – have largely been occluded by the dominant forms and debates of Irish history is an effect of the organizing concerns of official history: the formation of the nation and of the state; the narrative of political institutions and state apparatuses; in short, the modernization of Ireland. Accordingly, the very social processes, the continual transformation that take place not only within the purview of the state and the political sphere but also in its shadow, have been obscured.' My aim in this chapter is to present postcolonial Irish fiction working to shine a light on the social movements undergirding the 1916 Easter Rising.
2 Margot Gayle Backus, '"More Useful Washed and Dead": James Connolly, W.B. Yeats, and the Sexual Politics of "Easter 1916."' *Interventions* 10.1 (2008): 69.

3 According to Suzanne Knudsen, intersectionality is an emerging concept in feminist studies, which can be used to analyze 'how social and cultural categories intertwine. The relationships between gender, race, ethnicity, disability, sexuality, class and nationality are examined.' p. 61. For further reading on the concept of intersectionality, see Patricia Hill Collins's *Black Feminist Thought: Knowledge, Consciousness and the Politics of Empowerment* (London: Routledge Classics, 2008); Leslie McCall's 'The Complexity of Intersectionality,' *Journal of Women in Culture and Society* 30.3 (2005): 1771–1800; Susanne V. Knudsen's 'Intersectionality: A Theoretical Inspiration in the Analysis of Minority Cultures and Identities in Textbooks,' *Caught in the Web or Lost in the Textbook?* Ed. Eric Bruillard, et. al. 2006. Web. 22 January 2010. pp. 61–76.
4 Brian Lewis, 'The Queer Life and Afterlife of Roger Casement.' *Journal of the History of Sexuality* 14.4 (2005): 367. Ruth Dudley Evans, a noted revisionist historian and Unionist, speculated that Pearse was an 'unconscious homosexual.' She drew her conclusions based upon suggestive poetry he had written about young boys – particularly, 'A Mhic Bhig na gCleas' (Little Lad of the Tricks). See R.D. Evans. *The Triumph of Failure* (London: Victor Gollancz Ltd, 1990). See also Elaine Sisson. *Pearse's Patriots: St. Endas and the Cult of Boyhood* (Cork: Cork University Press, 2004).
5 Sisson, *Pearse's Patriots*.
6 Doug Ireland, 'Review of Brian Lacey's *"Terrible Queer Creatures": A History of Homosexuality in Ireland.*' *Gay City News*. 6 February 2009. http://hnn.us/roundup/entries/61344.html. 3 December 2009. p. 26.
7 Backus, 'Washed and Dead,' 72.
8 Agitation for Catholic Emancipation began in 1823, when Daniel O'Connell (1775–1847) set up the Catholic Association – a non-violent group that collected 'rent' in support of a proposed Catholic Emancipation Act. The Act passed in April 1829, allowing Catholic M.P.s to sit at Westminster and making Catholics eligible to hold most public offices.
9 John Banville, 'On the Road to Revolution.' *Guardian*, 24 September 2005. n. pag. www.guardian.co.uk/books/. 13 January 2010.
10 A number of documentaries and films gained the Irish public's attention and led to the Commission to Inquire into Child Abuse (CICA), including *States of Fear* (1991), a documentary series produced by Mary Raftery for Radio Telefís Éireann (RTÉ); and *Sex in a Cold Climate* (1998), a documentary directed by Steve Humphries. Later, in 2002, Peter Mullan wrote and directed the popular film, *The Magdalene Sisters*, which was based on Humphries's documentary. The film won the prestigious Golden Lion at the 2002 Venice Film Festival.

11 Thomas Inglis, *Moral Monopoly: The Rise and Fall of the Catholic Church in Modern Ireland*. 2nd edn (Dublin: University College Dublin Press, 1998), p. 217.
12 According to the *Ryan Report* issued on 20 May 2009 by the Commission to Inquire into Child Abuse (CICA), over 200 Catholic-run institutions – including state-sponsored childcare facilities such as reformatories and industrial schools – were governed by over 800 known abusers. Similarly, the Department of Justice and Law Reform's *Murphy Report* reveals the findings of public inquiries conducted by the Irish government into the sexual abuse scandal in the Catholic archdiocese of Dublin. An edited version of the report was released on 26 November 2009. The investigation considers the mishandling of allegations of sexual abuse against 46 Catholic priests between 1975 and 2004, when it was found 320 people were abused. The report accuses four archbishops of covering up the abuses: John Charles McQuaid, Dermot Ryan, Kevin McNamara, and Desmond Connell. On 20 March 2010, Pope Benedict XVI apologized to the victims of these abuses and acknowledged the significance of the sexual abuse scandal in Ireland: 'You have forfeited the esteem of the people of Ireland and brought shame and dishonour upon your confreres.' He added, 'Together with the immense harm done to victims, great damage has been done to the Church and to the public perception of the priesthood and religious life' ('Pastoral Letter to the Catholics of Ireland,' p. 19). These recent exposés have influenced a worldwide investigation into similar abuses.
13 Quoted in Richard Allen Greene, 'Ashamed to Be Irish: Abuse Angers Nation.' *CNN.com*. 20 March 2010. www.cnn.com/2010/WORLD/europe/03/20/ireland.abuse.voices/index.html. 20 March 2010.
14 Mary Kenny, *Goodbye to Catholic Ireland*. Revised and updated edn (Dublin: New Island Books, 2000), p. 309.
15 Terrence Brown, *Ireland: A Social and Cultural history 1922–2002* (London: Harper Perennial, 2004), p. 373.
16 Brown, *Ireland*, p. 372. For more on Irish homosexuality, see Brian Lacey's *Terrible Queer Creatures: A History of Homosexuality in Ireland* (Dublin: Wordwell, 2008).
17 Article 50 of the 1937 *Constitution of the Republic of Ireland* reads, 'Laws enacted before, but expressed to come into force after, the coming into operation of this Constitution, shall, unless otherwise enacted by the Oireachtas, come into force in accordance with the terms thereof.' The Supreme Court upheld the Criminal Law Amendment Act of 1885 on the grounds that it was not inconsistent with the Constitution's Christian moral teaching (Norris v. Ireland).
18 Section 11 of Henry Du Pré Labouchère's (1831–1912). *Criminal Law Amendment Act* reads, 'Any male person who, in public or private,

commits, or is a party to the commission of, or procures or attempts to procure the commission by any male person, any act of gross indecency with another male person, shall be guilty of a misdemeanor, and being convicted thereof shall be liable at the discretion of the court to be imprisoned for any term not exceeding two years.' The far-reaching consequence was that this act criminalized male homosexual acts, whether consensual or otherwise, and was given the broadest possible interpretation. It was for the violation of this law that the Irish playwright Oscar Wilde was convicted to two years of hard labor in 1895.

19 Marguerite Corish, 'Aspects of the Secularisation of Irish Society.' In Eoin G. Cassidy, ed., *Faith and Culture in the Irish Context* (Dublin: Veritas, 1996), p. 151.
20 Central Statistics Office, *Quarterly National Household Survey*, December 2000. www.cso.ie/qnhs/spe_mod_qnhs.htm. 22 January 2010.
21 Central Statistics Office, *Quarterly National Household Survey*.
22 Backus, 'Washed and Dead,' 69.
23 Jacques Derrida, *Spectres of Marx*, 1993. Trans. Peggy Kamuf (New York: Routledge Classics, 2006), p. 61.
24 Qtd. in Derrida, *Specters of Marx*, p. 135.
25 Derrida, *Spectres of Marx*, p. 137.
26 Derrida, *Spectres of Marx*, pp. 135–136.
27 In 1798 the United Irishmen, inspired by the American and French revolutions, unsuccessfully rebelled against British rule in Ireland. The defeat of the United Irishmen signaled the end of the Protestant Ascendancy's rule in Ireland. The 1800 Act of Union abolished the Irish parliament and moved the authority over Ireland back to the parliament in London.
28 Derrida, *Spectres of Marx*, pp. 140–141.
29 Luke Gibbons, *Transformations in Irish Culture* (Cork: Cork University Press, 1996), p. 5.
30 See Michael G. Cronin, '"He's My Country": Liberalism, Nationalism, and Sexuality in Contemporary Irish Gay Fiction.' Éire-Ireland 39.3–4 (2004): 250–267; Joseph Valente. 'Race/Sex/Shame: The Queer Nationalism of *At Swim, Two Boys*.' Éire-Ireland 40.3–4 (2005): 58 – 84; and Jodie Medd, '"Patterns of the Possible": National Imaginings and Queer Historical (Meta)Fictions in Jamie O'Neill's *At Swim, Two Boys*.' GLQ 13.1 (2006): 1–31.
31 Cronin, 'He's My Country,' 263.
32 Valente, 'Race/Sex/Shame,' 58.
33 Medd, 'Patterns of the Possible,' 4, 5.
34 Jamie O'Neill, *At Swim, Two Boys* (New York: Scribner, 2002), p. 200.
35 Valente, 'Race/Sex/Shame,' 59.
36 Valente, 'Race/Sex/Shame,' 61. Joseph Valente claims that the underlying theme of *At Swim, Two Boys* is O'Neill's declaration of Ireland

Ancient warriors, modern sexualities 125

as a 'queer nation,' in which 'the insistent, inextricable linkage of the problematics of Irish national identity and queer sexuality' are simultaneously and equally present in the national consciousness (59). Valente stops short of explaining how O'Neill's representation of the boys' commitment to founding a 'queer Ireland' relies entirely on 'the insistent, inextricable linkage' of the Easter Rising rebels with the Spartan 300. O'Neill uses Anthony MacMurrough to introduce the narrative technique of the past-haunted-present, which authenticates Jim's and Doyler's dual identity as gay Irish rebels and Greek homosexual lovers.

37 O'Neill, *At Swim, Two Boys*, 388.
38 O'Neill, *At Swim, Two Boys*, 172.
39 O'Neill, *At Swim, Two Boys*, 61.
40 O'Neill, *At Swim, Two Boys*, 315.
41 W.B. Yeats and Lady Augusta Gregory, 'Cathleen ni Houlihan.' *The Yeats Reader*. Ed. Richard J. Finneran. Rev. edn (New York: Scribner, 2002), p. 160.
42 The play ends as Michael Gillane abandons his fiancée Delia Cahel, 'to join the French' in rising up against the British in the failed 1798 Rebellion. His father Peter and his younger brother Patrick see Michael's sacrifice in these two different lights. Peter asks, 'Did you see an old woman going down the path?' To which Patrick responds, 'I did not, but I saw a young girl, and she had the walk of a queen' (Yeats 165).
43 Linda Dowling, *Hellenism and Homosexuality in Victorian Oxford* (Ithaca, NY: Cornell University Press, 1994), p. xiv.
44 Dowling, *Hellenism and Homosexuality*, p. xv.
45 Dowling, *Hellenism and Homosexuality*, pp. 81, 134. Pater tutored Wilde at Oxford, and his principles of the esthetic movement, which he established in *The Renaissance: Studies in Art and Poetry*, had a lasting effect on Wilde's work. In addition to his work with Pater, 'Wilde began a correspondence with John Addington Symonds while he was still at Trinity College, Dublin. In the notebooks he kept at Oxford, Wilde, who considered Symonds' prose to be the equal of Pater's and Ruskin's, copied numerous passages from Symonds' work, especially his *Studies of the Greek Poets* (1873). A key figure in both aestheticism and Oxford Hellenism, Symonds was also one of the most important Victorian homosexual apologists, the author of *A Problem in Greek Ethics* (1883) and *A Problem in Modern Ethics* (1891)' (New York University Library).
46 Dowling, *Hellenism and Homosexuality*, p. 36.
47 O'Neill creates a heroic homosexual narrative upon which a queer nation can be established because, as Timothy Brennan explains, 'Nations ... are imaginary constructs that depend for their existence on an apparatus of cultural fictions in which imaginative literature plays a decisive role': Brennan, 'The National Longing for Form.' *Nation and*

Narration. Ed. Homi K. Bhabha. (London: Routledge, 1990), p. 49. That is to say, queer Ireland requires a queer national origin story.
48 Dowling, *Hellenism and Homosexuality*, p. 36.
49 Thomas Osborne Davis (1814–1845), founder and poet of the Young Ireland movement (a nationalist organization that petitioned the 1800 Act of Union), wrote 'A Nation Once Again' in the mid-1840s to lobby for Irish Home-Rule.
50 Thomas Osborne Davis, 'A Nation Once Again.' *The Celtic Lyrics Collection*. 2009. www.celtic-lyrics.com/. 7 December 2009.
51 O'Neill, *At Swim, Two Boys*, 267.
52 Dowling, *Hellenism and Homosexuality*, p. xv.
53 O'Neill, *At Swim, Two Boys*, 540–541.
54 W.B. Yeats, 'Easter, 1916.' *The Collected Poems of W.B. Yeats*. 2nd edn. Ed. Richard J. Finneran (New York: Scribner, 1996), lines 75–76.
55 O'Neill, *At Swim, Two Boys*, 294.
56 Valente, 'Race/Sex/Shame,' 59.
57 O'Neill, *At Swim, Two Boys*, 287.
58 O'Neill, *At Swim, Two Boys*, 294.
59 O'Neill, *At Swim, Two Boys*, 295.
60 O'Neill, *At Swim, Two Boys*, 389.
61 For similar anti-nationalist arguments see for instance Sean O'Casey's *Three Dublin Plays* (London: Faber & Faber, 1998).
62 O'Neill, *At Swim, Two Boys*, 540.
63 Doyle's invention of Henry Smart is based, in part, on Ernie O'Malley's autobiography, *On Another Man's Wound* (London: Kimble & Bradford, 1936). Doyle credits O'Malley as a source on page 382 of *A Star Called Henry*.
64 Roddy Doyle, *A Star Called Henry* (New York: Penguin, 1999), p. 3.
65 'The State recognises [sic] the special position of the Holy Catholic Apostolic and Roman Church as the guardian of the Faith professed by the great majority of the citizens' (*Bunreact na hÉireann*, article 44.2).
66 Constance Markievicz, 'From Irish Citizen 23 Oct. 1915.' *In Their Own Voice: Women and Irish Nationalism*. Ed. Margaret Ward (Cork: Attic Press, 2001), pp. 52–53.
67 Doyle, *A Star Called Henry*, 41.
68 Doyle, *A Star Called Henry*, 72.
69 Doyle, *A Star Called Henry*, 27, 118.
70 Doyle, *A Star Called Henry*, 102.
71 James Drewett, 'An Interview with Roddy Doyle.' *Irish Studies Review* 11.3 (2003): 346.
72 Fearghal McGarry, *The Rising: Ireland: Easter 1916* (Oxford: Oxford University Press, 2010), p. 165. To be fair, McGarry goes on to indicate that 'a more accurate portent of the place of women in the Irish Republic that ultimately emerged was the experience of the many

women who spent Easter week out of sight in the G.P.O., confined to the kitchen at the back of the building: "we were very busy and we did not get invitations to come down" [BMH WS 216 (Louise Gavan Duffy)],' p. 165. Of course, as we'll see, Miss O'Shea directly rejects this subjugation: 'I didn't come here to make stew, Henry' (Doyle, *A Star Called Henry*, 138).
73 Constance Markievicz, 'From *Cumann na mBan* Vol. II, No. 10. Easter 1926.' *In Their Own Voice: Women and Irish Nationalism*. Ed. Margaret Ward (Cork: Attic Press, 2001), p. 35.
74 Markievicz, 'From *Cumann na mBan*,' p. 35.
75 Doyle, *A Star Called Henry*, 295.
76 Drewett, 'An Interview with Roddy Doyle,' 345. Doyle, who lists *On Another Man's Wound* as a source for his novel, would have also been made aware of this link between *Cumann na mBan*, *Fianna Eireann*, and ancient mythology by Ernie O'Malley: 'Fianna Eireann had been started by the Countess Markievicz. They were scouts trained to the use of arms, modeled somewhat on the ancient Fianna of the legends,' p. 62.
77 Margaret Skinnider, *Doing My Bit for Ireland* (New York: The Century Co, 1917), p. 6.
78 Jo Fox, 'Women of the Celts in Myth, Legend, and Story.' *SkyeViews* 8 (1996): n. pag. www.pabay.org/skyeviews.html. 29 December 2009.
79 Skinnider, *Doing My Bit for Ireland*, p. 67.
80 Sinéad McCoole, *No Ordinary Women: Irish Female Activists in the Revolutionary Years, 1900–1923* (Madison, WI: University of Wisconsin Press, 2003), p. 42.
81 Skinnider, *Doing My Bit for Ireland*, p. 148.
82 Sinéad McCoole, 'Seven Women of the Labour Movement 1916.' *Labour*. 2010. www.labour.ie/seven_women_of_the_labour_movement1916.pdf. 4 January 2010.
83 Doyle, *A Star Called Henry*, 81.
84 Doyle, *A Star Called Henry*, 124.
85 Doyle, *A Star Called Henry*, 149. Miss O'Shea's insistence that she can 'fire a gun as well as any man' echoes Nancy Wyse-Power's assertion that 'The promoters [of Cumann na mBan] may have had in mind an auxiliary association of women acting under the general instructions of the Volunteer executive but the organization immediately declared itself to be an independent organization of women determined to make its own decisions' [BMH WS 541 (Nancy Wyse-Power)] (Qtd. in McGarry, *The Rising*, p. 61). Ernie O'Malley substantiates Wyse-Power's claim: 'Cumann na mBan, the League of Women, had been organized as an auxiliary to the Volunteers ... They were not controlled by the volunteer executive' (*On Another Man's Wound*, p. 61).
86 Doyle, *A Star Called Henry*, 305.

87 Doyle, *A Star Called Henry*, 371.
88 See for instance Brian Donnelly, 'Roddy Doyle: From Barrytown to the G.P.O.' *Irish University Review* 30.1 (2000): 17–31; Lorraine Piroux, '"I'm Black an' I'm Proud": Re-Inventing Irishness in Roddy Doyle's "The Commitments."' *College Literature* 25.2 (1998): 45–57; and Åke Persson, 'Between Displacement and Renewal: The Third Space in Roddy Doyle's Novels.' *Nordic Irish Studies* 5.1 (2006): 59–71.
89 Doyle, *A Star Called Henry*, 104.
90 Doyle, *A Star Called Henry*, 119.
91 McGarry, *The Rising*, p. 29.
92 Doyle, *A Star Called Henry*, 134–135.
93 For a detailed comparison of Henry Smart to J.M. Synge's playboy of the Western world Christy Mahon, see Charlotte Jacklein's 'Rebel Songs and Hero Pawns: Music in *A Star Called Henry*.' *New Hibernia Review* 9.4 (2005): 129–143.
94 Doyle, *A Star Called Henry*, 136.
95 Doyle, *A Star Called Henry*, 102.
96 Doyle, *A Star Called Henry*, 138.
97 Rosemarie Tong, *Feminist Thought*. 3rd edn (Boulder, CO: Westview Press, 2009), p. 4.
98 McGarry, *The Rising*, p. 29.
99 Doyle, *A Star Called Henry*, 149.
100 Doyle, *A Star Called Henry*, 196.
101 Doyle, *A Star Called Henry*, 198.
102 Doyle, *A Star Called Henry*, 196.
103 Doyle, *A Star Called Henry*, 300.
104 Doyle, *A Star Called Henry*, 301.
105 Doyle, *A Star Called Henry*, 295.
106 Markievicz, 'From *Cumann na mBan*,' p. 75.
107 Doyle, *A Star Called Henry*, 305.
108 Roddy Doyle, 'Revel Rebel: Interview with Róisin Ingle.' *Irish Times*, 28 August 1999. www.tcd.ie/irishfilm/. 30 December 2009, p. 2.
109 Markievicz, 'From *Cumann na mBan*,' p. 35.
110 Jose Lanters, 'Demythicizing/Remythicizing the Rising: Roddy Doyle's *A Star Called Henry*.' *Hungarian Journal of English and American Studies* 8.1 (2002): 248.
111 Derrida, *Spectres of Marx*, p. 138.

4

Gothic inheritance and the Troubles in contemporary Irish fiction

On 10 April 1998, the British and Irish governments signed the Good Friday Agreement, marking the official end of the Troubles in Northern Ireland – though not the cessation of violence. A year earlier, Jeffrey Glenn, a 46-year-old librarian in Ballynahinch, County Down, submitted an essay for a retrospective collection, *Children of The Troubles: Our Lives in the Crossfire of Northern Ireland*. In it, he recalls the pangs of terror he regularly experienced while growing up in a Belfast suburb in the 1950s:

> As a young child, I used to look carefully under my bed every night before saying my prayers. The Irish Republican Army campaign of the fifties was in full swing and I was checking for bombs. Even if I couldn't see one, I still lay quaking with fear for what seemed like hours every night.[1]

Glenn's variation on this common childhood anxiety of 'monsters under the bed' highlights the particular paranoia caused by Irish paramilitary violence that threatened to erupt into domestic spaces. Glenn was a prisoner in his own 'suburban stronghold.'[2] Outside, he recalls, 'Buses, trucks, cars, and construction equipment formed blazing barricades and groups of angry-faced men were busy hi-jacking more.'[3] Later, Belfast was to be divided by more permanent 'peace lines' constructed of iron, brick, and steel, and topped with metal netting that reached a height of twenty-five feet. These barriers separated Catholic from Protestant neighborhoods, and turned Belfast streets into labyrinthine passages flanked by crumbling, bombed-out buildings – Glenn uses Gothic tropes to describe the Belfast cityscape and the 'endlessly repetitive pattern of attrition [throwing] their shadow[s] over everyday life.'[4]

Irish writers have long been obsessed with, and haunted by, Ireland's troubled history, and have regularly turned to Gothic evocations of ghosts and vampires as a means of negotiating Ireland's uncanny historical repetitions.[5] In 1996, historian Kevin Whelan observed, 'In Ireland, an appeal to the past inevitably worried old wounds on which the scar tissue had never fully congealed.'[6] And in her 1999 study, *The Gothic Family Romance*, Margot Backus identified Ireland's fascination with historical unrest as particularly Gothic: 'In Ireland, the Gothic, with its necromantic interest in the transmission of things – property, capital, curses, guilt – across generations, has had precisely the effect of "worrying old wounds."'[7] Contemporary Irish novelists, including John Banville, Emma Donoghue, and Patrick McCabe, have turned to the Gothic as a vehicle for picking at Ireland's colonial scabs. And Seamus Deane in *Reading in the Dark* (1996) and Anna Burns in *No Bones* (2001) have employed elements of the Gothic to represent the psychological burden caused by the return of Ireland's Troubles.[8]

In *Reading in the Dark* and *No Bones*, Deane and Burns both use child narrators who, through Gothic tropes, relate their personal accounts of the Northern Troubles. This common narrative choice highlights recurrent psychological damage caused by transgenerational acts of retributive violence in the North. The contemporary Gothic in Ireland generally serves to shadow the progress of Irish modernity with narratives that expose the underside of postcolonial nationhood – the ongoing struggle for a 32-county Republic, and recurring debates about whether Protestantism or Catholicism constitutes the 'true' Irish national character. By reimagining ancestral voices that endorse absolution rather than retribution, Deane and Burns break from popular political and social discourse that draws upon Ireland's ghosts as a way of justifying recurrent political violence. Both authors employ the familiar trope of the-past-haunting-the-present, but reverse typical outcomes. By focusing on the domestic consequences of the Troubles, specifically trauma experienced by children, both authors imagine a new generation of haunted individuals struggling to regain self-possession.

The Gothic in Ireland is a spectral genre. Like the Troubles, a seemingly revenant historical event, the Gothic is ghostly: it is a genre obsessed with the eruption of the past into the present, and therefore it most accurately represents the historical ghosts that 'remain always to come and to come-back.'[9] According to Kelly Hurley, 'The Gothic is rightly, if partially, understood as a cyclical genre that reemerges in times of cultural stress in order to negotiate anxieties for its readership by working through them in displaced (sometimes supernaturalized) form.'[10] With its litany of recurrent characters, themes, and narrative devices, the Gothic began, and continues, as a narrative mode of responding to continual social crisis.

The earliest Gothic novels – Horace Walpole's *The Castle of Otranto* (1765), Clara Reeve's *The Old English Baron* (1777) – established characters, settings, and props that quickly became the recurring and guiding tropes of the genre: gloomy mansions, evil doubles, wild landscapes, religious anxiety, psychosis, and rampaging mobs are used to comment on the sociopolitical anxiety over aristocratic privilege and the fear that the lower classes might overthrow the decadent and amoral aristocracy. Following the beginning of the French Revolution (1789–1799), additional conservative voices, like Anne Radcliffe (1764–1823), continue the tradition of replacing 'evil' aristocrats with their more gentle and mannered (i.e., English) counterparts. But while Radcliffe's paragons of female virtue – Emily in *The Mysteries of Udolpho* (1794), Ellena in *The Italian* (1797) – are members of aristocratic families, the values, ideals, and morals they display are clearly those of the rising English *middle* class. Recurrent themes of transgression and excess, threatened damnation, pursuit, persecution, and tyranny abound.[11] E.J. Cleary observes that the overtly didactic program of early Gothic literature is in line with the eighteenth-century pragmatic theory of the novel: Gothic novels aim to scare individuals into moral, virtuous behavior. Matthew Lewis's *The Monk* (1796), however, takes Walpole's influence in another direction, crafting grotesque scenes meant not only to terrify but also to disturb and titillate his readers. Jean Paul Riquelme notes that at the end of the eighteenth century, these established elements of the genre began to appear in national writing beyond the pale: after the French Revolution, 'the characteristics and issues apparent in Gothic writing of the eighteenth century carry forward into the nineteenth and twentieth centuries, but they are significantly transformed, intensified, and disseminated by interactions with national literatures and political events outside England.'[12] In Ireland, for instance, a number of nineteenth-century novelists turn to the Gothic as a useful narrative mode for commenting upon colonial oppression.

At the outset of the nineteenth century, Gothic modes crept into Irish fiction in works like Maria Edgeworth's *Castle Rackrent*

(1800) and Sydney Owenson's *The Wild Irish Girl* (1806); both texts employed recurrent narrative devices such as multiple and unreliable narrators, opaque narratives, and use of the fantastic to evoke horror in order to deal with the anxieties of a usurped aristocracy. It is, however, Irish-born Charles Robert Maturin's *Melmoth the Wanderer* (1820) that many critics claim 'as the last – and possibly the greatest – of the Gothic novels in the line from Walpole through Radcliffe and Lewis.'[13] Maturin's novel, according to David Punter, 'casts a bitter eye over the whole process of history and historical narration as he *and* Ireland have seen it.'[14] Maturin offers sociopolitical commentary on the inescapable suspension between theological and social narratives, as between Catholicism and Protestantism; on surveillance, suggesting Ireland's colonial condition under English domination; and on historical uncertainty, highlighted by Ireland's long, convoluted historiographical debate between nationalist and loyalist historians and fiction writers.

Later in the century, as a part of what has been termed the Second Wave Gothic, these same 'themes about the unreliability of history and the perverseness of power'[15] run through works by Irish writers, including J.S. Le Fanu's *Uncle Silas* (1864) and *In a Glass Darkly* (1872; site of the vampiric 'Carmilla'), Oscar Wilde's *The Picture of Dorian Gray* (1890/1891), and Bram Stoker's *Dracula* (1897). Each work 'regularly present[s] aspects of the Gothic translated to locations in which agents of empire experience disturbing encounters with nature and with indigenous peoples that challenge their sanity and their ideas about civilization.'[16]

Stoker's *Dracula*, perhaps the most popularly recognized Gothic novel, has undergone numerous permutations in modern film, has an uninterrupted print history, and maintains far-reaching influence over contemporary science fiction, fantasy, and horror narratives. But despite its popular success, its fantastic supernatural elements (the shape-shifting count), and its sensationalism (a trio of sexually aggressive vampireses), *Dracula* also articulates serious sociopolitical agendas. As Raphael Ingelbien points out,[17] the Count has been read by Irish Studies scholars such as Terry Eagleton and Seamus Deane as an aristocratic landlord of the failing Protestant Ascendancy, incapable of transitioning into modernity (1089); conversely, Bruce Stewart casts the Count as a Catholic middle-class Land Leaguer intent on taking back Ireland through the use of political violence,[18] which reinforces Stephen Arata's observation that *Dracula* relies upon traditional Gothic tropes such as wild landscapes, alluring wickedness, and the unbalancing of hierarchies of masculinity and femininity as well as of good and evil to comment upon the 'Late-Victorian nightmare of reverse colonization.'[19]

In the opening chapter, Jonathan Harker's description of the horrors of the Transylvanian forest, complete with wolves, darkness, a ghostly blue flame, and a mysterious coachman illustrate common English fears of Ireland 'beyond the pale' – a space where numerous rebellions against the Act of Union had originated.[20] This fear of recurrence, of some thing *coming back*, is, according to Siobhán Kilfeather, the most distinctive feature of the Irish Gothic.[21] In Ireland, historical repetition (and the specters that accompany recurrence) is more horrifying than stock Gothic machinery such as diabolical laughter, malevolent monks, or inquisition prisons. The Gothic, therefore, has remained particularly attractive to Irish novelists who have continued to use it throughout the twentieth century as a vehicle for constructing and contesting distinctions between nationalists and unionists, Catholics and Protestants – cultural divisions that mere modernity cannot resolve.

A number of Irish texts concerned with the Northern Troubles employ the Gothic to express feelings of anxiety and inherited psychological trauma caused by the conflict's 'uncanny' return despite claims that the Gothic genre was dying out at the end of the twentieth century. I think of Patrick McCabe's *Breakfast on Pluto* (1998) in which a Catholic priest rapes his housekeeper, who then gives birth to a son that grows up to be a self-proclaimed 'high-class escort girl' looking to unravel the mystery of his ancestry. And Colm Tóibín's *The Heather Blazing* (1992), which evokes Ireland's wild costal and political landscapes – equally treacherous – as setting for a series of haunting memories that conflate long-dead relatives with the living, and bygone wars with contemporary terrorism. Despite these and other examples of contemporary Irish Gothic texts, Fred Botting declares at the conclusion of his genre study, *Gothic* (1996), that Francis Ford Coppola's filmed adaptation of Bram Stoker's *Dracula* (1992) unequivocally staked the heart of the genre: 'With Coppola's *Dracula*,' Botting argues, 'Gothic dies, divested of its excesses, of its transgressions, horrors and diabolical laughter, of its brilliant gloom and rich darkness of its artificial and suggestive forms.'[22] He admits, however, that 'dying, of course, might just be the prelude to other spectral returns,'[23] a clever echo of Jonathan

Harker's observation early on in Stoker's novel that 'the old centuries had, and have, powers of their own which mere "modernity" cannot kill.'[24] The past – whether undead vampire, historical event, or literary form – is not static.

Seamus Deane and Anna Burns employ the standard machinery of the Gothic in their Troubles fiction, but set it in a recurring, transgenerational framework. Extreme mental disturbance emerges in both *Reading in the Dark* and *No Bones* in the figure of the Gothic specter, a manifestation of psychological trauma caused by the inherited curse of transgenerational violence in Ireland.[25] Deane and Burns therefore invoke critiques of inheritance offered by the Gothic in order to suggest alternative ways of imagining the narratives that come to us from the past. They use the necromantic capabilities of the Gothic to show how confrontation with the past (and the specters that are part and parcel of it) can lead to a stoppage of unproductive, malevolent haunting.

As John Paul Riquelme notes, the Gothic 'is frequently a vehicle for staging and challenging ideological thinking rather than a means of furthering it.'[26] In *Reading in the Dark* and *No Bones*, the Gothic mode is used not merely to illuminate Ireland's haunted predicament, but to stage encounters with Irish history that both haunt and exorcise contemporary Ireland at the same time. Both novels illustrate just how comprehensive and habitual the social machinery of vengeance has become in Northern Ireland, and offer requested haunting as a way of breaking the pattern of psychological trauma passed down from a troubled past that is anything but dead and gone.

In previous chapters, I've drawn upon Jacques Derrida's understanding of specters, especially their ability to transgress temporalities, in order to suggest a similar way of understanding how historians and literary artists have imagined the relationship between Ireland's past and present and therefore how authors are able to manipulate those histories. Derrida writes of ghosts, 'no one can be sure if by returning [the ghost] testifies to a living past or to a living future ... A ghost never dies, it remains always to come and to come-back.'[27] This is precisely the specter that haunts Ireland: an ever-present historical narrative that, like a palimpsest, is not erased, but written over; the past becomes a deferred threat of violence waiting to reappear. And here, too, is one of the distinctive features of the Irish Gothic, which speaks of history as, in the words of David Punter, 'inevitably involved in specific modes of ghostly persistence which may occur when, particularly in Scotland and Ireland, national aspirations are thwarted by conquest or by settlement, as they have been so often.'[28] In contemporary Irish fiction, writers call upon rather than attempting to exorcize the past. The Irish Gothic works to think through and to critique Irish historical unrest as much as it works to represent it.

At 10:40pm on 7 May 1966 a man threw a petrol bomb at a Catholic-owned storefront in Upper Charleville Street, between Belfast's Shankill and Crumlin Roads. He missed, and the bomb exploded inside the next-door home of Matilda Gould, a 77-year-old Protestant widow. She later died in the hospital from severe burns.[29] Although this attack was targeted at Catholics, because a Protestant woman died the act was taken for one of Catholic aggression. Two weeks after the bombing, on 21 May 1966, The Ulster Volunteer Force (UVF), a loyalist paramilitary organization that formed in response to a perceived revival of the Irish Republican Army (IRA), and to prime minister Terence O'Neill's promise of reform for Northern Ireland's minority Catholic population, issued a declaration of war: 'From this day, we declare war against the IRA and its splinter groups. Known IRA men will be executed mercilessly and without hesitation.'[30] In response to increased UVF activity, the Provisional IRA (PIRA) formed in early 1970 and quickly established itself as the defender of the nationalist community in the North. The Provos, as they became known, were also determined to revive armed struggle against British rule in Northern Ireland.

Officially, then, the Troubles in Northern Ireland can be said to have begun in 1966.[31] Yet, in 'Sins of Our Fathers,' the aptly titled introduction to *'We Wrecked the Place': Contemplating an End to the Northern Irish Troubles*, Jonathan Stevenson observes that

> As with everything Irish, centuries of history animate the present and recent past. The island's heritage is speckled with violent events, which serve as justifications for more violence. Depending on the context, republicans and loyalists will assert that relevant history starts at the Norman conquest (1171), the Irish rebellion in Ulster against Protestants (1641), Oliver Cromwell's evangelistic terror against Catholics (1649), King William's victory at the Battle of the Boyne (1690), Wolfe Tone's United Irishmen rebellion (1798), the Easter Rising (1916), partition (1921), the founding of the new UVF (1966), the Catholic civil rights movement (1968), the August riots in Belfast (1969), or the IRA split (1970).[32]

The popular assumption that unless we know the past we are condemned to repeat it often appears reversed in Ireland. According to Irish historical novelist Tom Flanagan, 'In Ireland, in fact, it could be argued that it is knowledge of history, history speaking in ancestral voices, rather than ignorance, which enforces its repetition.'[33] Stevenson's list of retributive events certainly justifies Flanagan's claim. The case of the past-haunting-the-present is often made to justify the escalating violence at the end of the 1960s. Many historians, in fact, see 1966 as the beginning of the end of the half-century-long Troubles. For instance, historian Jack Holland observes in 'Return of the Gunman 1966–1969,' 'The Troubles, most assumed, were a thing of the past, a name given to the turmoil of the early 1920s when the Irish Republican Army fought to drive the British out of Ireland.'[34] The IRA succeeded, however, in securing only twenty-six of the thirty-two counties. For the minority nationalist community in the North, the Troubles therefore signified the unfinished business of the 1916–1921 anti-colonial campaign.

For the purpose of this book, which recognizes contemporary Irish novelists' obsession with historical unrest and their call for the past to haunt the present, 1966 – which marked the 50th anniversary of the Easter Rising and saw the founding of the new UVF amidst rumors of the IRA revival – serves as a clear demarcation of both the return of overt anti-Catholic sentiment and of Ireland's revolutionary spirit. And like previous conflicts in Ireland, the two warring factions bifurcated predominantly along Catholic nationalist and Protestant unionist lines.

Nationalist historians tend to color the Troubles as the revived fight for Ireland's moral right to a thirty-two-county sovereignty. This argument is laid out by historians and cultural theorists such as Desmond Fennell (*The State of the Nation: Ireland Since the Sixties* [1983]), Eamonn McCann (*McCann: War and Peace in Northern Ireland* [1998]), Tim Pat Coogan (*The Troubles* [2002]), and Peter Beresford Ellis (*Eyewitness to Irish History* [2004]). On the other hand, Revisionist accounts of the reemergent violence in the North typically argue for Northern Ireland's justified struggle to retain union with the British commonwealth: Roy Foster's *Paddy and Mr. Punch: Connections in Irish and English History* (1993), Garret Fitzgerald's *Towards a New Ireland* (1972), Conor Cruise O'Brien's *States of Ireland* (1974), Claire O'Halloran's *Partition and the Limits of Irish Nationalism: An Ideology Under Stress* (1987), and Ruth Dudley Edwards's *Patrick Pearse: The Triumph of Failure* (2006).

Gothic inheritance and the Troubles

Despite ideological division, however, both nationalist and unionist writers regularly couch their observations in terms of Gothic repetition and recurrence – the Northern Troubles are repeatedly represented as a conflict from the past that will not stay past, the past that had in fact never disappeared. Such a pattern of recurrence becomes even more striking when viewed through Derrida's theories of spectral presence: 'They are always *there*, specters, even if they do not exist, even if they are no longer, even if they are not yet.'[35] What this means for post-peace process Northern Ireland is that both the spirit of revolution (the desire for freedom) and the specter of revolution (the use of violence to obtain it) continue to contaminate the seemingly peaceful present. Or, said another way, sectarian violence will inevitably return because political and cultural differences still haunt Northern Ireland.

For instance, at the end of Belfast-born playwright Anne Devlin's *The Long March* (1984), protagonist Helen Walsh reflects on the People's Democracy march from Belfast to Derry in 1969, and contemplates the spectral nature of Irish history:

> I still remember that time when we thought we were beginning a new journey: the long march. What we didn't see was that it had begun a long time before with someone else's journey; we were simply getting through the steps in our own time.[36]

Walsh implies that her 'long march' is a revenant event populated by different participants. Devlin's play brings the specter of Irish oppression at the hands of British soldiers during the Irish Revolution (1916–1921) into the historical space of Catholic civil-rights protests in Northern Ireland in 1969 as a way of critiquing the Royal Ulster Constabulary (RUC) attacks on peaceful demonstrators. Walsh's contemplation of historical return illustrates a consistent Gothic trope in contemporary Irish fiction, namely the use of historical ghosts – or being haunted by history – as a way of placing turn-of-the-century Ireland in conversation with the traumatic events of its historical past. Estheticized responses to the Troubles, such as Devlin's play, present sectarian conflict as a revenant event that draws upon Ireland's traumatic colonial history. Seamus Deane and Anna Burns continue to employ the Gothic (its formal innovations, tropes, and critical register) as the most precise narrative mode through which to both depict and critique the conflict's 'uncanny' reappearance.

Sigmund Freud argues that the 'uncanny' evokes fear from individuals who are confronted by a repressed memory – in this case, memory of revolution. He writes, 'the uncanny is that species of the frightening that goes back to what was once well known and had long been familiar,'[37] but has become (through repression) unfamiliarly horrifying. Revolution in Ireland evokes feelings of home and normalcy, while simultaneously illustrating that home has changed utterly, bringing with it a sense of uncertainty.

Seamus Deane's first novel is set near the border of Derry/Londonderry (Northern Ireland) and Donegal (Republic of Ireland) in post-World War II Northern Ireland, where the restless ghosts of the 1920s Troubles haunt geographical and generational borders. Against the backdrop of the impending Troubles, Deane's unnamed narrator spends his childhood trying to uncover his family's buried past by piecing together the incomplete and obfuscated facts of his Uncle's mysterious disappearance in April, 1922 – facts that the boy's parents and grandparents have tried, and failed, to forget:

> Hauntings are, in their own way, very specific. Everything has to be exact, even the vaguenesses. My family's history was like that too. It came to me in bits, from people who rarely recognized all they had told. Some of the things I remember, I don't really remember. I've just been told about them so now I feel I remember them, and want to the more because it is so important for others to forget them.[38]

The boy explains that his curiosity about familial ghosts was born of others' desire to forget them, or in Gothic terms, the boy's parents and grandparents have attempted to make the familiar history of their family unfamiliar.

Deane populates his novel with Gothicized figures from Celtic folklore (heroic ghosts, malevolent fairies, and secret passages) and juxtaposes them with more realistic, psychological hauntings (faded memory, violent trauma, and torturous uncertainty) as a way of compounding myth and reality, past and present, and domestic and social conflicts. In Deane's novel, the Gothic clearly exists, in part, to use Freudian terminology, as a way of collapsing what should be *heimlich* into the *unheimlich*. It acts, in other words, as a spectral genre in which temporalities, events, or peoples are enjambed as a way of placing twenty-first-century Ireland in conversation with the traumatic events of its historical past to show how confrontation with the past might attenuate malevolent haunting in the present.

Reading in the Dark, originally published on 3 October 1996 in the midst of a stalled peace process, questions failed and failing attempts to resolve the conflict in Northern Ireland.[39] Deane uses domestic anxieties – such as the feared, anticipated, and much hated return of familial specters which threaten to completely unravel the narrator's already dysfunctional family – to illustrate the more far-reaching social anxieties in Northern Ireland: the feared, anticipated, and much hated return of sectarian violence. Written at a time in Northern Ireland when peace still seemed elusive, *Reading in the Dark* illustrates the maddening escalation of transgenerational religious and political intolerance.

The novel's pointed and meta-textual use of the Gothic shows that putting an end to the Troubles does not necessitate abandoning the past. In fact, in *Reading in the Dark*, Deane adopts standard Gothic machinery – ghosts, dysfunctional families, psychological violence, revolutionary anxieties, and dangerous curiosity – to argue the opposite. He calls forth specters from Ireland's past troubles to put more recent violent political conflict on full display. Doing so seems to exorcise or resist patterns of ideologically influenced retribution that have historically led to psychological and physical violence within the nation. In Ireland, looking backwards often uncovers a clear pattern of retributive violence stemming from colonial trauma. The first step towards ending this tradition, Deane's novel suggests, is to invite ancestral voices to speak in the present, to preserve the voices so that they are not forgotten, and to translate them so that they can speak with a revised significance to end, rather than continue, Ireland's unproductive Troubles.[40]

Over the course of the novel, the narrator works to learn his family's secrets in order to reconstruct the truth about his paternal uncle Eddie's disappearance. The narrator's maternal grandfather, mother, and father have all produced theories concerning Eddie's whereabouts. The father assumes his brother died a hero of the IRA; the narrator's grandfather claims he absconded to America. The family secret – known only to the narrator's grandfather, mother, and a man named Crazy Joe, is that the grandfather (a lieutenant in the IRA during the earlier Troubles) ordered Eddie's execution because the narrator's mother had (inaccurately) fingered him as a police informant. 'And then she had married [Eddie's brother], closing herself in forever, haunted forever.'[41] She has incarcerated herself in that most Gothic of prisons, her mind.

In the novel's opening scene, 'Stairs: February 1945,' Deane introduces stock Gothic conventions in order to attune his readers to the way in which he will use spectral tropes throughout the novel. Traditionally, the Gothic has been employed to arouse a strong affective response of anxiety, fear, and recoil from its readers; Deane, however, uses it to intrigue, thereby asking his readers to become critics. The novel employs the Gothic in a meta-critical way, calling attention to its use in the novel as a generic convention.

Reading in the Dark begins with the narrator's description of the staircase upon which he first learns that his house is haunted: 'It was a short staircase, fourteen steps in all, covered in lino from which the original pattern had been polished away to the point where it had the look of a faint memory.'[42] The boy's description of the faded linoleum upon the stairs as resembling a faint memory both calls attention to the frustration he encounters while trying to conjure the ghost and betrays his mother's anxiety over the fact that the ghost is actually her faint memory of Eddie, which she cannot escape. In the dialogue that follows, the boy clearly defines his objective to call his family's ghosts into full view, while his mother denies his request to be haunted:

> 'Don't move,' my mother said from the landing. 'Don't cross that window.' I was on the tenth step, she was on the landing. I could have touched her. 'There's something there between us. A shadow. Don't move.' I had no intention. I was enthralled. 'There's somebody there. Somebody unhappy. Go back down the stairs, son.'[43]

The boy is ordered back down the stairs without further explanation, but he yearns to experience the feeling of being haunted, which he imagines is 'a bit like the smell of damp clothes.'[44] His mother denies his fantasy: 'Don't talk yourself into believing it.'[45] But it is too late, the boy is possessed with excitement: 'We were haunted! We had a ghost, even in the middle of the afternoon.'[46] His response reverses our expectation that ghosts terrify, that they are to be avoided. He spends the rest of his childhood trying to encounter this domestic specter instead of trying to escape from it.

The novel illustrates that nervous abhorrence of the past versus intense curiosity as to how that past continues to influence the present is the difference between perpetual animosity and the possibility of healing old wounds. This distinction is important because it suggests that a careful examination and reinvention of history is necessary to successfully recalibrate the present. Steven Bruhm maintains, 'The Gothic's basic investment in ravaging history and fragmenting the past meshes with our own investments now as we attempt to reinvent history as a way of healing the perpetual loss in modern existence.'⁴⁷ Such examinations of the past are particularly poignant in Northern Ireland where, for so long, established patterns of loyalty and animosity have caused more violence to erupt.

Deane casts Northern Ireland as a place echoing with the cries of the past, where the individual and political are delicately interwoven, and personal and national histories rely upon both folklore and the supernatural as a means of explaining trauma. He exploits the Gothic's recurrent structural devices that include interrupted and incomplete narratives, not to reinforce these inherited gaps or secrets, but to illustrate their latent dangers. In a recent article, Daniel Ross contrasts *Reading in the Dark* with traditional Irish bildungsroman such as James Joyce's *A Portrait of the Artist as a Young Man*: 'Deane's story inverts the pattern that we have come to expect from the Irish bildungsroman, where the son rebels against the mother.'⁴⁸ In Joyce's text Stephen Dedalus flees from his biological mother and mother Ireland. Rather than flee, the boy in *Reading in the Dark* attempts to heroically exorcize the family ghosts by calling on them to make their secrets known, thereby neutralizing their ability to terrorize. Ross, therefore, identifies Joyce and Deane as unsuccessful exorcists:

> Joyce's highly autobiographical fiction testifies to his unsuccessful attempt to bury his Dublin past – replete with all its quarrels with family and friends – forever. It is little wonder that Deane, on whom the Joycean influences are clear, uses a similar technique.⁴⁹

While Ross correctly notes Joyce's influence on Deane, their similarity, I argue, is not that they both attempt to bury Irish history, but that they call forth Ireland's specters to put them on full display. Both *A Portrait* and *Reading in the Dark* illustrate that what allows historical specters to terrorize the present is not necessarily forgetting the past, but ignoring it. Ultimately, Deane's focus upon one family's obscured past in *Reading in the Dark* implies that Ireland's political history is similarly opaque.

The boy's obsession with his family's past, and the relationship between past and present, is typical of the Gothic, which is further invoked by his description of the family's home as a prison. While the boy waits for his mother to descend the stairs with news of the ghost, he describes his gloomy home complete with 'cobweb tremors' and 'moiling darkness,' 'the clock in the bedroom' counting down what seems to be a prison sentence while he 'stared into the redness locked behind the bars of the range.'⁵⁰ The boy calls our attention to the bars of the fireplace, suggesting the Gothic nature of his situation: both mother and child are prisoners in this house – the mother because she is faced with constant reminders of a traumatic past that she so badly wants to forget, and the curious boy because he wants to know completely his family's secrets, but cannot.

In her article that explores 'the feared, half-anticipated and much hated return of the Troubles in Northern Ireland,'[51] Maeve Davey raises the question that I see lying below the surface of *Reading in the Dark*:

> How is this long and bloody conflict meant to be finally and lastingly resolved if everyone, from the public to politicians, journalists, playwrights and novelists, is too busy looking the other way to address the disturbing legacy it has left behind?[52]

Davey's question implies that ignoring the legacy of the Troubles has led to Ireland's imprisonment within repetitive acts of sectarian violence. Deane's novel makes a similar argument, and further implies that the older generations who have inherited divisive ideology will have to rely upon their children to be tolerant of political and religious difference in Northern Ireland.

Reading in the Dark suggests actively conjuring the spectral past in order to come to terms with it – to divest the past of its ability to terrorize. The instant the boy's mother appears at the bottom of the stairs he asks, 'did you see anything?'[53] Even though she insists, 'No, nothing, nothing at all ... There's nothing there,'[54] the boy rushes to the window to see for himself. He is certain that the ghost is there: 'I felt someone behind me and turned to see a darkness leaving the window.'[55] The mother's insistence that no ghost exists, and the boy's certainty that *something* is there, reinforces the divide between those who silence their ghosts – and therefore grant them the authority to terrorize – and those who confront the past, and therefore deprive the past of its ability to instill fear in the haunted. The boy's mother is terrorized by the threat of the past erupting into the present and reigniting familial and paramilitary feuds. On the other hand, the boy actively calls forth and untangles his family's convoluted and veiled history with the IRA in an attempt to heal his parents' tortured relationship. *Reading in the Dark* reimagines the way individuals interact with domestic and political history by suggesting, via the boy's curiosity, that haunting can be productive. Individuals can call upon the past not to reinforce or justify acts of retributive violence, but to condemn them.

Deane's most poignant warning against abandoning the past takes shape in the character of the boy's mother at the novel's conclusion. Deane returns us to the stairs – the site of the first haunting:

> She took to the lobby window again. But she disliked anyone standing with her there to talk, most especially me. There she was with her ghosts. Now the haunting meant something new to me – now I had become the shadow.[56]

At this point, her son is the only person left that knows her secret, and his presence becomes the haunting reminder of what she has done. She goes mad with anticipation that the boy will tell her secret, that she is responsible for the execution of an innocent man (Eddie) and for the escape of an informant (McIlhenny). She asks her son, guardian of this secret, to leave. She hopes that his absence will mean the absence of this ghost in the lobby window. The novel, however, does not endorse this view. Rather, it suggests that confronting one's ghosts is the key to exorcizing them.

In 1959, when all the other holders of her secret have died or been locked in the asylum at Gransha, the boy asked his mother what she would like for her birthday: '"Just for that day," she answered, "just for that one day, the seventeenth of May, to forget everything. Or at least not to be reminded of it. Can you give me that?"'[57] He cannot, for as Derrida's theory of spectrality reminds us, 'they are always *there*, specters, even if they do not exist, even if they are no longer, even if they are not yet.'[58] The Gothic signals the specter's imminent return: 'This, the thing ("this thing") will end up coming. The *revenant* is going to come.'[59] How one responds to the specter, with curiosity or recoil, dictates whether the return is productive – as represented by the boy's curiosity and use of the past as a healing agent – or destructive – as represented by the mother's fear of the past and ultimate insanity.

Seamus Deane juxtaposes these two opposing responses to specters – curiosity and madness – in his most consciously Gothic episode of the novel: 'Grianan, September 1950.' The boy spends his summer holidays racing around and staging mock battles at the Grianan Aileach, a stone fortress in County Donegal that dates back to the rule of early Irish chieftains (c. 800 BCE).[60] 'Once,' he reports, 'my friends – Moran, Harkin, Toland – locked me in [its] secret passage.'[61] The boy's description of the place, combined with his incarceration in a secret, haunted passage, depicts the Irish architectural past in Gothic terms:

> Grianan was a great stone ring with flights of worn steps on the inside leading to a parapet that overlooked the countryside in one direction and the coastal sands of the lough in the other. At the base of one inside wall, there was a secret passage, tight and black as you crawled in and then briefly higher at the end where there was a wishing-chair of slabbed stone. You sat there and closed your eyes and wished for what you wanted most, while you listened for the breathing of the sleeping warriors of the legendary Fianna who lay below.[62]

According to the Fenian (or Ossianic) myth Cycle, Finn MacCool, King Cormac's bravest soldier, rose to mythological status along with his band of warriors – the Fianna. They are said to have possessed extraordinary skill in battle, including the supernatural ability to communicate with the Celtic otherworld. In modern Ireland, the most popular mythology surrounding the Fianna is that they lie below Ireland, ready to reawaken and defend the land in the hour of its greatest need – usually perceived as the final battle between Ireland and England. This myth remains particularly attractive to those who see the Northern Troubles as the result of continued British occupation and governance.

The Fianna myth reverses the Gothic theme of the dreaded return as well as the Gothic image of corruption beneath a desirable façade. Whereas the undead are typically thought of as malevolent creatures to be feared, Deane draws upon a myth that establishes spectral warriors as the heroic defenders of Ireland. However, in a double-reversal, Deane's narrator, who has already been identified as one who invites ghosts to haunt him, admits that he fears those heroic ghosts who are believed to fight on behalf of Ireland and its people:

> They were waiting there for the person who would make that one wish that would rouse them from their thousand-year sleep to make final war on the English and drive them from our shores forever ... I was terrified that I might, by accident, make that special wish and feel the ground buckle under me and see the dead faces rise, indistinct behind their definite axes and spears.[63]

The boy's anxiety that he might accidentally summon the Fianna seems uncharacteristic, yet this scene is juxtaposed with his earlier motivation for actively calling forth ancestral voices to haunt from beyond the grave. He conjures the dead, such as his uncle Eddie, to gain insight into his family's and Ireland's troubled histories. Here, though, he is terrified of accidentally conjuring the Fianna because he does not want to 'worry those old [colonial] wounds.'[64] Deane's narrator, incarcerated in this Gothic passageway, offers an alternate reading of the Fianna myth that imagines a dreaded return rather than a desired final battle between Ireland and England.[65] For him, the Fianna represent a retributive force that would perpetuate the cycle of violence in the North, not bring it to an end. On the other hand, he believes that the conjuration of Eddie's ghost would at least ease the tensions between him and his parents, if not between his mother and father. The boy's knowledge of his uncle's fate, however, estranges him from both parents. He observes, 'Every time [my mother] saw me she felt exposed, even though I made it clear I would never say anything;'[66] 'staying loyal to my mother made me disloyal to my father.'[67] The absence of Eddie's ghost terrorizes the entire family: the mother because she fears the truth that its return might deliver, the father because he does not know the truth about his brother's whereabouts, and the boy because he knows the truth but cannot speak it. The narrator's fear of being responsible for perpetrating the continuation of Troubles-related violence (by accidentally wishing for the Fianna to return) testifies to his motivation for seeking out ghosts earlier in the novel, which was to deny them the power to terrorize. In short, exorcising the specter of the Irish past in one context can stop cycles of violence; in another it can perpetuate them.

Aware of the psychological dangers of repressing history and its attendant specters, the boy performs a sort of exorcism inside the secret passage. He refuses the Fianna legend's efficacy by calling it to haunt him and subsequently exorcizing it by deconstructing the mythology of the legend. His action serves as a direct critique of those who try to ignore their specters, and who therefore suffer psychological trauma.

While locked in the underground passage, he does not try to block out the haunting sounds of the Fianna as might be expected. Rather, he sits in the wishing-chair concentrating on the emaciated ghost sounds within the passage:

> I imagined I could hear the breathing of the sleeping Fianna waiting for the trumpet call that would bring them to life again to fight the last battle ... If you concentrated even further, you would scent the herbal perfumes of the Druid spells and you would hear the women sighing in sexual pleasure – yes-esss-yes-esss ... I could hear the wind, or maybe it was the far-off sea. That was the breathing Fianna. I

could smell the heather and the gorse tinting the air; that was the Druid spells. I could hear the underground waters whispering; that was the women sighing.[68]

The boy conflates past myth and present reality by recognizing that the haunting sound of the breathing Fianna is also the wind, or perhaps the waves echoing in the underground passage; the perfumes are both the lingering presence of a supernatural spell, and the heather and gorse growing in the ground just above him; the sighing women are simultaneously the whispering waters of underground creeks. We can turn once again to Derrida's theory of spectrality to aid our understanding of Deane's textual logic:

> [There] is [a] fold of 'a striking difference,' Derrida maintains, between two modalities or two temporalities in the conjuration of the dead, in the evocation or convocation of the specter. One has to admit that they resemble each other. They contaminate each other.[69]

Like a palimpsest, two paintings on one canvas, the Gothic (this spectral genre) brings together two modalities and two temporalities in one moment – the myth is made real; the past is made present. The narrator instructs readers how to recognize, and perhaps more importantly how to accept, radical heterogeneity.[70]

Reading in the Dark suggests, therefore, that competing narratives always occupy the same space. Another example of this can be found in the 'Reading in the Dark' chapter, which opens with an allusion to James Murphy's *The Shan Van Vocht: A Story of the United Irishmen* (1889). Its green cover signals Irish heritage; the boy's mother's maiden name penned on the flyleaf signals domestic tradition. The two coalesce in the physical object of the book about Old Mother Ireland who calls for the men of the nation to fight for independence during the 1798 rebellion. Here Deane not only brings together social and domestic spheres (national troubles and familial troubles), but he also disrupts temporal boundaries by equating past failed rebellions with the current Troubles (1798, 1916, and 1966–1998).

Deane's novel does more than simply dramatize Northern Ireland's traumatic experience. By bringing the history of Celtic mythology into the historical space of the Northern Irish Troubles, the Grianan episode invites multiple competing and seemingly discordant narratives to coexist.[71] Deane refuses to enter the recurring debate about what constitutes the 'true' Irish national character because he rejects the notion that such a character exists. The novel's use of the Gothic return can be read as a critique of repetitive acts of violence aimed at defining Irishness. The return – of Eddie, of the Fianna, of the Troubles – is feared because these specters bring with them threats of intense psychological and physical violence. Deane puts the consequences of haunting on full display to argue for a new way of encountering the past. In the Grianan episode, Deane explores the possibility of pardoning those who do us wrong. He depicts the boy's incarceration, symbolic of constraining transgenerational violence, as a prank that does not require revenge: 'Eventually, someone came and rolled the stone back and I scrambled out into the sunshine, dazed by the light, unsteady when I walked, as though all my blood had collected around my ankles.'[72] He does not seek retribution; he simply rejoins the races and mock battles. The boy's willingness to call Ireland's ghosts into full view empowers him to deny their ability to haunt, thereby symbolically challenging the pattern of transgenerational violence into which he was born.

Deane then illustrates that by ignoring the past one inherits its specters. On their way home from Grianan, the boys encounter 'water rats,' which one of the friends, Brendan Moran, explains is the 'nickname given to customs officers.' The narrator then relates a story told to him by his father about a customs official who was also imprisoned in Grianan's haunted passageway. This incarceration, however, was not a joke among friends, but a violent political act – and as a result of the trauma, the official goes mad:

> My father told me the smugglers caught [a customs officer] one night near Grianan and they took his customs jacket off, tied him up and closed him inside the passage. It was nearly two days before they found him, and he was stark, staring mad when they got him out. He's still in the asylum at Gransha and they say he's always cold; never warmed up since. Never will.[73]

The customs official represents an older generation who, the novel suggests, typically ignores the repercussions of these repeated acts of violence, and is therefore driven mad by his incarceration. The boy reports, 'He's always cold; never warmed up. Never will.'[74] By first introducing us to the Gothic passage through the eyes of the curious young boy, however, our experience is shaped by the boy's composure throughout a potentially maddening situation. And by inviting the ghosts within the passage to haunt, thereby denying them the ability to terrorize, the boy avoids common psychological trauma associated with Troubles violence.

The customs official's misery mirrors that of the boy's mother. Haunted by the knowledge that her husband's brother was mistakenly executed as an informant on the orders of her own father, this woman's guilt is illustrative of political conflict contaminating domestic space. The incident at Grianan serves as another example of political treachery that has been passed down unchecked through generations. The mistrust of public officials has been a recurring theme in Irish history, reaching back to the nationalist hatred for fellow Irishmen who enlisted in the British Army during World War I, and who worked in the British-run police force (Royal Irish Constabulary, RIC) after the war. The families of those who took jobs in the RIC have not been trusted since, never will.

The repetition of the word 'never' is at odds with the Fianna myth's claim to an imminent 'last battle' and 'final war': it insinuates Ireland's continual subordination to England. Throughout the novel, only the narrator gives welcome to both familial and political pasts to haunt him; he actively seeks them out in order to make sense of them in relation to one another, and therefore is the only character in the novel that is able to reconcile the personal with the political. The others – his family members, police officers, and clergy – refuse to let go of centuries-old political and religious divisions that have become integral to their sense of Irishness.[75] In actuality, Deane clearly warns against abandoning personal identity for political cooperation. His novel illustrates that the anxiety about adopting new identities is actually what perpetuates the conflict. Neither side wants to recalibrate their ideals of Irishness. *Reading in the Dark* suggests that this is in fact not the way to end the Troubles; in a *Fortnight* interview Deane insists, '[If we] forget the past, [we will] forget Ireland.'[76] Deane, therefore, draws upon spectral qualities of the Gothic that are indicative of productive (or didactic) haunting: haunting that suggests a non-violent, if still conflicted, response to acts of terror. His reversal of a repetitive esthetic strategy – the Gothic return – counteracts common justification for continued violence in Northern Ireland.

Anna Burns's debut novel *No Bones* combines the psychological terror and neuroses that Seamus Deane exploits in *Reading in the Dark* with the more sensational machinery on display in earlier Gothic novels such as *Dracula*: terrifying wilderness, extreme psychosis resulting in unstable narrative time and space, and graphic sexual aggression.[77] Like Deane's eerie rural Derry, where the ghosts of executed IRA informants and the legendary Fianna continue to haunt the living, Burns transforms her native Belfast into a Gothic nightmare narrated (in part) by Amelia Lovett.[78] Chronologically, Burns's novel begins where *Reading in the Dark* leaves off (at the 'beginning' of the Troubles in Northern Ireland), and follows a similar coming-of-age structure that charts the maturation of Amelia from the age of seven in 1969 to the age of thirty-two in 1994. Over the course of twenty-five years, Amelia's best friend is blown up by a car bomb, her sister commits suicide, and she is nearly the victim of an incestuous rape. By internalizing the violence experienced in Belfast's Catholic neighborhood of Ardoyne, Amelia suffers severe anorexia and alcoholism, and finally a complete mental breakdown resulting in confinement at a London insane asylum. The novel, divided into twenty-three interrupted and incomplete episodes told through the eyes of multiple confused narrators, mirrors Amelia's psychosis.

Burns's use of the Gothic return highlights an ever-present historical narrative that is continuously written over by increasingly violent acts, thereby creating a culture of revenge in which the past manifests in the present. Burns' protagonists meta-textually recognize elements of the Gothic in their surroundings, and are therefore able to undermine and reverse typical 'revenge' plots by exposing the machinery that produces unending acts of retribution. *No Bones* illustrates just how all-encompassing and internalized vengeance has become in Northern Ireland. Judith Grossman observes, 'The driving force of *No Bones* is a passionate indictment of the decades-long rule of sociopathic killers in Belfast's neighborhoods, and of the deluded families willing to pitch child after child into that deadly arena.'[79] This culture of revenge in Northern Ireland, which *No Bones* works to overturn, becomes particularly clear in an early chapter titled 'Somethin' Political' in which Amelia outlines her mother's fighting rules: 'Rule Number One: (a) Don't start fights. (b) If someone else starts them, get stuck in, for you've got to save face no matter what ... Rule Number Two: Never run away.'[80] Thus, as Margot Backus observes of Glenn Patterson's *Burning Your Own* (1988), *No Bones* is a novel that 'explores the position of children within a transgenerational familial and national system that appropriates them into a priori patterns of loyalty and animosity.'[81] Children in the novel are made to suffer the consequences of their ancestors' actions, a particularly Gothic plot device. Amelia and her siblings are ordered to 'get stuck in' the cycle of sectarian violence. Both of Amelia's older siblings – her brother Mick, a PIRA operative, and her older sister Lizzie, who solves every conflict with her fists – 'very much resembled her parents, at least as they used to be, before they'd become useless and afraid.'[82] Amelia, on the other hand, refuses her role in the recurring drama.

In a narrative shift similar to that executed by Seamus Deane in *Reading in the Dark*, Burns's use of the Gothic rejects firmly established patterns of Ireland's historical unrest. She suggests an alternative way of dealing with the persistent call for retribution by placing Amelia at odds with familial ideology. Amelia questions Rule Number Two's promotion of recurrent acts of retributive violence at any cost: 'I just couldn't come to grips with that Rule Number Two at all. It seemed to me there was something terribly wrong with it.'[83] Her mother admits, 'It may not be much but when you've been murdered, and you will be, you'll at least have done your best and you won't have run away.'[84] But Amelia insists, 'Grown-ups never understood. They were stupid, distracted, mindless sorts of beings. They never had a clue. They always got it wrong.'[85] Amelia attempts to break this transgenerational system of loyalty and animosity by simply ignoring the conflict around her.

Amelia's refusal to participate in the conflict, however, initially results in psychotic fragmentation: Amelia experiences a mental breakdown that bifurcates her into what she refers to as 'dual realities'[86] – she simultaneously exists in Belfast and in London, in the past and in the present. She refuses to be sacrificed to a transgenerational pattern of violence that would, at the very least, effectively kill her capacity to think and act independently. While Amelia successfully retreats from the physical dangers of numerous schoolyard and workplace riots, and later escapes from Ardoyne to Camden Town, she eventually goes mad. Her attempt to ignore the external political madness of troubled Belfast causes the physical violence from the streets to manifest as psychological violence.

Burns's most direct commentary on the extreme states of mental disturbance caused by the inescapable recurring violence in Northern Ireland, and her clearest articulation of what she thinks will end Troubles-related psychosis, comes in two later chapters ('Triggers, 1991' and 'No Bones, 1991–1992') in which she draws heavily upon the Gothic to narrate the spectral return of two ghosts from Amelia's past: her childhood friend Roberta, who was killed by a car bomb in 1975, and her sister Liżzie, who committed suicide in 1989.

No Bones reinforces the popular assumption that Ireland is a place of recurrent traumas, a 'strange country' (Deane) where 'the old centuries had, and have, powers of their own which mere "modernity" cannot kill.'[87] The Troubles, after all, continuously (re)appear as a series of violent events, which serve as justifications for more violence. We can thus think of Burns's use of the Gothic as a means of critiquing the unwillingness to challenge seemingly irrepressible forces from the past that continue to tyrannize the present; however, Amelia Lovett does offer a challenge of sorts – she escapes to London. Like the mother in Deane's *Reading in the Dark*, Amelia hopes to ignore her past, and as a result suffers a mental breakdown. The specters from her Belfast past cross the Irish Sea as easily as they transgress temporal and metaphysical borders:

> She was having dual realities again, right here in front of her. As well as being in Camden Town in London, she was also on Belfast's Crumlin Road ... Something else was starting to bother her. It turned out to be Roberta McKeown who, at that moment, was walking by. Roberta shouldn't have been walking by and Amelia had no business to be seeing her, for Roberta'd been blown up by a car bomb in 1975. 'That can't be Roberta,' said Amelia, knowing it for a fact because she remembered that she'd forgotten, deliberately, to go to Roberta's funeral. After all, just how many funerals was one expected to attend?[88]

Here, Burns illustrates the danger of 'looking the other way,' by exposing her protagonist to the Gothic's 'unwanted return.'[89] The return of Roberta's specter, in other words, is caused by Amelia's refusal to attend the funeral, or to even acknowledge the violent death of her friend at all. Therefore Amelia, though not physically present in Belfast, is still mentally imprisoned there: haunted. She cannot escape from its terrifying atmosphere.

There seem to be multiple meanings for Roberta's return: personal, national, and transnational. Burns reminds her readers, via Amelia's haunting, that sectarian violence in Belfast was not restricted to Northern Ireland. In this passage, Burns equates 1975 Belfast with London in 1991, where the IRA detonated explosives on five different occasions.[90] At the time *No Bones* was published the violence had largely ended, yet the novel asks us to recognize that the legacy of the Troubles cannot simply be left behind.[91] Amelia announces that she deliberately forgets to attend Roberta's funeral, insinuating that any life taken in the conflict was not martyred but squandered. *No Bones* implies that the victims of the Troubles want their deaths to be productive, not fruitless. To be productive, individuals such as Amelia will have to look at their ghosts and reflect on what has happened. As we will see, the ghosts in *No Bones* are not there to terrorize; they come back to warn against the dangers of continual acts of retribution.

Burns keys in on the Gothic mechanics of inheritance in which families sacrifice their children to the transgenerational conflict. Amelia recalls with horror the expectation (at both the familial and the national levels) that she become responsible for the 'sins of her father.'[92] The climax of her breakdown in a public shopping center in Camden Town is triggered by the presence of children:

> Amelia panicked when she heard them. The sound of children was like the sound of terrorists. She hadn't known there were children and she knew that this was the time, if ever there was one, to run. Her brain and her nervous system, her heart, couldn't cope with children. They were the ones who became the adults and she slipped into powerless frightened childhood every time.[93]

Amelia is frozen with horror. It is at this moment in the novel that she realizes – despite being insane – that 'she could never get away.'[94] All of her defense mechanisms (alcohol, anorexia, sex, humor, and emigration) have failed to help her escape the Troubles' consuming system of compulsory violence, provoking the questions, 'How could she fall to her knees? How could she surrender?'[95] The answer comes in the following chapter while Amelia is heavily drugged in a London asylum, and all of her ghosts come back to her.[96]

'No Bones, 1991–1992' opens upon a traditionally Gothic landscape near Belfast. Amelia, unconscious in the London asylum, dreams that she is in a graveyard in the Glens of Antrim along with the specter of Roberta:

> Amelia went up the Glens in the dead of night. She had just reached the white slabs of the old famine graveyard, when something made her stop and turn around. Roberta McKeown was standing on the edge of the cliff.[97]

The setting collapses what should be *heimlich* into the *unheimlich*. Roberta's specter states, 'I'm lost. This isn't Belfast. I don't know this place.'[98] The same is true of Amelia; she is mentally displaced.

Burns illustrates the extent to which Belfast is closed off from the rest of Northern Ireland during the Troubles. Despite the girls' uncertainty about their surroundings, there is something familiar about the unfamiliarity of the Glens. Amelia describes the environment in terms that evoke images of the conflict in Belfast, thus tying together the more traditionally Gothic landscapes that are 'desolate, alienating and full of menace'[99] with the contemporary Gothic cityscape:

> Crashing and banging were coming from out there. It was the wind. It threw itself onto the rocks, whipped itself into caves, howled around inside them, then screamed its way out again ... animals cried and killed each other in the night. It was dark.[100]

'Crashing and banging' recalls the sound of the car bomb that killed Roberta; the howling and screaming transports readers back into the chaos of the Lovett household from earlier chapters where the siblings nearly killed one another daily; the animals here evoke images of paramilitary terrorists in Belfast, killing each other in the night.

Amelia's initial reaction is to try, once again, to escape from these images: 'Amelia felt they were familiar and not at all welcome so, in order to get away, she stepped back without hesitation and fell off the edge of the cliff.'[101] For a brief moment she wakes up from her dream and becomes cognizant of her bed in the asylum before falling back asleep and involuntarily returning to the nightmare. Her attempt to retreat from memories of the past is useless. Like the narrator's mother in *Reading in the Dark*, who takes to the lobby window again and again to commune with Eddie, Amelia is similarly transported back to the cliff where Roberta is waiting for her:

> 'Now why'd ye do that for?' said Roberta, her hands on her hips, getting herself ready, as she used to, for fights. 'Something on your conscience Amelia Lovett? Something you're not facing up to? Something, for example, you don't want to be reminded of?'[102]

In fact there is. Amelia had, after all, 'forgotten, deliberately, to go to Roberta's funeral.'[103]

Following Roberta's question about the state of Amelia's conscience, Amelia's repressed memory of that particular day resurfaces. That afternoon in 1975, on their way home from school, Amelia and Roberta had made plans to go dancing at Toby's Disco. The past infects the present, and she relives that moment:

> 'Are you gonna call on me or am I gonna call on you?' ... 'Come on Amelia,' said Roberta. 'Answer me. Are you gonna call on me, or am I gonna call on you?' ... 'You call on me Bert,' [Amelia] said.[104]

Roberta's question works on two levels. First, it serves to remind Amelia of the events that took place in 1975, when Roberta asked her where they would meet-up on their way to the disco. Secondly, the question refers to the later haunting: Roberta asks, 'are you gonna call on me?' In other words, will Amelia invite Roberta to come back, or will the haunting be another dreaded return? Either way, the specter of Roberta is going to come back: 'You can't get away Amelia Boyd Lovett. You have to go on. And you won't get rid of me you know, unless I decide to go.'[105] Amelia's only hope for regaining her sanity is to respond to her ghosts – like Deane's narrator in *Reading in the Dark* – with curiosity and tolerance.

She surrenders to the past, to the fact that she needs her ghosts. She recognizes that they are part of her identity, and ultimately she asks to be haunted. In doing so Amelia begins the process of reinventing the way in which histories of the Troubles are reconciled with the present. She begins to understand that she cannot control Roberta's coming and going, but she can control her own response to the specter's presence:

> She started up after her old friend to give her a good talking to, but stopped when something in her mind jarred and fell into place. It was a memory and remembering it, Amelia lifted her head and stared up the staircase at Roberta McKeown above her ... 'About time too,' said Roberta after a silence.[106]

What she remembers in that moment are the exact details of what happened the night Roberta died – Amelia went dancing despite having known that a car bomb had killed her best friend. As Amelia begins actively to remember events that she has deliberately forgotten from her Belfast childhood, she slowly becomes more mentally stable.

Until this moment in the novel, Amelia is a character that orders ghosts away, or at least tries to do so. Here, Amelia begins the process of calling those ghosts back to her:

> It was crowded. They were all in here with her, including her parents and her brother and all the others she had forgotten. Lizzie said, 'Ye've got to get it into your head Amelia. We can't do it all y'know. *We didn't come back to get you. You came back to get us.*' (Emphasis added)[107]

Gothic inheritance and the Troubles   155

The realization that she requested her haunting cures Amelia of her psychosis. She awakes from the nightmares permanently, and in the novel's concluding chapters, 'Safe House,' and 'A Peace Process,' goes on to lead a relatively normal life. In both chapters, title and content are decidedly more optimistic, implying progress toward individual and national recovery. Amelia's regained sanity suggests that recovery from those 'old wounds' is dependent upon welcoming spirits of the dispossessed who have returned to argue, in words that echo historian Jonathan Stevenson, that 'Northern Ireland needs to make room for the inevitable unforgiving,'[108] for 'even without contrition, ceasefires are welcome.'[109]

Burns uses the Gothic specter, specifically designed to rouse curiosity even as it terrifies, as a tool for grappling with larger questions of what it means to be a child of the Troubles: Is there a more treacherous and ambivalent virtue than that of inherited loyalty? This idea of loyalty underscores the larger issue of unending retributive acts of violence. Amelia breaks this cycle by reimagining the way individuals interact with domestic and political tradition. She suggests, via her conjuration of Roberta and Lizzie, that haunting can be productive. Individuals can call upon the past not to reinforce or justify acts of retributive violence, but to condemn them. It is only after she confronts her specters and returns to Belfast that Amelia successfully removes herself from the conflict, and therefore regains her sanity. As I observed with reference to the narrator in *Reading in the Dark*, individuals are only ever terrorized by their own willingness to grant authority to that which haunts. Amelia realizes this, and refuses to grant her specters the authority to frighten her. Rather, she invites them to communicate with her. Central to Burns's challenge of the Gothic motif of involuntary recurrence, then, is the idea of invitation.

Literary historian Jim Hansen recently observed, 'Literary genres participate in confronting and negating certain socio-historical problems and, to some degree, in preserving those very problems in and for subsequent contexts.'[110] This seems to be particularly evident in the genres artists manipulate in addressing the problems of Northern Ireland, including Deane and Burns, who turn to the Gothic to narrate the Troubles. Both *Reading in the Dark* and *No Bones* take up and reverse a repetitive esthetic strategy – the Gothic return – used, within political and social discourse by nationalists and loyalists alike, to justify violence in Ireland. Both novels argue for a new rhetoric of the past-haunted-present, one to be embraced, even called forth, rather than feared.

Throughout this chapter, I have illustrated how both Deane and Burns use the Gothic trope of the past-haunted-present in a new way: to negate the pattern of generationally deferred threats of retributive violence in Northern Ireland, while simultaneously preserving the horrors of the Troubles in order to help liberate individuals from a great deal of latent grief. In a recent article, 'Don't talk about the Troubles,' Malachi O'Doherty observes the anxiety in Northern Ireland over how 'easily' the Troubles had ended,[111] and points out that as a result, people have been afraid to 'scrutinize how they ended or to test the compromises by which they ended, in case we bring them back.'[112] What Deane and Burns illustrate, via the Gothic, is that the Troubles, though officially ended, have not gone away. To ignore their latent presence will 'bring them back'; however, to 'scrutinize how they ended' will, in fact, lay them to rest.

The casualties of the Troubles continue to haunt, and both novels explore productive ways of interacting with those specters. For as Carla Freccero maintains, 'The goal of spectral thinking is ... not to immure, but to allow to return, to be visited by a demand, a demand to mourn and a demand to organize.'[113] *Reading in the Dark* and *No Bones* offer a model of spectral thinking, a model for productively coming to terms with the consequences of the Troubles, as well as providing a productive lens through which to examine recurrent sociohistorical problems in Northern Ireland without prompting yet another cycle of violence.

Notes

1 Jeffrey Glenn, 'Surviving the Troubles: A View from the Suburbs.' *Children of 'The Troubles': Our Lives in the Crossfire of Northern Ireland*. Ed. Laurel Holliday (New York: Pocket Books, 1997), p. 79.
2 Glenn, 'Surviving the Troubles,' p. 78.
3 Glenn, 'Surviving the Troubles,' p. 80.
4 Glenn, 'Surviving the Troubles,' p. 84.
5 Siobhán Kilfeather, 'Terrific Register: The Gothicization of Atrocity in Irish Romanticism.' *boundary 2* 31.1 (2004): 53.
6 Kevin Whelan, *The Tree of Liberty: Radicalism, Catholicism, and the Construction of Irish Identity, 1760–1830* (South Bend, IN: University of Notre Dame Press, 1996), p. 37.

7 Margot Gayle Backus, *The Gothic Family Romance: Heterosexuality, Child Sacrifice, and the Anglo-Irish Colonial Order* (Durham, NC: Duke University Press 1999) p. 243–244.
8 Seamus Deane's *Reading in the Dark* is traditionally read as a neo-Gothic novel. In this chapter, I will offer further evidence in support of such readings, and introduce Anna Burns's *No Bones* as yet another example of the Irish Gothic revived.
9 Jacques Derrida, *Specters of Marx* (New York: Routledge Classics, 2006), p. 123.
10 Kelly Hurley, 'British Gothic Fiction, 1885–1930.' *The Cambridge Companion to Gothic Fiction*. Ed. Jerrold E. Hogle (Cambridge: Cambridge University Press, 2002), p. 194.
11 Richard Haslam, 'Irish Gothic: A Rhetorical Hermeneutics Approach.' *Irish Journal of Gothic and Horror Studies* 2 (2007): n. pag.
12 John Paul Riquelme, 'Toward a History of Gothic and Modernism: Dark Modernity from Bram Stoker to Samuel Beckett.' *Modern Fiction Studies* 46.2 (2000): 586.
13 Chris Baldick, Introduction. *Melmoth the Wanderer*. By Charles Robert Maturn. Ed. Chris Baldick (Oxford: Oxford University Press, 1989), p. ix. In 'Irish Gothic: A Rhetorical Hermeneutics Approach,' Richard Haslam offers an exhaustive list of Gothic conventions, themes, and narrative devices which he has collected from studies ranging from the rise in Gothic criticism during the 1970s through the present: 'Recurrent characters, settings, and props in eighteenth- and nineteenth-century Gothic fiction include Faust/Cain/Wandering Jew or Prometheus-like protagonists, Mephistophelean tempters, virtuous heroines, dysfunctional families, gloomy mansions, evil doubles, eerie portraits, wild landscapes, Inquisition prisons, incarcerating monasteries, malevolent monks, rampaging mobs, labyrinthine underground passages, graveyards, corpses, skeletons, crumbling buildings, and crumbling manuscripts (ruins and runes). Recurrent themes and situations include representation of physical and psychological violence, transgression and excess, explicit and implicit sectarianism, revolutionary anxieties, alluring wickedness, dangerous curiosity, threatened damnation, pursuit, persecution, and insanity; in addition to the unbalancing of (contemporaneously accepted) hierarchies of good and evil, free will and predestination, tyranny and liberty, and masculinity and femininity. Recurrent narrative devices include multiple narrators, interrupted – sometimes incomplete – manuscripts or accounts (wholly or partly encased sub-narratives), and the alternation of incidents designed to provoke terror with those designed to provoke horror.' Richard Haslam, 'Irish Gothic: A Rhetorical Hermeneutics Approach.' *Irish Journal of Gothic and Horror Studies* 2 (2007): n. pag., para. 7.

14 David Punter, 'Scottish and Irish Gothic.' *The Cambridge Companion to Gothic Fiction*. Ed. Jerrold E. Hogle (Cambridge: Cambridge University Press, 2002), p. 123.
15 Punter, 'Scottish and Irish Gothic,' p. 123.
16 Riquelme, 'Toward a History of Gothic and Modernism,' 588.
17 Raphael Ingelbien, 'Gothic Genealogies: Dracula, Bowen's Court, and Anglo-Irish Psychology.' *ELH* 70.4 (2003): 1089–1105.
18 Bruce Stewart, 'Bram Stoker's Dracula: Possessed by the Spirit of the Nation?' *Irish University Review* 29.2 (1999): 255.
19 Stephen D. Arata, 'The Occidental Tourist: *Dracula* and the Anxiety of Reverse Colonization.' *Dracula*. Ed. Nina Auerbach and David J. Skal (New York: W.W. Norton, 1997), p. 465.
20 The Pale was originally the fenced-in territory established around Dublin by the invading English in the medieval period, a border between English civilization and Celtic foreignness. In later usage, the phrase, 'beyond the pale' came to have a purely metaphoric meaning – to stand outside the conventional boundaries of law, behavior, or social class.
21 Kilfeather, 'Terrific Register,' 71.
22 Fred Botting, *Gothic* (London: Routledge, 1996), p. 180.
23 Botting, *Gothic*, p. 180.
24 Bram Stoker, *Dracula*. Ed. Nina Auerbach and David J. Skal (New York: W.W. Norton, 1997), p. 41.
25 Chris Baldick maintains that all Gothic fiction is 'concerned with extreme states of mental disturbance,' p. x.
26 Riquelme, 'Toward a History of Gothic and Modernism,' 588.
27 Derrida, *Specters of Marx*, p. 123.
28 Punter, 'Scottish and Irish Gothic,' p. 105.
29 Andrew Boyd, *Holy War in Belfast* (Tralee: Anvil Books, 1969), p. 187.
30 Qtd. in Peter Taylor, *Loyalists* (London: Bloomsbury Publishing, 2000), p. 41.
31 The official beginning to the Troubles in Northern Ireland varies from historian to historian, but is traditionally accepted to be between 1966 and 1969.
32 Jonathan Stevenson, *'We Wrecked the Place': Contemplating an End to the Northern Irish Troubles* (New York: The Free Press, 1996), p. 7.
33 Thomas Flanagan, *There You Are: Writings on Irish and American Literature and History*. Ed. Christopher Cahill (New York: New York Review of Books, 2004), p. 444.
34 Jack Holland, 'Return of the Gunman 1966–1969.' *Hope Against History: The Course of Conflict in Northern Ireland* (New York: Henry Holt & Co., 1999), p. 4. For a comprehensive history of the origins of the Troubles reaching back to the early twentieth century, see Simon Prince's *Northern Ireland's '68: Civil Rights, Global Revolt and the Origins of the Troubles* (Dublin: Irish Academic Press, 2007).

Gothic inheritance and the Troubles 159

35 Derrida, *Specters of Marx*, p. 221.
36 Anne Devlin, *The Long March*. In *Ourselves Alone, with A Woman Calling and The Long March* (London: Faber, 1986), p. 155. The long march to which Walsh refers is the Belfast-Derry march that began on Wednesday 1 January 1969. According to reports, 'Approximately 40 members of People's Democracy (PD) began a four-day march from Belfast across Northern Ireland to Derry. The Northern Ireland Civil Rights Association (NICRA) and some nationalists in Derry had advised against the march. The march was modeled on Martin Luther King's Selma to Montgomery march. The first day involved a walk from Belfast to Antrim. [Over the next four days the number of people on the march grew to a few hundred. The march was confronted and attacked by Loyalist crowds on a number of occasions, the most serious attack occurring on 4 January 1969.]'. See Martin Melaugh, 'The People's Democracy March: Chronology of Main Events.' *Conflict Archive on the Internet, University of Ulster*. 16 December 2009.
37 Sigmund Freud, *The Uncanny*. Trans. David McLintock (New York: Penguin Classics, 2003), p. 124.
38 Seamus Deane, *Reading in the Dark* (New York: Vintage, 1996), pp. 236–237.
39 The first IRA ceasefire of 31 August 1994 had ended on 9 February 1996 when the PIRA exploded a bomb in the London Docklands killing two and injuring forty people. The second, and permanent, ceasefire would not take place until 19 July 1997. At the time of the novel's publication, then, no one could be sure if the peace process had failed, and even with the signing of the Good Friday Agreement on 10 April 1998 and complete IRA disarmament on 23 October 2001, peace is still precarious. In the epilogue to his study of the Northern Irish peace process, *A Secret History of the IRA* (London: W.W. Norton, 2002), p. 492, Irish journalist Ed Moloney observes, 'After nineteen years of difficult, secret, and often dangerous diplomacy, Northern Ireland had finally arrived at a sort of peace. A new government, fairer than anything that had preceded it, was striving to make its roots grow, and Northern Ireland's deeply divided population was struggling to come to terms with a new political order, one in which each side had been obliged to abandon some strongly held beliefs in return for a chance at building stability.'
40 See, for instance, Postcolonial literary theorist Robert Young's observation concerning historical revisionism: 'The racism and intolerance to which such holistic conceptions of the nation inevitably lead means that postcolonial intellectuals ... have tried to think of the nation differently, to propose alternative accounts of the nation which begin not with an idealized version of how it might be, but with how it is'. Young, *Postcolonialism* (Oxford: Oxford University Press, 2003), p. 63.

41 Deane, *Reading in the Dark*, 242.
42 Deane, *Reading in the Dark*, 3.
43 Deane, *Reading in the Dark*, 3.
44 Deane, *Reading in the Dark*, 4.
45 Deane, *Reading in the Dark*, 4.
46 Deane, *Reading in the Dark*, 4.
47 Steven Bruhm, 'Contemporary Gothic: Why We Need It.' *The Cambridge Companion to Gothic Fiction*. Ed. Jerrold E. Hogle (Cambridge: Cambridge University Press, 2002), p. 274.
48 Daniel Ross, 'Oedipus in Derry: Seamus Deane's *Reading in the Dark*.' *New Hibernia Review* 11.1 (2007): 25.
49 Ross, 'Oedipus in Derry,' 26.
50 Deane, *Reading in the Dark*, 4.
51 Meave Davey, '"The Strange Heart Beating": Bird Imagery, Masculinities and the Northern Irish Postcolonial Gothic in the novels of Sean O'Reilly and Peter Hollywood.' *The Irish Journal of Gothic and Horror Studies* 5 (2008): n pag. http://irishGothichorrorjournal.homestead.com/NorthernIrishPostcolonialGothic.html. 21 February 2010.
52 Davey, 'The Strange Heart Beating.'
53 Deane, *Reading in the Dark*, 4.
54 Deane, *Reading in the Dark*, 4.
55 Deane, *Reading in the Dark*, 4.
56 Deane, *Reading in the Dark*, 228.
57 Deane, *Reading in the Dark*, 235.
58 Derrida, *Specters of Marx*, 221.
59 Derrida, *Specters of Marx*, 4.
60 The original fortress was destroyed in 1101 by Muirchertach Ua Briain, then King of Munster, and was reconstructed in 1878 by Dr. Walter Bernard. See Bettina Linke, 'Dr. Bernard's Restoration of Grianan Aileach from 1874–1878.' *Inishowen*. 10 July 2006.
61 Deane, *Reading in the Dark*, 57.
62 Deane, *Reading in the Dark*, 56.
63 Deane, *Reading in the Dark*, 56.
64 Whelan, *The Tree of Liberty* p. 37; Backus, *Gothic Family Romance* p. 244.
65 St. Columcille's prophecy foretells that the band of warriors would rise again to wage 'the final war on the English' … 'after which the one remaining English ship would sail out of Lough Foyle and away from Ireland forever.' Seamus Deane, *Strange Country: Modernity and Nationhood in Irish Writing since 1790*. Oxford: Clarendon, 1997, pp. 56, 57.
66 Deane, *Reading in the Dark*, 234.
67 Deane, *Reading in the Dark*, 236.
68 Deane, *Reading in the Dark*, 57–58.

69 Derrida, *Specters of Marx*, p. 138.
70 Gothic critic Steven Bruhm maintains, 'We need [the Gothic] because the twentieth century has so forcefully taken away from us that which we once thought constituted us – a coherent psyche, a social order to which we can pledge allegiance in good faith, a sense of justice in the universe – and that wrenching withdrawal, that traumatic experience, is vividly dramatized in the Gothic'. 'Contemporary Gothic,' p. 273.
71 According to Peter Mahon, 'The reader-narrator of Deane's text stakes out a site where a non-hierarchical framework or system of incomplete narratives can flourish because no story has the ability to cancel out any other, and it is this site that marks the text's main contribution to the debate on the political situation in Northern Ireland'. Mahon, 'In the Crypt of the Sun.' *Partial Answers: Journal of Literature and the History of Ideas* 5.1 (2007): 118.
72 Deane, *Reading in the Dark*, 58.
73 Deane, *Reading in the Dark*, 58–59.
74 Deane, *Reading in the Dark*, 59.
75 Andrew O'Hehir maintains, 'Here and there, Deane makes explicit the analogy between this broken family and the slowly disintegrating political community of Northern Ireland, where decades of Protestant domination and Catholic resentment led inexorably to the outbreak of the contemporary "Troubles" in 1968. While *Reading in the Dark* is a tender-hearted book, it is also fatalistic. Deane implies that the warring tribes of Derry are so deeply enmeshed in their stories of hating one another that they would virtually have to abandon their identities in order to stop'. O'Hehir, 'Irish Ghost Stories.' *Salon Magazine*. 11 April 1997: 5.
76 Carol Rumens, 'Reading Deane.' *Fortnight* July/August (1997): 30. Here Deane echoes Joyce's call in *Finnegans Wake*, 'Go away, we are deluded; come back, we are disghosted.'
77 Anna Burns was born in Belfast in 1962 and moved to the Notting Hill district of London in 1987. *No Bones* is her first novel, and was shortlisted for the 2002 Orange Prize, which is awarded annually to a female author for the best original English-language novel published in the United Kingdom.
78 The name Amelia Lovett calls to mind the fifteen-year-old Ann Lovett, who hid her pregnancy and died giving birth alone in a grotto for the Virgin Mary in 1984. Burns relies on this story, in which personal tragedy became national scandal, to suggest Amelia suffers similar horrors.
79 Judith Grossman, Review. *No Bones*, by Anna Burns. *The Women's Review of Books* 20.1 (2002): 10.
80 Anna Burns, *No Bones* (New York: W.W. Norton, 2002), pp. 99–100.
81 Backus, *Gothic Family Romance*, p. 2.

82 Burns, *No Bones*, 148.
83 Burns, *No Bones*, 100.
84 Burns, *No Bones*, 100.
85 Burns, *No Bones*, 63.
86 Burns, *No Bones*, 284.
87 Stoker, *Dracula*, 41.
88 Burns, *No Bones*, 284–285.
89 Davey, 'How is this long and bloody conflict meant to be finally and lastingly resolved if everyone, from the public to politicians, journalists, playwrights and novelists, is too busy looking the other way to address the disturbing legacy it has left behind?'
90 On 7 February, at 10 Dowling Street; 18 February, at Victorian Station; 14 December, at a shopping center; 15 December, at the National Gallery; 16 December, at a railway line in South London.
91 For as Stevenson observes, 'The fruitlessness of the conflict is hard truth for the Northern Irish. But unlike the mythologies of the past, the revelation might offer some lessons about the futility of runaway righteousness and hypersensitivity to history.' '*We Wrecked the Place,*' p. 257.
92 This phrase is often used to represent the transgenerational nature of the Troubles. See for instance Stevenson's introduction to '*We Wrecked the Place.*' See also the 1994 film by Jim Sheridan, *In the Name of the Father*, in which the title refers both to the religious context of the Troubles, and also to the pattern of violence inherited by the main protagonist from his biological father.
93 Burns, *No Bones*, 288–289.
94 Burns, *No Bones*, 289.
95 Burns, *No Bones*, 289.
96 Amelia's mental breakdown is not uncommon. In *IRA Man: Talking with the Rebels*, Douglass McFerran (Westport, CT: Praeger, 1997) speaks with volunteers about their experience of the Troubles. One in particular, Rory, 'talked about his own time in a British jail. He had never been physically mistreated, he said, but there was every effort to break him psychologically,' p. 115.
97 Burns, *No Bones*, 291.
98 Burns, *No Bones*, 291.
99 Botting, *Gothic*, 2.
100 Burns, *No Bones*, 291–292.
101 Burns, *No Bones*, 292.
102 Burns, *No Bones*, 292.
103 Burns, *No Bones*, 285.
104 Burns, *No Bones*, 293.
105 Burns, *No Bones*, 294.
106 Burns, *No Bones*, 299.

107 Burns, *No Bones*, 315.
108 Burns, *No Bones*, 252.
109 Burns, *No Bones*, 258.
110 Jim Hansen, *Terror and Irish Modernism: The Gothic Tradition from Burke to Beckett* (Albany, NY: State University of New York Press, 2009), p. 7.
111 Malachi O'Doherty, 'Don't talk about the Troubles.' *Fortnight* 457 (2008): 12.
112 O'Doherty, 'Don't talk about the Troubles,' 13.
113 Carla Freccero, 'Queer Spectrality: Haunting the Past.' *A Companion to Lesbian, Gay, Bisexual, Transgender, and Queer Studies*. Ed. George Haggerty and Molly McGarry (Oxford: Blackwell, 2007), p. 196.

Conclusion: Famine and the Western Front in Samuel Beckett's *Waiting for Godot*

Throughout this book I've traced the common employment of what I have identified as spectral tropes through nearly a dozen works of contemporary Irish fiction, from James Joyce's *Finnegans Wake* (1939) to Anna Burns's *No Bones* (2002). In novel after novel, we've witnessed how twentieth-century Irish authors have called upon Ireland's historical ghosts to establish Irish history and national identity as more complex and convoluted than popular conceptions of Ireland's historical narrative have previously admitted. But, as in any exploratory undertaking, one important piece of work remains to be completed – for while discovery is generally valuable, it is of far greater value to find use for such discoveries. Allow me now to offer two potential uses to the reader armed with this new understanding of the specter imbuing contemporary Irish fiction; and let me then extend briefly into a discussion of where I believe contemporary Irish fiction, building upon the work of the last fifteen years, may be headed.

The discovery of a spectral register in contemporary Irish historical fiction can, at the minimum, sharpen one's reading of these works, as in the example of Sebastian Barry's *The Whereabouts of Eneas McNulty* and *The Secret Scripture*. The specter provides us with both the theoretical framework and precise language for discussing Ireland's historical ghosts, and for placing twenty-first-century Ireland in conversation with the traumatic events of its historical past. Moreover, the specter, which Derrida defines as, among other things, 'what one imagines, what one thinks one sees and which one projects – on an imaginary screen where there is nothing to see,'[1] points us to sites of imaginative reinvention of Ireland's historical narrative and cultural myths – as when Jamie O'Neill and Roddy

Doyle re-mythologize the Easter Rising in both queer and feminist terms, giving this iconic historical event new social meaning in the present. Such reinvention offers us insight into the psychology of contemporary Ireland more than it answers long-standing questions about complex historical events.

Spectrality, as a theoretical lens, can also heighten our awareness of reemergent cultural factors (colonial trauma, gender and sexual discrimination, political insularity) that originally led to the Irish artist's dual esthetic and political identity during the late nineteenth and early twentieth centuries, and give us a glimpse into how contemporary Irish writers use fiction to respond to the long-standing identification of the Irish artist as politically vested. The novelists discussed in *Haunted historiographies* all imbue their works with layers of social, political, and cultural significance. Recall, for instance, Nuala O'Faolain and Joseph O'Connor's use of the Irish Famine to draw connections between nineteenth-century Irish hunger and later twentieth-century transnational dispossession. Their novels highlight the reciprocity between historical events and literary discourse to influence the ways in which Ireland is remembered, and therefore suggest what sorts of international positioning Ireland will undertake in the future.

Furthermore, drawing upon Jacques Derrida's theories of historical spectrality in *Specters of Marx* (tropes, modes, themes, and forms that bring multiple histories and fictions into dialogue with one another), I have been able to trace the varied ways in which a striking number of contemporary Irish novels revisit and expose the partisan architecture of Ireland's founding mythology. I then argue that many writers adopt a similar blueprint to construct the scaffolding for Ireland's liberal reinvention at the turn of the twenty-first century. By juxtaposing a wide spectrum of recent historical novels, *Haunted historiographies* exposes a ubiquitous project of cultural reinvention cutting across contemporary Irish fiction of (re)mythologizing the nation. However, the noticeable difference between modernist texts that revise and overwrite the Irish historical narrative and the contemporary historical novels explored in this book is that these more recent novels tend to announce – almost didactically, in fact – that their participation in reinventing Ireland constitutes a radical restructuring of the Republic's foundational mythology. More often than not, these efforts have been in support of Ireland's social and political liberalization, as in Seamus

Deane's *Reading in the Dark* and Anna Burns's *No Bones*, both of which re-imagine ancestral voices endorsing absolution rather than retribution in the North, thereby breaking from extremist political and social discourse that draws upon Ireland's ghosts as a way of justifying recurrent political violence. Many contemporary Irish artists have refashioned and brought into focus this dual esthetic and political identity by crafting novels that seek to both reflect and influence Ireland's changing political, economic, and social circumstances. Keeping in mind how in the previous fifteen years Irish authors have successfully blurred the lines of seemingly mutually exclusive dichotomies – nationalist vs. unionist, past vs. present, fiction vs. history – I will now offer a case study that underscores this dual identity in action in order to delineate where Irish studies scholars stand with spectrality as a critical lens for analyzing the present and coming fiction about twenty-first-century Ireland. Samuel Beckett's *Waiting for Godot* (1949, trans. 1953) is a particularly useful example because it fluently theorizes this dual esthetic and political identity, thereby bridging the high modernism of James Joyce and the postcolonial spectrality of *Haunted historiographies*' Post-Celtic Tiger authors.

In his 1907 lecture 'Ireland, Island of Saints and Sages,' Joyce challenged the Celtic Revivalist assertion that Irish history and culture should be sterilized to fit a homogenous romantic ideal: 'Our civilization is an immense woven fabric in which very different elements are mixed ... In such a fabric, it is pointless searching for a thread that has remained pure, virgin and uninfluenced by other threads nearby.'[2] A century later, in 2008, Sebastian Barry similarly observed, 'The fact is, we are missing so many threads in our story that the tapestry of Irish life cannot but fall apart. There is nothing to hold it together.'[3] The evolution of this tapestry metaphor signals the shift in national identity politics from a debate about the necessity or possibility of homogenization to a program that establishes dispossession as the one crucial characteristic of Irishness in both the twentieth and twenty-first centuries – 'there is nothing to hold it together' but nothingness, specters.

Though, '[i]t is well known that [Samuel Beckett] became a writer through apprenticeship to James Joyce, acting as his amanuensis in Paris in the late 1920s while *Work in Progress* was in progress,'[4] we cannot be sure if Beckett inherited his interest in spectrality as a trope for circular and overlapping temporalities from

Joyce. His creative and critical involvement with *Finnegans Wake*, however, should at least point our attention to the spectral elements of Beckett's work. And when we do read Beckett through a spectral lens, it becomes clear that *Waiting for Godot*, much like Sebastian Barry's *The Whereabouts of Eneas McNulty*, reverses Fianna Fáil's implicit enlistment of the Irish Famine as rationale for non-engagement in World War II. Famine imagery operates within the play's carefully crafted subtext as a means of critiquing Irish neutrality during the war.[5] By juxtaposing imagery from the Great Famine and World War II, I argue that Beckett's placement of these tragedies in conversation with one another defines them as very different, yet similarly avoidable, transnational traumas.

After surveying eight postcolonial Irish novels, we can more easily interpret Beckett's Famine subtext as a critique of Irish non-engagement. Though critics have noted Beckett's use of the Famine in his play, and others the use of World War II imagery, no one has yet consolidated these two observations in order to locate a critique of Irish neutrality in the play's spectral register – the site where presence and non-presence, generality and specificity overlap. *Waiting for Godot*'s ambiguity invites us to bring various contexts and subtexts into contention with one another in an arena bereft of specificity.

Waiting for Godot contains imagery that brings the history of the Famine into the historical space of World War II. These overlapping histories present nineteenth-century Irish trauma as rationale not for neutrality, but for engagement. That is to say, when read in a specifically Irish context, it is possible to see how *Godot* rejects the long-standing nationalist use of the Famine narrative as an argument for separation from England and therefore the wider European community. Beckett's imagery creates a palimpsest upon which the Irish trauma of Famine suffering and emigration is overlaid with the twentieth-century trauma of Jewish displacement and persecution. Identifying this spectral register allows contemporary readers to study the play not only as an abstract examination of existential humanism, but also as a critique of Irish non-engagement in the face of crisis. To be sure, W.J. McCormack insists that one 'impact of the twentieth-century scientific revolution on Beckett was existential or (to use an old word in the old ways) *moral*.'[6]

When read in an Irish context, *Waiting for Godot* can be understood as a critique of the ways in which the Republican government employed specters of the past to constitute an isolationist foreign policy during World War II. Beckett's play is the product of a haunting in which he allows Ireland's colonial past to inform and influence his sense of personal responsibility during transnational conflict. His underlying argument in *Waiting for Godot* – 'Let us do something, while we have the chance!'[7] – can be read not merely as an abstract existential meditation, but also as a critique of the immorality of Irish neutrality.

In 1937, at the age of 31, Samuel Beckett left Ireland for Paris, which became his permanent home until he died in 1989. Two years later, war seemed all but inevitable, and as Neville Chamberlain pledged Britain to defend Poland, Beckett pledged his allegiance to France: 'If there is a war, as I fear there must be soon, I shall place myself at the disposition of this country.'[8] When Hitler invaded Poland on 1 September 1939, and both Britain and France declared war on Germany two days later, Beckett was visiting his mother in neutral Ireland. He returned to France the following day. According to biographer James Knowlson, '[Beckett] had followed the rise of Nazism in the 1930s with fascination, growing disgust, and, finally, horror,'[9] and on 1 September 1941 he formally joined a non-combat arm of the French Resistance called Gloria SMH.[10]

In the Resistance, Beckett was involved in gathering intelligence. Specifically, he was responsible for compiling and translating reports of intercepted German communication detailing military movement. Knowlson observes, 'Although he did not run the same risks as agents or couriers, Beckett's own involvement was still highly dangerous.'[11] In 1942, in fact, German authorities infiltrated Gloria SMH and a number of Beckett's close friends were arrested. He and his girlfriend Suzanne Deschevaux-Desmesnil (whom he married in 1961) escaped to the village of Roussillon where Beckett worked as a farm hand, concealed armaments, and aided Ally supply chains for the duration of the war. As Mark and Juliette Taylor-Batty have observed, his experience as a refugee informs *Waiting for Godot*:

> In their escape to Roussillon, Beckett and Suzanne walked long distances by night and slept during daylight in haystacks and ditches. The image of a mutually dependent couple, disoriented and bereft of social context, able to both irritate and console one another, uncertain of their future, alternately clutching at straws of hope and sunk by fear and despair, is clearly central to the expression of *Waiting for Godot*.[12]

Beckett's and Suzanne's situation, and the ways in which they reportedly interacted with one another during their time in the Resistance, is echoed by the relationship between Vladimir (Didi) and Estragon (Gogo) in the play. Neither couple, however, is 'disoriented and bereft of social context.' A careful reading of Beckett's use of Famine imagery in the play suggests that, like himself and Suzanne, Didi and Gogo may be placed in war-torn France with the intent of resisting anti-Semitic groups and to lend aid to suffering Jewish refugees.

Beckett's involvement with the French Resistance during the war rejected Ireland's policy of neutrality and worked to establish an Irish cosmopolitanism that would help integrate Ireland into the transnational European community. Reflecting on Beckett's speech from a 10 June 1946 radio address titled 'The Capital of the Ruins,' in which Beckett juxtaposed his understanding of colonial violence in Ireland with the equally violent occupation of France in the twentieth century, Lois Gordon observes that Beckett's recognition of the similarities between occupied France and colonial Ireland necessitated *involvement*, not neutrality. Gordon maintains that

> Fighting an enemy of uncontested and categorical evil enabled Beckett to respond to a pain that he had carried since childhood, namely, the experience of Ireland's Civil War, which introduced him at an early age to the depths of human suffering.[13]

The Irish Civil War (1922–1923) was fought over disagreements concerning the contents of the Anglo-Irish Treaty. The treaty divided the Irish Republic's leadership over two issues: declaring allegiance to the British crown and the partition of Ulster.[14] Beckett's first-hand experience of suffering underscores the presence of past colonial abuses in his play. The landscape in *Waiting for Godot* reflects the site of Ireland's greatest colonial atrocity, the Famine, and brings it to bear upon the battlefields of France. This overlapping invites readers to interpret Beckett's general call 'to do something' to alleviate human suffering as an argument for Ireland's participation in the broader European community via a juxtaposition of similar international moments of crisis.

Immediately following the war, Beckett volunteered for a project arranged through a transnational partnership between the Irish and French Red Crosses to help build a hospital in Saint-Lô, France. Gordon comments,

As a man of specific place and origin – always rooted in this world and certainly not an artist-would-be-god or an unworldly aesthete – Beckett stresses [in his radio address] that the Irish in Saint-Lô demonstrated the best part of human nature, that quality that seeks not to dominate or desolate but rather to heal and console.[15]

Gordon's description of Beckett 'as a man of specific place and origin' calls attention to Beckett's Irishness. Ireland's traumatic history gave him a distinct perspective of World War II ethnic abuses and consequently provoked from him an empathetic humanitarian response by which he sought 'not to dominate or desolate but rather to heal and console.'

In the wake of world war, and following his involvement with the French Resistance and subsequent humanitarian efforts in Saint-Lô, Beckett began writing *En Attendant (Waiting)* between 9 October 1948 and 29 January 1949. He later rewrote it in English as *Waiting for Godot* in 1953. His decision to originally craft the play in French spurred Hugh Kenner's assertion that Beckett 'is not Irish as Irishness is defined today by the Free State ... [He was] willing to be the last Anglo-Irishman.'[16] As such, Beckett was not politically attached to de Valera's nationalist mandate of neutrality, and in fact seems to have been alienated from it by virtue of his particular background. And by originally writing *Waiting for Godot* in the affiliated language of action he had linguistically established his political beliefs.

In light of Kenner's comments, critics have analyzed *Waiting for Godot*'s landscape as that of wartime France, and thus indicative of a specific locale; and still others have focused on the distinctively Irish dimensions of the play – usually pointing to Beckett's use of idiomatic language constructions that privileged the 'Dubalin man'[17] or stage constructions that allude to the Great Irish Famine – as a way of situating *Godot* in the Irish dramatic tradition as represented by Yeats, Synge, and O'Casey.[18] However, no critic has yet consolidated these two observations in order to locate a critique of Irish neutrality in the play's spectral register – the site where presence and non-presence, generality and specificity overlap.

In *From Burke to Beckett*, W.J. McCormack provides a brief catalogue of Irish references in Beckett's work: 'detailed streetscape and suburban hinterland of Dublin in *More Pricks than Kicks*, the abandoned Irish cities in *Murphy*, the retreat to unnamed but (to the incurably initiated) recognizable asylums in Foxrock of *Watt* and *All that Fall*. And so on.'[19] McCormack's list excludes mention of allusions to barren Connemara in *Waiting for Godot*. Yet we can identify echoes of the Famine in the play within the bombed-out French landscape if we read Vladimir and Estragon as Irishmen. Reading Didi and Gogo in this way allows us to consider Beckett's play in a new light: as a challenge to Irish neutrality. Didi and Gogo, Irish volunteers stationed in France, reflect Beckett's own engagement with relief efforts during the war, and seem to suggest that Ireland should promote its sovereignty through participation in, rather than isolation from, global affairs.

Marjorie Perloff's 2005 article, 'In Love with Hiding: Samuel Beckett's War,' is the most recent in a line of scholarship that refutes the dominant reading of *Godot* as a decontextualized, existential meditation on the human condition. It follows Eric Bentley's 1967 linking of *Godot* to a World War II context in which he equates Vladimir and Estragon to Holocaust prisoners in Auschwitz and Buchenwald waiting for rescue, and also builds upon Hugh Kenner's 1973 assertion that Didi and Gogo are, like Beckett himself, French Resistance operatives. Kenner maintains,

> It is curious how readers and audiences do not think to observe the most obvious thing about the world of the play, that it resembles France occupied by the Germans, in which its author spent the war years. How much waiting must have gone on in that bleak world; how many times must Resistance operatives – displaced persons when everyone was displaced, anonymous ordinary people for whom every day renewed the dispersal of meaning – have kept appointments not knowing whom they were to meet, with men who did not show up and may have had good reasons for not showing up, or bad or may even have been taken.[20]

Kenner's explication of the play's specific setting is echoed in Beckett's authorized biography, *Damned to Fame* (1996). In it, James Knowlson relates Beckett's intimate engagement with the traumas of war and its aftermath, which manifested in his work not as a response to the abstract human condition, but as an urgent and contemporary crisis. Beckett often claimed, 'I produce an object. What people make of it is not my concern.'[21] Yet he once asserted of his duos from *Endgame* and *Godot*, 'You must realize that Hamm and Clove are Didi and Gogo at a later date, at the end of their lives ... Actually they are Suzanne and me.'[22] Though Beckett was probably talking more generally about his difficult marriage – he and Suzanne drove each other mad, but they could not part – his comment allows readers to draw connections between the landscapes in which his characters wait, and his own experience in Roussillon.

Readers can also bring an Irish context to bear upon *Godot's* bombed-out French landscape by identifying images and tropes from the Great Famine. 'Look at this muckheap!' Estragon wildly exclaims, 'I've never stirred from it!'[23] Gogo's observation, when taken in accord with his previous explanation to Pozzo – whom Kenner identifies as Prussian Gestapo,[24] and whom we can also come to identify as a representation of nineteenth-century Anglo-Irish landlords – that 'We're not from these parts,'[25] seems paradoxical. He and Didi are neither 'from these parts' nor ever having stirred from them. Here, Beckett crafts a spectral landscape in which Vladimir's and Estragon's present muckheap (France) can be read as the reappearance of the nineteenth-century Irish muckheap that pervades their national consciousness. Though they are palimpsestuously present in a different time and place, they have not stirred from this sort of landscape.

In addition to tracing allusions to World War II, a number of critics have also established that the landscape of *Waiting for Godot* resembles Ireland during the Famine.[26] Joseph Roach, for instance, observes Beckett's use of Famine imagery to narrate lingering Irish domestic trauma:

> Like the 'Abode of Stones' of which Lucky speaks in his thrice-repeated naming of Connemara [*Godot*, 37], rural Ireland is haunted by dead voices. To anyone who is prepared to listen, they speak of the consequences of the potato famine, or the Great Hunger, the effects of which endured long after its deadliest years, 1845–1851.[27]

Roach, and others, have plumbed the depths of Beckett's imagery, but have stopped short of connecting it to the seemingly more obvious World War II landscape. If we bring these two critical approaches together, we can locate another interpretation of the play that understands spectral contamination, or historical overlap between moments of conflict, as a critique of inaction at times of great crisis.

The potential specificity with which *Waiting for Godot* testifies to the context from which it was produced is often overshadowed by Beckett's effective demonstration of the limits of language. Critics regularly read Beckett's manipulation of these limits as evidence of his texts' universal humanism. Mark and Juliette Taylor-Batty, for instance, maintain, 'In *Waiting for Godot*, the

Famine in Beckett's Waiting for Godot

audience's attention is constantly drawn to the unreliability, the pointlessness or the simple non-referentiality of language.'[28] This abstraction, according to Martin Esslin, reinforces Beckett's interest in generalities: 'Beckett gradually reduces the realistic original material, in order to extract the deeper, eternal, essential human situation – so that the play can become truly universal.'[29] Yet, as is often the case in Beckett's work, the dialogue, while abstract, can be read within a specific context. For readers of *Godot*, it may be particularly useful to read the play as a site of amalgamation wherein obfuscated references to Irish history resonate within the context of occupied France.

At the beginning of Act II, for instance, Vladimir and Estragon engage in a conversation that narrates their equation of Jewish holocaust victims and victims of the Irish Famine:

VLADIMIR: You're a hard man to get on with, Gogo.
ESTRAGON: It'd be better if we parted.
VLADIMIR: You always say that and you always come crawling back.
ESTRAGON: The best thing would be to kill me, like the other.
VLADIMIR: What other? [*Pause.*] What other?
ESTRAGON: Like billions of others.
VLADIMIR: [*sententious*] To every man his little cross. [*He sighs.*] Till he dies. [*Afterthought.*] And is forgotten.
ESTRAGON: In the meantime let us try and converse calmly, since we are incapable of keeping silent.
VLADIMIR: You're right, we're inexhaustible.
ESTRAGON: It's so we won't think.
VLADIMIR: We have that excuse.
ESTRAGON: It's so we won't hear.
VLADIMIR: We have our reasons.
ESTRAGON: All the dead voices.
VLADIMIR: They make a noise like wings.
ESTRAGON: Like leaves.
VLADIMIR: Like sand.
ESTRAGON: Like leaves.
[*Silence.*][30]

A number of critics have referenced this conversation for various reasons: Hugh Kenner observes Beckett's use of 'spaced and measured silences' to reinforce the feeling of waiting;[31] Barbara Reich Gluck highlights the passage's repetitious and circular design which reflects the play's overall structure;³² Michael Worton calls upon 'all the dead voices' to reference the souls in Dante's *Purgatory*, thus speculating on the theme of hope;³³ Mark and Juliette Taylor-Batty draw on this conversation to illustrate that, for Beckett, 'language is terminally evasive and inconclusive.'³⁴ Other possible interpretations arise, however, if we read *Godot* as an Irish play in which Beckett's depiction of World War II reflects elements of the Great Famine, and thereby offers a retroactive challenge to de Valera's non-engagement policy.

Vladimir twice asks Estragon, 'What other?' And Estragon's rather vague response, 'Like billions of others,' prompts the reader to ask, what others? Who are these others? On one hand, recalling Beckett's involvement in the French Resistance and the time period in which *Godot* was written, we can read these others as all the dead voices of World War II.³⁵ On the other hand, Beckett provides a number of references that allude to the billions of Irish who suffered the Great Famine and its far- and long-reaching consequences. He describes the voices as sounding 'like wings,' 'like leaves,' 'like sand.' Each of these words should suggest, to Irish scholars, images of emigration. The sound of *wings* paired with the word *leaves*, read as a verb rather than a noun, can be read as a reference to the Flight of the Wild Geese, which Declan Kiberd explains were 'those Irish rebels who sought training in the armies of Catholic Europe after 1691 in hopes of returning to expel the occupier.'³⁶ According to John McGurk and Henry Gráinne, the term is also used more broadly to refer to Irish soldiers who left the island to serve in Continental European armies in the seventeenth and eighteenth centuries, and the British Army in the twentieth century.³⁷ Furthermore, the word *sand*, followed by the second mention of *leaves*, is another allusion to the desolate fields that forced departure in the nineteenth century, thereby juxtaposing military migration with Famine emigration.

In this particular reading, the play argues for Irish involvement in World War II through its protagonists' sense of Ireland's traumatic past. Estragon instructs Vladimir to 'converse calmly, since we are incapable of keeping silent.' In concert with other indicators, we can read the pair's loquaciousness as conventionally Irish.³⁸ *Godot* trades on this stereotype to identify the pair as Irishmen disturbed by de Valerean neutrality, which ignores similarities between calls for help by Famine victims and victims of the War.

This conflation of voices affords readers the opportunity both to see a new perspective of the echoes of Irish history and to obtain a clearer understanding of Ireland's moral responsibilities in the present. Michael Worton maintains,

> In order to understand how Beckett's texts work, we must accept that there is always a *presupposition* of reference. Every Beckett text is built on the premise that whenever we speak or write, we are using someone else's thoughts and language. We are condemned or 'damned' to construct ourselves through the discourses of others, whether we like it or not. And each time we write, we are rewriting and therefore transforming (and deforming!) what we and others previously wrote.[39]

Beckett crafts the abstract action of *Waiting for Godot* as a haunting wherein the Irish past can erupt into the Jewish present as a *continued* trauma, as a *presupposition* of reference (as Worton puts it). The repetition of ethnic trauma mandates Irish commitment to the Allied cause based on dispossession.

In fact, the play provides readers the opportunity to recognize disarticulation and dispossession as central to the identity of both Irish Famine victims and displaced Jews. In addition to juxtaposing poor Catholic emigrants with Jewish émigrés, for instance, we can also trace parallels between the decline and fall of the Anglo-Irish aristocracy during the nineteenth and early twentieth centuries and displaced Europeans during the war years. Beckett was, after all, an Anglo-Irish Protestant, and therefore attuned to the deterioration of the Aristocracy.[40] As I mentioned above, Hugh Kenner's identification of Beckett's willingness to be 'the last Anglo-Irishman'[41] highlights, for us, Beckett's attention to Famine-related difficulty for Ascendency landlords, not only for their tenants.

Pozzo – whom a number of critics, including Marjorie Perloff, have identified as a Gestapo officer – also exhibits characteristics of an Ascendency landlord accompanying his malnourished tenant to procure passage to America. Pozzo explains his position to Vladimir and Estragon,

> I do [want to get rid of Lucky]. But instead of driving him away as I might have done, I mean instead of simply kicking him out on his arse, in the goodness of my heart I am bringing him to the fair, where I hope to get a good price for him. The truth is you can't drive such creatures away. The best thing would be to kill them. [*Lucky weeps.*][42]

Pozzo's dialogue offers readers another example of the myriad of possibilities for interpreting the play. Here, in the play's spectral register, Pozzo and Lucky can be read as simultaneously Gestapo and Jew as well as landlord and tenant – unsettling both in their ambiguity.

Our understanding of Pozzo's explanation for getting rid of Lucky depends upon how we read this ambiguous passage. Literally, Pozzo is travelling to a fair in order to sell Lucky at a slave auction. Contextualizing the pair in the historical space of World War II, however, Michael Bentley and Hugh Kenner have read Pozzo as a Gestapo officer transporting his prisoner to a work camp. Additionally, the play offers another context in which Famine suffering and emigration is overlaid with the trauma of Jewish persecution and displacement. Pozzo claims that he is attempting to help Lucky, like a number of landlords who, rather than simply kicking their tenants out on their arses, paid for their transatlantic passage. Pozzo announces that through the goodness of his heart (or at least for the concern of his pocket-book) he is taking Lucky, whom it is possible to identify as his starving tenant, to the fair – which, when heard by an audience rather than read on the page, can be construed as *fare*, or food. Furthermore, Pozzo states that he hopes 'to get a good price for him': as a landlord paying for Lucky's emigration, Pozzo would hope to negotiate a reasonable fee for his transatlantic passage.

In the above passage from Act I, we can recognize Pozzo as an Ascendancy landlord who harbors a clear sense of Anglo-Irish social decline in nineteenth-century Ireland – he admits, following a vibrant speech about the sky, 'I weakened a little towards the end.'[43] Pozzo, of course, means that his speech faltered at the end, but this line may also allude to failing Anglo-Irish estates during the Famine years and after. In Act II, when the pair returns, Pozzo and Lucky, respectively blind and mute, have metaphorically fallen and literally fall. They are unable to rise without the aid of Vladimir and Estragon, and Pozzo's repeated cries for 'Help!'[44] are heard in concert with the cries of helpless Jews that were seized and executed during the war.

On 10 February 1966, Beckett recalled for Alec Reid his reaction to the execution of Jewish hostages, some of whom he knew personally: 'you simply couldn't stand by with your arms folded.'[45] In *Waiting for Godot*, Beckett directly critiques inaction during times of crisis through Vladimir's own rationale for helping Pozzo and Lucky:

Famine in Beckett's Waiting for Godot 177

> VLADIMIR: Let us not waste our time in idle discourse! [*Pause. Vehemently.*] Let us do something, while we have the chance! It is not every day that we are needed. Not indeed that we personally are needed. Others would meet the case equally well, if not better. To all mankind they were addressed, those cries for help still ringing in our ears! But at this place, at this moment of time, all mankind is us, whether we like it or not. Let us make the most of it, before it is too late! Let us represent worthily for once the foul brood to which a cruel fate consigned us! What do you say? [*Estragon says nothing.*]⁴⁶

Vladimir's call for action stems from 'all the dead voices' manifested in Pozzo's plea for 'Help!' He seems to offer a stinging critique of neutrality in general, and given Beckett's heritage and war experience, of Irish neutrality in particular. If we are to read 'the foul brood' – which Didi claims he and Gogo represent – as Irish, it is possible to identify the 'cruel fate' as the Famine, which established within the Irish character such dejection. Like his author, Vladimir can't simply stand by with his arms folded. And though 'Estragon says nothing,' his very presence might be read as a protest against the isolationism that resulted from Famine trauma. When Vladimir insists, then, 'What are we doing here, *that* is the question,'⁴⁷ the textual answer is that they are waiting for Godot. One of the larger questions, however, is about the ethics of Irish neutrality.

At almost every turn, Beckett critiques the very inaction that his play *seems* to depict. On the surface, Didi and Gogo do nothing. They wait. And while this literal inaction is maddening, it represents an immorality central to the play. *Waiting for Godot* argues that ignoring any call for help, be it from Irish tenant, Anglo-Irish landlord, French farmer, Jewish hostage, or fallen traveler is inhumane. Vladimir's motivation for helping the fallen Pozzo represents Beckett's rejection of inaction:

> VLADIMIR: We wait. We are bored. [*he throws up his hand.*] No, don't protest, we are bored to death, there's no denying it. Good. A diversion comes along and what do we do? We let it go to waste. Come, let's get to work! [*He advances towards the heap, stops in his stride.*] In an instant all will vanish and we'll be alone once more, in the midst of nothingness! [*He broods.*]⁴⁸

Vladimir's lamentation that 'In an instant all will vanish and we'll be alone once more' can be read as an echo of popular postwar concerns in Ireland about the consequences of neutrality. *Waiting for Godot* suggests that participation is always a better answer to international humanitarian crises than non-engagement, which in an Irish context sounds like pointed critique of de Valera's policy of neutrality.

In an editorial piece from *The Bell* in 1945, Sean O'Faoláin predicted that neutral Ireland's postwar relationships with the Allied nations would be troubled: 'We emerge a little dulled, bewildered, deflated. There is a great leeway to make up, many lessons to be learned, problems to be solved which, in those six years of silence, we did not even allow ourselves to state.'[49] When Beckett's main characters finally act – they assist the fallen Pozzo and Lucky – perhaps they do so as a direct challenge to de Valera's mandate of neutrality, the manifestation of his belief that past colonial trauma necessitated Ireland's removal from the war.

Beckett adopts and adapts particularly Irish trauma and then turns the apprehension of that trauma into a lens through which to view and engage with international conflict. In doing so, he offers readers a narrative that complicates Irish nationalist rhetoric that insists upon sovereignty predicated upon isolation. Reading *Godot* as a particularly Irish text exposes neutrality as shortsighted both in the moment and historically, and offers us another way of understanding each text as an argument for an ethics of Irish engagement based upon a productive haunting of the World War II moment by the Famine past. Ultimately, we are able to uncover another possible interpretation of *Waiting for Godot*, one in which the play compares individual and national response and offers an explicit argument against 'waiting' for someone else to answer a cry for help.

Haunted historiographies has juxtaposed past and present Ireland, historical and fictional representations of national history, and nationalist and unionist debates over the 'true' nature of Irish identity. It is a project, in other words, that articulates the creative reimaginings of Irish history and identity in terms of spectral repetition. Joyce and Barry serve as the theoretical bookends for a literary project that, over the course of the twentieth century, has conjoined artistic representation and political transformation of the Irish historical narrative. In the process, Irish novelists have significantly reshaped a political debate and helped solve a question (what is Irishness?) that a generation ago seemed relatively insoluble. It only remains to be seen, as time and circumstance add more layers to the Irish national story, how specters such as Finn McCool, Sgathaich,

Famine in Beckett's Waiting for Godot 179

or even Dracula will again be reawakened and reinvoked to help guide a people whose very identity will always be interwoven with the political, ideological, and mythological ghosts of the past.

Notes

1. Jacques Derrida, *Specters of Marx*. 1993. Trans. Peggy Kamuf (New York: Routledge Classics, 2006), p. 125.
2. James Joyce, 'Ireland: Island of Saints and Sages.' *James Joyce: Occasional, Critical, and Political Writing*. Ed. Kevin Barry. Trans. Conor Deane (Oxford: Oxford University Press, 2000), p. 118.
3. Sebastian Barry, *The Secret Scripture* (New York: Viking, 2008), p. 183.
4. W.J. McCormack, *From Burke to Beckett: Ascendancy, Tradition and Betrayal in Literary History* (Cork: Cork University Press, 1994), p. 380. See also James Knowlson and Elizabeth Knowlson, eds., *Beckett Remembering Beckett* (New York: Arcade Publishing, 2011): p. 45. Beckett recalls, '[James Joyce] dictated some pages of Finnegan's Wake to me at one stage' (p. 45). He also reports, 'It was at [Joyce's] suggestion that I wrote "Dante ... Bruno. Vico ... Joyce" because of my Italian. And I spent a lot of time reading Bruno and Vico in the magnificent library, the Bibliothèque of the Ecole Normale. We must have had some talk about the "Eternal Return," that sort of thing' (p. 45).
5. To be clear, neither Beckett nor I am comparing or suggesting any sort of similarity between the Irish Famine and World War II. The Nazis actively destroyed a group of people and made it their national mission to commit genocide. The Famine, it can be argued, arose from incompetence, malaise, and unresponsiveness. The Nazis were interested in the active destruction and annihilation of an entire people; the British were simply shrugging their shoulders. One nation set up death camps to murder people by the trainload, the other let a natural disaster run its course.
6. McCormack, *From Burke to Beckett*, p. 382.
7. Samuel Beckett, *Waiting for Godot*. In *Samuel Beckett: The Grove Centenary Edition*. Vol 3. Ed. Paul Auster (New York: Grove Press, 2006), p. 72.
8. James Knowlson, *Damned to Fame: The Life of Samuel Beckett* (New York: Grove Press, 1996), p. 273.
9. Knowlson, *Damned to Fame*, p. 278.
10. According to a letter written on 20 May 1992 by Gervase Cowell, British Special Operations Executive Adviser, to James Knowlson, 'The letters reversed the initials of "His Majesty's Service"... [and] "Gloria" was also the code name by which one of the founders of the group, Jeannine Picabia, was known' (qtd. in Knowlson, *Damned to Fame*, p. 279).

11 Knowlson, *Damned to Fame*, p. 283.
12 Mark Taylor-Batty and Juliette Taylor-Batty, *Samuel Beckett's Waiting for Godot* (London: Continuum, 2008), p. 4.
13 Lois Gordon, *Reading Godot* (New Haven, CT: Yale University Press, 2002), p. 48.
14 For example, Mr. Sean MacEntee declares, 'I am opposed to this Treaty because it gives away our allegiance and perpetuates partition. By that very fact that it perpetuates our slavery; by the fact that it perpetuates partition it must fail utterly to do what it is ostensibly intended to do – reconcile the aspirations of the Irish people to association with the British Empire' (MacEntee). And Mr. O'Ceallaigh insists, 'For my own part, war or no war, having taken an Oath of Allegiance twice over to the Republic, and administered it, in the face of heaven and by your command, to scores of my colleagues, no consideration on earth will induce me voluntarily to declare allegiance or lip fidelity to the King of a country whose instruments of Government have oppressed and traduced our people for seven centuries and a half' (O'Ceallaigh). See also Bill Kissane, *The Politics of the Irish Civil War* (Oxford: Oxford University Press, 2005).
15 Gordon, *Reading Godot*, p. 54.
16 Hugh Kenner, *A Colder Eye: The Modern Irish Writers* (New York: Knopf, 1983), p. 270.
17 A.J. Leventhal, Beckett's secretary, observed, 'The real innovation in the Irish production [of *Waiting for Godot*] lies in making the two tramps speak with the accent of O'Casey's Joxer tempered by Myles na gCopaleen's [Flann O'Brien] "Dubalin" man'. A.J. Leventhal, 'Dramatic Commentary.' *Dublin Magazine* 31.1 (1956): 53.
18 For Irish dimensions of Beckett's plays, see John P. Harrington, *The Irish Beckett*, James Knowlson's *Damned to Fame*, Mary Junker's *Beckett: The Irish Dimension* (Dublin: Wolfhound, 1995), and Anthony Cronin's *Beckett: The Last Modernist* (Cambridge, MA: Da Capo Press, 1999).
19 McCormack, *From Burke to Beckett*, p. 398.
20 Hugh Kenner, *A Reader's Guide to Samuel Beckett* (New York: Farrar, Straus and Giroux, 1973), p. 30.
21 Colin Duckworth, ed. *Samuel Beckett: En Attendant Godot* (London: Harrap, 1966), p. xxiv.
22 Deirdre Bair, *Samuel Beckett: A Biography* (London: Vintage, 1990), p. 495.
23 Beckett, *Waiting for Godot*, 53.
24 'We can easily see why a Pozzo would be unnerving. His every gesture is Prussian. He may be a Gestapo official clumsily disguised.' Kenner, *A Colder Eye*, p. 30.
25 Beckett, *Waiting for Godot*, 17.

26 See Eoin O'Brien, *The Beckett Country* (Dublin: Black Cat Press, 1986), J.C.C. Mays, 'Irish Beckett, A Borderline Instance,' in *Beckett in Dublin*. Ed. S.E. Wilmer (Dublin: Lilliput Press, 1992), and Rodney Sharkey, 'Irish? Au Contraire! The Search for Identity in the Fictions of Samuel Beckett.' *Journal of Beckett Studies* 3.2 (1994): 1–18.
27 Joseph Roach, 'All the Dead Voices: The Landscape of Famine in Waiting for Godot.' *Land/Scape/Theater*. Eds. Elinor Fuchs and Una Chaudhuri (Ann Arbor, MI: University of Michigan Press, 2002), p. 88.
28 Taylor-Batty and Taylor-Batty, *Samuel Beckett's Waiting for Godot*, p. 4.
29 Martin Esslin. 'Waiting for Godot: Western and Korean.' *The Samuel Beckett On-Line Resources and Links Pages*. 1988, p. 2.
30 Beckett, *Waiting for Godot*, 54–55.
31 Kenner, *A Reader's Guide*, p. 34.
32 Barbara Reich Gluck, *Beckett and Joyce: Friendship and Fiction* (London: Associated University Press, 1979).
33 Michael Worton, '*Waiting for Godot* and *Endgame*: Theatre as Text.' *The Cambridge Companion to Beckett*. Ed. John Pilling (Cambridge: Cambridge University Press, 1994).
34 Taylor-Batty and Taylor-Batty, *Samuel Beckett's Waiting for Godot*, p. 47.
35 Taylor-Batty and Taylor-Batty, *Samuel Beckett's Waiting for Godot*.
36 Declan Kiberd, *Inventing Ireland: The Literature of the Modern Nation* (Cambridge, MA: Harvard University Press, 1997), p. 327. The Wild Geese left Ireland following the 3 October 1691 signing of the Treaty of Limerick, which ended the Jacobite War in Ireland (1688–1691).
37 Henry Gráinne, 'Women "Wilde Geese," 1585–1625: Irish Women and Migration to European Armies in the Late Sixteenth and Early Seventeenth Centuries.' *Irish Women and Irish Migration*. Ed. Patrick O'Sullivan (London: Leicester University Press, 1995); John McGurk, 'Wild Geese: The Irish in European Armies (Sixteenth to Eighteenth Centuries).' *Patterns of Migration*. Ed. Patrick O'Sullivan (London: Leicester University Press, 1997).
38 According to Irish novelist John McGahern, 'In 1934, Virginia Woolf wrote to Katherine Arnold-Forster "[Ireland] is a lovely country, but very melancholy, except that the people never stop talking"': McGahern, *Love of the World: Essays* (London: Faber & Faber, 2009) p. 28.
39 Worton, '*Waiting for Godot* and *Endgame*,' p. 81.
40 For Beckett, a professed Atheist, Protestantism was more of a cultural marker than a religious devotion.
41 Kenner, *A Colder Eye*, p. 270.
42 Beckett, *Waiting for Godot*, 25.

43 Beckett, *Waiting for Godot*, 31.
44 Beckett, *Waiting for Godot*, 73.
45 Knowlson, *Damned to Fame*, p. 279.
46 Beckett, *Waiting for Godot*, 72.
47 Beckett, *Waiting for Godot*, 72.
48 Beckett, *Waiting for Godot*, 73.
49 Sean O'Faoláin, 'The Price of Peace,' *Bell* 10.4. (1945), p. 288. Later, in 1984, Political theorist James Raymond similarly reported Ireland's difficult foreign policy objectives in the immediate postwar era: 'The ending of partition was clearly preeminent, closely followed by Ireland's need to restore favorable economic relations with the United Kingdom. The third objective was the restoration of friendly relations with the United States, and the fourth and final was membership of the United Nations.' James Raymond. 'Irish Neutrality: Ideology or Pragmatism?' *International Affairs*. Winter (1983/84): p. 35.

Bibliography

Anderson, Amanda. *The Power of Distance: Cosmopolitanism and the Cultivation of Detachment.* Princeton, NJ: Princeton University Press, 2001. Print.

Anderson, Benedict. *Imagined Communities.* London: Verso, 1991. Print.

Arata, Stephen D. 'The Occidental Tourist: *Dracula* and the Anxiety of Reverse Colonization.' *Dracula.* Ed. by Nina Auerbach and David J. Skal. New York: W.W. Norton, 1997. pp. 462–470. Print.

Attridge, Derek and Marjorie Howes. *Semicolonial Joyce.* Cambridge: Cambridge University Press, 2000. Print.

Backus, Margot Gayle. *The Gothic Family Romance: Heterosexuality, Child Sacrifice, and the Anglo-Irish Colonial Order.* Durham, NC: Duke University Press, 1999. Print.

———. '"More Useful Washed and Dead": James Connolly, W.B. Yeats, and the Sexual Politics of "Easter 1916."' *Interventions* 10.1 (2008): 67–85. Print.

Bair, Deirdre. *Samuel Beckett: A Biography.* London: Vintage, 1990. Print.

Baldick, Chris. Introduction. *Melmoth the Wanderer.* By Charles Robert Maturn. Ed. Chris Baldick. Oxford: Oxford University Press, 1989. pp. vii–xix. Print.

Banville, John. 'On the Road to Revolution.' *The Guardian*, 24 September 2005. n. pag. www.guardian.co.uk/books/. 13 January 2010.

Barry, Sebastian. 'A Conversation With Sebastian Barry.' Afterword. *The Whereabouts of Eneas McNulty.* Sebastian Barry. New York: Penguin, 1998. pp. 5–9. Print.

———. 'A Conversation with Sebastian Barry.' *Penguin.com (USA).* 2008. n. pag. http://us.penguingroup.com/static/rguides/us/secret_scripture.html. 5 June 2010.

——. Man Booker Interview. *The Man Booker Prize for Fiction YouTube Channel.* 15 October 2008. www.youtube.com/user/TheManBookerPrize. 8 December 2010.
——. *The Secret Scripture.* New York: Viking, 2008. Print.
——. *The Steward of Christendom.* London: Methuen Publishing, 2001. Print.
——. *The Whereabouts of Eneas McNulty.* New York: Penguin, 1998. Print.
Bauerle, Ruth, ed., *The James Joyce Songbook* (New York: Garland Publishers, 1982).
Beckett, Samuel. 'Dante ... Bruno. Vico ... Joyce.' *Samuel Beckett: The Grove Centenary Edition.* Vol. 4. Ed. Paul Auster. New York: Grove Press, 2006. pp. 495–510. Print.
——. *Waiting for Godot. Samuel Beckett: The Grove Centenary Edition.* Vol. 3. Ed. Paul Auster. New York: Grove Press, 2006. Print.
Beine, Joseph. 'Ships Arriving at the Port of New Orleans from Belfast, Liverpool and Londonderry.' *NARA Microfilm.* May 2000. www.genesearch.com/neworleans/. 16 December 2009.
Bell, J. Bowyer. *The Secret Army.* 1974. Revised and Expanded. Piscataway, NJ: Transaction Publishers, 1997. Print.
Benedict XVI. 'Pastoral Letter of the Holy Father Pope Benedict XVI to the Catholics of Ireland.' 'Pope Says "Sorry" for Irish Church Abuse.' *CNN.com.* 20 March 2010. http://edition.cnn.com/2010/WORLD/europe/03/20/. 20 March 2010.
Benjamin, Walter. 'On the Concept of History.' *Walter Benjamin: Selected Writings (1938–1940).* Vol. 4. Ed. Howard Eiland and Michael W. Jennings. Cambridge, MA: Belknap, 2003. pp. 389–400. Print.
Bentley, Eric. 'Postscript 1967.' *Samuel Beckett: The Critical Heritage.* Eds. Lawrence Graver and Raymond Federman. London: Routledge & Kegan Paul, 1979. 119–120. Print.
Bentley, Michael. *Modern Historiography: An Introduction.* London: Routledge, 1999. Print.
Bhabha, Homi K. 'DissemiNation: Time, Narrative, and the Margins of the Modern Nation.' *Nation and Narration.* Ed. Homi K. Bhabha. London: Routledge, 1990. pp. 291–322. Print.
Bishop, John. *Joyce's Book of the Dark: Finnegans Wake.* Madison, WI: University of Wisconsin Press, 1993. Print.
Bloy, Marjie. 'The Irish Famine: 1845–9.' *The Victorian Web.* 11 October 2002. n. pag. www.victorianweb.org/history/famine.html. 24 May 2010.
Botting, Fred. *Gothic.* London: Routledge, 1996. Print.

Bourke, Angela, ed. *The Field Day Anthology of Irish Writing: Irish Women's Writing and Traditions*. New York: New York University Press, 2002. Print.
Boyd, Andrew. *Holy War in Belfast*. Tralee: Anvil Books, 1969. Print.
Brennan, Timothy. 'The National Longing for Form.' *Nation and Narration*. Ed. Homi K. Bhabha. London: Routledge, 1990. pp. 44–70. Print.
Brown, Terrence. *Ireland: A Social and Cultural History 1922–2002*. London: Harper Perennial, 2004. Print.
Bruhm, Steven. 'Contemporary Gothic: Why We Need It.' *The Cambridge Companion to Gothic Fiction*. Ed. Jerrold E. Hogle. Cambridge: Cambridge University Press, 2002. pp. 259–276. Print.
Burns, Anna. *No Bones*. New York: W.W. Norton, 2002. Print.
Campbell, Joseph and Henry Morton Robinson. *A Skeleton Key to Finnegans Wake*. Ed. Edmund L. Epstein. Novato, CA: New World Library, 2005. Print.
Caruth, Cathy. 'Interview with Gayatri Chakravorty Spivak.' *PMLA* 125.4 (2010): 1020–1025. Print.
——. *Unclaimed Experience*. Baltimore, MD: Johns Hopkins University Press, 1996. Print.
Casey, Maura J. 'Appreciations: Nuala O'Faolain.' *New York Times*. 13 May 2008. www.nytimes.com/. 24 October 2009.
Castle, Gregory. 'Ousted Possibilities: Critical Histories in James Joyce's *Ulysses*.' *Twentieth Century Literature* 39.3 (1993): 306–328. Print.
Central Statistics Office. *Quarterly National Household Survey*, December 2000. www.cso.ie/qnhs/spe_mod_qnhs.htm. 22 January 2010.
Cheng, Vincent J. *Joyce, Race, and Empire*. Cambridge: Cambridge University Press, 1995. Print.
Cleary. E.J. 'Introduction.' *The Castle of Otranto* by Horace Walpole. Ed. W.S. Lewis. New York: Oxford University Press, 2009. pp. vii–xxxiii. Print.
Cleary, Joe. *Outrageous Fortune: Capital and Culture in Modern Ireland*. Field Day Files I. Eds. Seamus Deane and Brendán Mac Suibhne. Dublin: Field Day Publications, 2007. Print.
Collins, Patricia Hill. *Black Feminist Thought: Knowledge, Consciousness and the Politics of Empowerment*. London: Routledge Classics, 2008. Print.
Commission to Inquire into Child Abuse (CICA). *The Ryan Report*. 20 May 2009. www.childabusecommission.ie/. 20 August 2010.
Conley, Thomas. 'Translator's Introduction: For a Literary Historiography.' Introduction. *The Writing of History*. By Michel de Certeau. Trans. Thomas Conley. New York: Columbia University Press,

1975. pp. vii–xxiv. Print.
Coogan, Michael D. et. al., eds. *The New Oxford Annotated Bible with Apocrypha: New Revised Standard Version*. 4th edn. New York: Oxford University Press, 2010.
Coogan, Timothy Patrick. *Ireland Since the Rising*. 2nd edn. Santa Barbara, CA: Greenwood Press, 1967. Print.
Corish, Marguerite. 'Aspects of the Secularisation of Irish Society.' *Faith and Culture in the Irish Context*. Ed. Eoin G. Cassidy. Dublin: Veritas, 1996. 138–172. Print.
Cronin, Anthony. *Beckett: The Last Modernist*. Cambridge, MA: Da Capo Press, 1999. Print.
Cronin, Michael G. '"He's My Country": Liberalism, Nationalism, and Sexuality in Contemporary Irish Gay Fiction.' *Éire-Ireland* 39.3–4 (2004): 250–267. Print.
Crowe, Sean. 'Easter 1916 Dublin Commemoration.' *Sinn Féin – Keep Left*. 5 April 2010. http://sinnfeinkeepleft.blogspot.com/2010. 30 August 2010.
Culler, Jonathan. 'Introduction: Critical Paradigms.' *PMLA* 125.4 (2010): 905–915. Print.
Cullingford, Elizabeth. 'Colonial Policing: *The Steward of Christendom* and *The Whereabouts of Eneas McNulty*.' *Èire-Ireland: A Journal of Irish Studies* 39.3–4 (2004): 11–37. Print.
——. *Ireland's Others: Ethnicity and Gender in Irish Literature and Popular Culture*. Notre Dame, IN: University of Notre Dame Press, 2001. Print. Field Day Monographs. 10.
Daly, Mary. *The Famine in Ireland*. Dundalk, IRE: Dundalgan Press, 1986. Print.
Davey, Meave. '"The Strange Heart Beating": Bird Imagery, Masculinities and the Northern Irish Postcolonial Gothic in the Novels of Sean O'Reilly and Peter Hollywood.' *Irish Journal of Gothic and Horror Studies* 5 (2008): n pag. http://irishgothichorrorjournal.homestead.com/NorthernIrishPostcolonialGothic.html. 21 February 2010.
Davis, Thomas Osborne. 'A Nation Once Again.' *The Celtic Lyrics Collection*. 2009. www.celtic-lyrics.com/. 7 December 2009.
Deane, Paul. 'Rebels Without a Cause: Sebastian Barry's *The Whereabouts of Eneas McNulty*.' *Notes on Modern Irish Literature* 13 (2001): 28–32. Print.
Deane, Seamus. *Celtic Revivals*. Winston-Salem: Wake Forest University Press, 1987. Print.
——. *Field Day Anthology of Irish Writing*. Ed. Seamus Deane. London: Faber & Faber, 1991. Print.
——. *Reading in the Dark*. New York: Vintage, 1996. Print.

———. *Strange Country: Modernity and Nationhood in Irish Writing since 1790*. Oxford: Clarendon Press, 1997.

———. 'Wherever Green is Read.' *Revising the Rising*. Eds. Máirín Ní Donnchadha and Theo Dorgan. Derry: Field Day, 1991. pp. 91–105. Print.

De Certeau, Michel. *The Writing of History*. Trans. Thomas Conley. New York: Columbia University Press, 1975. Print.

Department of Justice and Law Reform. 'Report by Commission of Investigation into Catholic Archdiocese of Dublin (The Murphy Report).' 26 November 2009. www.justice.ie/en/JELR/Pages/. 20 August 2010.

Derrida, Jacques. *The Gift of Death*. 1991. Trans. David Wills. Chicago: University of Chicago Press, 1996. Print.

———. *Specters of Marx: The State of the Debt, the Work of Mourning, and the New International*. 1993. Trans. Peggy Kamuf. New York: Routledge Classics, 2006. Print.

De Valera, Eamon. 'Article 44.2.' *Bunreact na hÉireann* (1937). 27 May 1999. www.constitution.ie/publications/irish-text.pdf. 10 February 2010.

———. *Ireland's Stand: Being a Selection of the Speeches of Eamon De Valera During the War (1939–1945)*. 2nd edn. Dublin: M.H. Gill and Son, Ltd, 1946. Print.

Devlin, Anne. *The Long March. Ourselves Alone, with A Woman Calling and The Long March*. London: Faber, 1986. Print.

'Dis, *prefix*.' Definition, *The Oxford English Dictionary Online*. 3rd edn. 2009. www.oed.com. 28 August 2010.

Donnelly, Brian. 'Roddy Doyle: From Barrytown to the GPO.' *Irish University Review* 30.1 (2000): 17–31. Print.

Dowling, Linda. *Hellenism and Homosexuality in Victorian Oxford*. Ithaca: Cornell University Press, 1994. Print.

Doyle, Richard. 'Union is Strength: John Bull.' 1846. *Punchcartoons.com*. n.d. www.punchcartoons.com/m49/Doyle,-Richard/. 20 August 2010.

Doyle, Roddy. *A Star Called Henry*. New York: Penguin, 1999. Print.

———. 'Revel Rebel: Interview with Róisin Ingle.' *Irish Times*, 28 August 1999. www.tcd.ie/ irishfilm/. 30 December 2009.

Drewett, James. 'An Interview with Roddy Doyle.' *Irish Studies Review* 11.3 (2003): 337–349. Print.

Duckworth, Colin, ed. *Samuel Beckett: En Attendant Godot*. London: Harrap, 1966. Print.

Dufferin, Lord K.P. *Irish Emigration and the Tenure of Land in Ireland*. 2nd edn. London: Willis, Sotheran, and Co., 1867. Print.

Eagleton, Terry. *Heathcliff and the Great Hunger: Studies in Irish Culture*. London: Verso, 1995. Print.

Edwards, R. Dudley and T. Desmond Williams, eds. *The Great Irish Famine: Studies in Irish History 1845–1852*. New York: New York University Press, 1957. Print.

Ellmann, Richard. *James Joyce*. Rev. edn, New York: Oxford University Press, 1982. Print.

Epstein, Edmund L., ed. *A Skeleton Key to Finnegans Wake*. Novato: New World Library, 2005. Print.

Esslin, Martin. '*Waiting for Godot*: Western and Korean.' *The Samuel Beckett On-Line Resources and Links Pages*. 1988. www.drama21c.net/text/Eesslin.htm. 19 December 2009.

Estévez-Saá, José Manuel. 'An Interview with Joseph O'Connor.' *Contemporary Literature* 46.2 (2005): 161–175. Print.

Evans, Ruth Dudley. *The Triumph of Failure*. London: Victor Gollancz, Ltd, 1990. Print.

Fanon, Frantz. 'On National Culture.' *The Wretched of the Earth*. Trans. Richard Philcox. New York: Grove Press, 2005. pp. 145–180. Print.

Fargnoli, A. Nicholas and Michael P. Gillespie, eds. *James Joyce A–Z: The Essential Reference to His Life and Writings*. Oxford: Oxford University Press, 1995. Print.

Ferriter, Diarmaid and Colm Toíbín. *The Irish Famine*. London: Profile Books, 2002. Print.

Finn, John. *New Orleans Irish: Famine Exiles*. Front Royal: Holy Family Church Press, 1997. Print.

Fitzgerald-Hoyt, Mary. 'Writing the Famine, Healing the Future: Nuala O'Faolain's My Dream of You.' *Ireland's Great Hunger: Relief, Representation, and Remembrance*, Vol. 2. Ed. David A. Valone. Lanham, MD: University Press of America, 2010. pp. 88–110. Print.

Flanagan, Thomas. *There You Are: Writings on Irish and American Literature and History*. Ed. Christopher Cahill. New York: New York Review of Books, 2004. Print.

Flannery, John Brendan. *The Irish Texans*. San Antonio, TX: Institute for Texan Cultures, 1995. Print.

Foster, R.F. *Modern Ireland: 1600–1972*. London: Penguin, 1988. Print.

Fox, Jo. 'Women of the Celts in Myth, Legend, and Story.' *SkyeViews* 8 (1996): n. pag. www.pabay.org/skyeviews.html. 29 December 2009.

Freccero, Carla. 'Queer Spectrality: Haunting the Past.' *A Companion to Lesbian, Gay, Bisexual, Transgender, and Queer Studies*. Ed. George Haggerty and Molly McGarry. Oxford: Blackwell Press, 2007. pp. 192–211. Print.

Freud, Sigmund. *The Uncanny*. New York: Penguin Classics, 2003. Print.

Gellman, Irwin F., 'The *St. Louis* Tragedy.' *American Jewish Historical Quarterly* 61.2 (1971): 144–157. Print.

Gibbons, Luke. *Transformations in Irish Culture*. Cork: Cork University Press, 1996. Print.

Gibbons, Luke and Michael Cronin, eds. *Reinventing Ireland: Culture, Society, and the Global Economy*. London: Pluto Press, 2002. Print.

Gilbert, Stuart and Richard Ellmann, eds. *Letters of James Joyce*. Vol. 3. New York: Viking, 1966. Print.

Glenn, Jeffrey. 'Surviving the Troubles: A View from the Suburbs.' *Children of 'The Troubles': Our Lives in the Crossfire of Northern Ireland*. Ed. Laurel Holliday. New York: Pocket Books, 1997. pp. 78–85. Print.

Gluck, Barbara Reich. *Beckett and Joyce: Friendship and Fiction*. London: Associated University Press, 1979. Print.

Goldman, Peter. 'Christian Mystery and Responsibility: Gnosticism in Derrida's *The Gift of Death*.' *Anthropoetics* 4.1 (1998): n. pag. www.anthropoetics.ucla.edu/ap0401/pg_DERR.htm. 26 September 2010.

Gonne, Maud. *Dawn*. 1900. *Lost Plays of the Irish Renaissance*. Eds Robert Hogan and James Kilroy. Newark: Proscenium Press, 1970. Print.

——. 'The Famine Queen.' *Irish Writing: An Anthology of Irish Literature in English 1789–1939*. Ed. Stephen Regan. Oxford: Oxford University Press, 2004. pp. 183–185. Print.

Gordon, Lois. *Reading Godot*. New Haven, CT: Yale University Press, 2002. Print.

Gráinne, Henry. 'Women "Wilde Geese," 1585–1625: Irish Women and Migration to European Armies in the Late Sixteenth and Early Seventeenth Centuries.' *Irish Women and Irish Migration*. Ed. Patrick O'Sullivan. London: Leicester University Press, 1995. pp. 23–40. Print.

Greene, Richard Allen. 'Ashamed to Be Irish: Abuse Angers Nation.' *CNN.com*. 20 March 2010. www.cnn.com/2010/WORLD/europe/03/20/ireland.abuse.voices/ index.html. 20 March 2010.

Gregory, Lady Augusta. 'Our Irish Theatre.' *Modern and Contemporary Irish Drama*. Ed. John P. Harrington. 2nd edn. New York: W.W. Norton, 2009. Print.

Grob-Fitzgibbon, Benjamin. *The Irish Experience During the Second World War: An Oral History*. Dublin: Irish Academic Press, 2004. Print.

Grossman, Judith. Review of *No Bones*, by Anna Burns. *Women's Review of Books* 20.1 (2002): 10–11. Print.

Hamacher, Werner. 'From 95 Theses on Philology.' *PMLA* 125.4 (2010): 994–1001. Print.

Hand, Derek. *A History of the Irish Novel*. Cambridge: Cambridge University Press, 2011. Print.

Hansen, Jim. *Terror and Irish Modernism: The Gothic Tradition from Burke to Beckett*. Albany, NY: State University of New York Press, 2009. Print.

Hardwick, Susan Wiley. *Mythic Galveston*. Baltimore, MD: Johns Hopkins University Press, 2002. Print.

Harrington, John P. 'The Irish Beckett.' *Modern and Contemporary Irish Drama*. Ed. John P. Harrington. New York: W.W. Norton, 2009. pp. 525–530. Print.

Haslam, Richard. 'Irish Gothic: A Rhetorical Hermeneutics Approach.' *Irish Journal of Gothic and Horror Studies* 2 (2007): n. pag. http://irishgothichorrorjournal.homestead.com/IrishGothicHaslam.html. 15 February 2010.

Higgins, Roisí. 'Projections and Reflections: Irishness and the Fiftieth Anniversary of the Easter Rising.' *Èire-Ireland* 42.3/4 (2007): 11–34. Print.

Hofheinz, Thomas C. *Joyce and the Invention of Irish History: Finnegans Wake in Context*. Cambridge: Cambridge University Press, 1995. Print.

Holland, Jack. 'Return of the Gunman 1966–1969.' *Hope Against History: The Course of Conflict in Northern Ireland*. New York: Henry Holt & Co., 1999. pp. 3–23. Print.

Hurley, Kelly. 'British Gothic Fiction, 1885–1930.' *The Cambridge Companion to Gothic Fiction*. Ed. Jerrold E. Hogle. Cambridge: Cambridge University Press, 2002. pp. 189–208. Print.

Hutcheon, Linda. *The Politics of Postmodernism*. New York: Routledge, 1989. Print.

Hyde, Douglas. 'The Necessity for De-Anglicising Ireland.' *Language, Lore and Lyrics: Essays and Lectures by Douglas Hyde*. Ed. Breandán Ó Conaire. Dublin: Irish Academic Press, 1986. Print.

Ingelbien, Raphael. 'Gothic Genealogies: Dracula, Bowen's Court, and Anglo-Irish Psychology.' *ELH* 70.4 (2003): 1089–1105. Print.

Inglis, Tomas. *Moral Monopoly: The Rise and Fall of the Catholic Church in Modern Ireland*. 2nd edn. Dublin: University College of Dublin Press, 1998. Print.

In the Name of the Father. Dir. Jim Sheridan. Perf. Daniel Day-Lewis, Pete Postlethwaite. Hell's Kitchen Films, 1994. DVD.

Ireland, Doug. 'Review of Brian Lacey's *"Terrible Queer Creatures": A History of Homosexuality in Ireland*.' *Gay City News*. 6 February

Bibliography 191

2009. http://hnn.us/roundup/entries/61344.html. 3 December 2009.
Irish Congress of Trade Unions. *Delivering Gender Equality 1999–2004: Fourth Equality Programme*. Dublin: Irish Congress, 1999. Print.
Jacklein, Charlotte. 'Rebel Songs and Hero Pawns: Music in *A Star Called Henry*.' *New Hibernia Review* 9.4 (2005): 129–143. Print.
Jameson, Fredric. 'Third-World Literature in the Era of Multinational Capitalism.' *Social Text* 15 (1986): 65–88. Print.
Joyce, James. *A Portrait of the Artist as a Young Man*. Ed. John Paul Riquelme. New York: W.W. Norton, 2007. Print.
——. *Finnegans Wake*. New York: Penguin, 1999. Print.
——. 'Ireland: Island of Saints and Sages.' *James Joyce: Occasional, Critical, and Political Writing*. Ed. Kevin Barry. Trans. Conor Deane. Oxford: Oxford University Press, 2000. pp. 108–126. Print.
——. *Letters of James Joyce*. Vol. 3. Ed. Richard Ellmann. New York: Viking Press, 1966. Print.
——. *Ulysses*. Ed. Hans Walter Gabler. New York: Vintage, 1986. Print.
Junker, Mary. *Beckett: The Irish Dimension*. Dublin: Wolfhound Press, 1995. Print.
Keating, Patrick. *A Singular Stance: Irish Neutrality in the 1980s*. Dublin: Institute of Public Administration, 1984. Print.
Kennedy-Andrews, Elmer. 'The Novel and the Northern Troubles.' *The Cambridge Companion to the Irish Novel*. Ed. John Wilson Foster. Cambridge: Cambridge University Press, 2006. Print.
Kenner, Hugh. *A Colder Eye: The Modern Irish Writers*. New York: Knopf, 1983. Print.
——. *A Reader's Guide to Samuel Beckett*. New York: Farrar, Straus and Giroux, 1973. Print.
Kenny, Mary. *Goodbye to Catholic Ireland*. Revised and updated ed. Dublin: New Island Books, 2000. Print.
Kiberd, Declan. *Inventing Ireland: The Literature of the Modern Nation*. Cambridge, MA: Harvard University Press, 1997. Print.
Kiberd, Declan. *Ulysses and Us: The Art of Everyday Living*. London: Faber & Faber, 2009. Print.
Kilfeather, Siobhán. 'Terrific Register: The Gothicization of Atrocity in Irish Romanticism.' *boundary 2* 31.1 (2004): 49–71. Print.
Kinealy, Christine. 'The Great Irish Famine: A Dangerous Memory.' *The Great Famine and the Irish Diaspora in America*. Ed. Arthur Gribben. Amherst, MA: University of Massachusetts Press, 1999. pp. 239–254. Print.
——. *The Great Irish Famine: Impact, Ideology and Rebellion*. New York: Palgrave, 2002. Print.

Kissane, Bill. *The Politics of the Irish Civil War*. Oxford: Oxford University Press, 2005. Print.

Kitcher, Philip. *Joyce's Kaleidoscope: An Invitation to* Finnegans Wake. Oxford: Oxford University Press, 2007. Print.

Klein, Richard. 'The Future of Literary Criticism.' *PMLA* 125.4 (2010): 920–923. Print.

Knowlson, James. *Damned to Fame: The Life of Samuel Beckett*. New York: Grove Press, 1996. Print.

Knowlson, James and Elizabeth Knowlson, eds., *Beckett Remembering Beckett*. New York: Arcade Publishing, 2011. Print.

Knudsen, Susanne V. 'Intersectionality: A Theoretical Inspiration in the Analysis of Minority Cultures and Identities in Textbooks.' *Caught in the Web or Lost in the Textbook?* Ed. Eric Bruillard et al. 2006. *www.caen.iufm.fr/colloque_iartem/pdf/knudsen.pdf*. 22 January 2010.

Konovitch, Barry J. 'The Fiftieth Anniversary of the *St. Louis*: What Really Happened.' *American Jewish History* 79.2 (1989–1990): 203–210. Print.

Labouchère, Henry Du Pré. 'Criminal Law Amendment Act.' 1885. *UK Law Online*. 9 July 2010. www.swarb.co.uk. 20 August 2010.

Lacey, Brian. *Terrible Queer Creatures: A History of Homosexuality in Ireland*. Dublin: Wordwell, 2008. Print.

Lanters, Jose. 'Demythicizing/Remythicizing the Rising: Roddy Doyle's *A Star Called Henry*.' *Hungarian Journal of English and American Studies* 8.1 (2002): 245–258. Print.

Laxton, Edward. *The Famine Ships: The Irish Exodus to America*. New York: Henry Holt, 1996. Print.

Lennon, Peter. *Rocky Road to Dublin*. 1967. London: BBC, 2006. DVD.

Leventhal, A.J. 'Dramatic Commentary.' *Dublin Magazine* 31.1 (1956): 52–54. Print.

Lewis, Brian. 'The Queer Life and Afterlife of Roger Casement.' *Journal of the History of Sexuality* 14.4 (2005): 363–382. Print.

Linke, Bettina. 'Dr. Bernard's Restoration of Grianan Aileach from 1874–1878.' *Inishowen*. 10 July 2006. http://unknownswilly.orgfree.com/grianan.html. 20 August 2010.

Lloyd, David. *Anomalous States: Irish Writing and the Post-Colonial Moment*. Dublin: Lilliput, 1993. Print.

———. *Ireland After History*. Critical Conditions: Field Day Essays and Monographs 9. Ed. Seamus Deane. Notre Dame, IN: University of Notre Dame Press, 1999.

Lynch, Diarmuid and Florence O'Donoghue. *The I.R.B. and the 1916 Rising*. Cork: The Mercier Press, 1957. Print.

Lyotard, Jean François. *The Postmodern Condition*. Minneapolis, MN: University of Minnesota Press. 1984. Print.
Macardle, Dorothy. *The Irish Republic*. 1937. Dublin: Wolfhound Press, 1999. Print.
Mageean, Deirdre M. 'Emigration from Irish Ports.' *Journal of American Ethnic History* 13.1 (1993): 6–30. Print.
Mahaffey, Vicki. *States of Desire: Wilde, Yeats, Joyce, and the Irish Experiment*. Oxford: Oxford University Press, 1998. Print.
Mahon, Peter. 'In the Crypt of the Sun: Towards the Narrative Politics of Seamus Deane's Reading in the Dark.' *Partial Answers: Journal of Literature and the History of Ideas* 5.1 (2007): 91–119. Print.
Malcolm, Elizabeth. '"On Fire." The Great Hunger: Ireland 1845–1849.' *New Hibernia Review* 12.4 (2008): 143–149. Print.
Mara, Miriam O'Kane. '(Re)producing Identity and Creating Famine in Nuala O'Faolain's *My Dream of You*.' *Critique* 48.2 (2007): 197–216. Print.
Markievicz, Constance. 'From *Cumann na mBan* Vol. II, No. 10. Easter 1926.' *In Their Own Voice: Women and Irish Nationalism*. Ed. Margaret Ward. Cork: Attic Press, 2001. pp. 33–35. Print.
——. 'From *Irish Citizen* 23 Oct. 1915.' *In Their Own Voice: Women and Irish Nationalism*. Ed. Margaret Ward. Cork: Attic Press, 2001. pp. 51–53. Print.
Mays, J.C.C. 'Irish Beckett, A Borderline Instance.' *Beckett in Dublin*. Ed. S.E. Wilmer. Dublin: Lilliput Press, 1992. Print.
McCall, Leslie. 'The Complexity of Intersectionality.' *Journal of Women in Culture and Society* 30.3 (2005): 1771–1800. Print.
McCoole, Sinéad. *No Ordinary Women: Irish Female Activists in the Revolutionary Years, 1900–1923*. Madison, WI: University of Wisconsin Press, 2003. Print.
——. 'Seven Women of the Labour Movement 1916.' *Labour*. 2010. www.labour.ie/seven_women_of_the_labour_movement1916.pdf. 4 January 2010.
McCormack, W.J. *From Burke to Beckett: Ascendancy, Tradition and Betrayal in Literary History*. Cork: Cork University Press, 1994. Print.
McDonald, Ronan. 'Beckett Review Essay.' *Irish Studies Review* 6.11 (1998): 87–89. Print.
McFerran, Douglass. *IRA Man: Talking with the Rebels*. Westport, CT: Praeger Publishing, 1997. Print.
McGahern, John. *Love of the World: Essays*. London: Faber & Faber, 2009. Print.
McGarry, Fearghal. *The Rising: Ireland: Easter 1916*. Oxford: Oxford University Press, 2010. Print.

McGill, Meredith L. and Andrew Parker. 'The Future of the Literary Past.' *PMLA* 125.4 (2010): 959–967. Print.

McGurk, John. 'Wild Geese: The Irish in European Armies (Sixteenth to Eighteenth Centuries).' *Patterns of Migration*. Ed. Patrick O'Sullivan. London: Leicester University Press, 1997. 36–62. Print.

Medd, Jodie. '"Patterns of the Possible": National Imaginings and Queer Historical (Meta) Fictions in Jamie O'Neill's *At Swim, Two Boys*.' *GLQ: A Journal of Lesbian and Gay Studies* 13.1 (2006): 1–31. Print.

Melaugh, Martin. 'The People's Democracy March: Chronology of Main Events.' *Conflict Archive on the Internet, University of Ulster*. 16 December 2009. www.cain.ulst.ac.uk/events/pdmarch/chron.htm. 12 February 2010.

Moloney, Ed. *A Secret History of the IRA*. London: W.W. Norton, 2002. Print.

Moynihan, Sinéad. '"Ships in Motion": Crossing the Black and Green Atlantics in Joseph O'Connor's *Star of the Sea*.' *Symbiosis: A Journal of Anglo-American Literary Relations* 12.1 (2008): 41–58. Print.

Murphy, James. *The Shan Van Vocht: A Story of the United Irishmen*. Dublin: M.H. Gill and Son, 1889. Print.

Naficy, Hamid. 'Framing Exile: From Homeland to Homepage.' Introduction. *Home, Exile, Homeland: Film, Media and the Politics of Place*. Ed. Naficy. London: Routledge, 1999. Print.

Niehaus, Earl F. *The Irish in New Orleans, 1800–1860*. Baton Rouge, LA: Louisiana State University Press, 1965. Print.

'Norris v. Ireland.' *European Court of Human Rights*. 26 October 1988. www.unhcr.org/refworld/. 31 August 2010.

Nutt, Kathleen. 'Irish Identity and the Writing of History.' *Eire-Ireland* 29.2 (1994): 160–172. Print.

New York University Library. 'Wilde at Oxford/Oxford Gone Wilde.' *Reading Wilde, Querying Spaces*. New York University, n.d. www.nyu.edu/library/bobst/research/fales/exhibits/wilde/. 31 August 2010.

O'Brien, Conor Cruise. *Ancestral Voices: Religion and Nationalism in Ireland*. Chicago, IL: Chicago University Press, 1995. Print.

O'Brien, Eoin. *The Beckett Country*. Dublin: Black Cat Press, 1986. Print.

O'Brion, Leon. *Dublin Castle and the 1916 Rising*. Rev. edn. New York: New York University Press, 1971. Print.

O'Casey, Sean. *Three Dublin Plays*. London: Faber and Faber, 1998. Print.

O'Connor, Catherine. '"The Smell of Her Apron": Issues of Gender and Religious Identity in the Oral Testimonies of Church of Ireland

Women in Ferns, 1945–1965.' *Anáil an Bhéil Bheo: Orality and Modern Irish Culture.* Eds Nessa Cronin et al. Newcastle upon Tyne: Cambridge Scholars, 2009. pp. 127–136. Print.
O'Connor, Joseph. *Star of the Sea.* New York: Harcourt Inc., 2002. Print.
Ó Corráin, Donnchadh. 'Emancipation, Famine & Religion: Ireland Under the Union, 1815–1870.' *Multi-text Project in Irish History.* 23 January 2006. http://multitext.ucc.ie/d/Emancipation. 10 October 2009.
O'Doherty, Malachi. 'Don't talk about the Troubles.' *Fortnight* 457 (2008): 12–15. Print.
O'Faolain, Nuala. *Are You Somebody?: The Accidental Memoir of a Dublin Woman.* New York: Holt, 1996. Print.
———. *My Dream of You.* New York: Riverhead Books, 2001. Print.
O'Faolain, Sean. *King of Beggars: A Life of Daniel O'Connell, The Irish Liberator.* London: Viking, 1938. Print.
———. 'The Price of Peace,' *Bell* 10.4. (1945): 288. Print.
O'Farrell, Patrick. *Ireland's English Question.* New York: Schocken Books, 1972. Print.
Office of the Houses of the Oireachtas. 'Dáil Debates Official Report: 22 December 1921.' *Parliamentary Debates.* n.d. http://historical-debates.oireachtas.ie/. 30 August 2010.
Ogilvie, Sarah A. and Scott Miller. *Refuge Denied: The St. Louis Passengers and the Holocaust.* Madison, WI: University of Wisconsin Press, 2006. Print.
O'Hehir, Andrew. 'Irish Ghost Stories.' *Salon Magazine.* 11 April 1997. www.salon.com/april97/reading970411.html. 18 December 2008.
O'Malley, Ernie. *On Another Man's Wound.* London: Kimble & Bradford, 1936. Print.
O'Neill, Jamie. *At Swim, Two Boys.* New York: Scribner, 2002. Print.
O'Rourke, John. *The History of the Great Irish Famine of 1847.* Charleston: BiblioLife, 2008. http://books.google.com/books. 24 May 2010.
Pater, Walter. *The Renaissance: Studies in Art and Poetry: The 1893 Text.* Ed. Donald E. Hill. Berkeley, CA: University of California Press, 1980. Print.
Pearse, Padraig. 'Little Lad of the Tricks.' 1909. *Gombeen Nation.* 30 July 2007. http://gombeennation.blogspot.com/2007. 20 August 2010.
Perloff, Marjorie. '"In Love With Hiding": Samuel Beckett's War.' *Iowa Review* 35.2 (2005): 76–103. Print.
Persson, Åke. 'Between Displacement and Renewal: The Third Space in Roddy Doyle's Novels.' *Nordic Irish Studies* 5.1 (2006): 59–71. Print.

Piroux, Lorraine. '"I'm Black an' I'm Proud": Re-Inventing Irishness in Roddy Doyle's "The Commitments."' *College Literature* 25.2 (1998): 45–57. Print.

Platt, Len. '"No Such Race": The *Wake* and Aryanism.' *Joyce, Ireland, Britain*. Eds Andrew Gibson and Len Platt. Gainesville, FL: University Press of Florida, 2006. pp. 14–41. Print.

Prendergast, Christopher. 'Derrida's Hamlet.' *SubStance* 34.1 (2005): 44–47. Print.

Prince, Simon. *Northern Ireland's '68: Civil Rights, Global Revolt and the Origins of the Troubles*. Dublin: Irish Academic Press, 2007. Print.

Punter, David. 'Scottish and Irish Gothic.' *The Cambridge Companion to Gothic Fiction*. Ed. Jerrold E. Hogle. Cambridge: Cambridge University Press, 2002. pp. 105–124. Print.

Quigley, Michael. 'Grosse Île: Canada's Famine Memorial.' *The Great Famine and the Irish Diaspora in America*. Ed. Arthur Gribben. Amherst, MA: University of Massachusetts Press, 1999. pp. 133–154. Print.

Rambo, Shelly. 'Haunted (by the) Gospel: Theology, Trauma, and Literary Theory in the Twenty-First Century.' *PMLA* 125.4 (2010): 936–941. Print.

Raymond, James. 'Irish Neutrality: Ideology or Pragmatism?' *International Affairs*. Winter (1983/84): 35. Print.

Renan, Ernest. 'What is a Nation?' *Nation and Narration*. Ed. Homi K. Bhabha. London: Routledge, 1990. Print.

Riquelme, John Paul. 'Toward a History of Gothic and Modernism: Dark Modernity from Bram Stoker to Samuel Beckett.' *Modern Fiction Studies* 46.2 (2000): 586–605. Print.

Roach, Joseph. 'All the Dead Voices: The Landscape of Famine in *Waiting for Godot*.' *Land/Scape/Theater*. Eds Elinor Fuchs and Una Chaudhuri. Ann Arbor, MI: University of Michigan Press, 2002. pp. 84–93. Print.

Robbins, Bruce. *Secular Vocations: Intellectuals, Professionalism, Culture*. London: Verso, 1983. Print.

Robinson, Mary. 'Cherishing the Irish Diaspora: An Address.' *Irish Diaspora*. 29 October 1995. www.rootsweb.ancestry.com/~irlker/diaspora.html. 12 October 2009.

Ross, Daniel. 'Oedipus in Derry: Seamus Deane's *Reading in the Dark*.' *New Hibernia Review* 11.1 (2007): 25–41. Print.

Rumens, Carol. 'Reading Deane.' *Fortnight* July/August (1997): 29–30. Print.

Rushdie, Salman. 'Imaginary Homelands.' *Imaginary Homelands*. New York: Penguin, 1992. Print.

Ryan, Desmond. *The Rising: The Complete Story of Easter Week*. 2nd edn. Dublin: Golden Eagle Books, 1949. Print.

Samuel, Raphael. 'Ancestor Worship.' *Island Stories: Unraveling Britain: Theatres of Memory*. Vol. 2. Ed. Alison Light, Sally Alexander, and Gareth Stedman Jones. London: Verso, 1999. pp. 272–275. Print.

Schork, R.J. *Joyce and Hagiography: Saints Above!* Gainesville, FL: University of Florida Press, 2000. Print.

Sea Tales: The Doomed Voyage of the St. Louis. Distributed by A & E Home Video, 1996. DVD.

Sex in a Cold Climate. Dir. Steve Humphries. Testimony Films, 1998. DVD.

Shakespeare, William. *Hamlet*. 2nd edn. Ed. Cyrus Hoy. New York: W.W. Norton, 1992. Print.

Sharkey, Rodney. 'Irish? Au Contraire!: The Search for Identity in the Fictions of Samuel Beckett.' *Journal of Beckett Studies* 3.2 (1994): 1–18. Print.

Shaw, George Bernard. 'George Bernard Shaw on "Irish Nonsense About Ireland."' *New York Times*. 9 April 1916. http://query.nytimes.com/gst/. 22 March 2010.

Sheehan, Ronan. 'Novelists on the Novel: Ronan Sheehan Talks to John Banville and Francis Stuart.' *The Crane Bag* 3.1 (1979): 76–84. Print.

Sisson, Elaine. *Pearse's Patriots: St. Endas and the Cult of Boyhood*. Cork: Cork University Press, 2004. Print.

Skinnider, Margaret. *Doing My Bit for Ireland*. New York: The Century Co, 1917. Print.

Smith, James M. *Ireland's Magdalen Laundries and the Nation's Architecture of Containment*. South Bend, IN: University of Notre Dame Press, 2007. Print.

Smyllie, R.M. 'Unneutral Neutral Éire.' *Foreign Affairs* 24.2 (1946): 316–326. Print.

Spivak, Gayatri Chakravorty. *In Other Worlds: Essays in Cultural Politics*. New York: Methuen, 1987. Print.

States of Fear. Prod. Mary Raftery. Radio Telefís Éireann, Dublin. 1991. Television.

Steedman, Carolyn. *Dust: The Archive and Cultural History*. New Brunswick, NJ: Rutgers University Press, 2001. Print.

Stevenson, Jonathan. *'We Wrecked the Place': Contemplating an End to the Northern Irish Troubles*. New York: The Free Press, 1996. Print.

Stewart, Bruce. 'Bram Stoker's *Dracula*: Possessed by the Spirit of the Nation?' *Irish University Review* 29.2 (1999): 238–255. Print.

Stoker, Bram. *Dracula*. Ed. Nina Auerbach and David J. Skal. New York: W.W. Norton, 1997. Print.
Szeman, Imre. 'Who's Afraid of National Allegory? Jameson, Literary Criticism, Globalization.' *South Atlantic Quarterly* 100.3 (2001): 803–827. Print.
Talbot v. Talbot: A Report of the Speech of Wm. Keogh, Esq., M.P., Solicitor General for Ireland, on Behalf of the Appellant, Before The High Court of Delegates. London: Thomas Blenkarn, 1855. Print.
Taylor, Peter. *Loyalists*. London: Bloomsbury Publishing, 2000. Print.
Taylor-Batty, Mark and Juliette Taylor-Batty. *Samuel Beckett's Waiting for Godot*. London: Continuum, 2008. Print.
The Double Crossing: The Voyage of the St. Louis. Holocaust Memorial Foundation of Illinois and Loyola University of Chicago. Distributed by Ergo Media, Inc., 1992. DVD.
The Magdalene Sisters. Dir. Peter Mullan. Miramax Home Entertainment, 2004. DVD.
The Talbot Judgment. House of Commons Sitting, 28 February 1856, series 3, Vol. 140, cc1544–63. n.d. http://hansard.millbanksystems.com/commons/1856/feb/28/case-of-talbot-v-talbot. 17 January 2010.
The Voyage of the St. Louis. Distributed by Galafilm, Inc., Montreal, Canada, 1995. DVD.
Tong, Rosemarie. *Feminist Thought*. 3rd edn. Boulder, CO: Westview Press, 2009. Print.
Townsend, Charles. *Easter 1916: The Irish Rebellion*. Lanham, MD: Ivan R. Dee, 2006. Print.
Trindle, Cath Madden. *Irish Emigration*. 2008. www.scchgs.org/meetinghandouts/Irishemigration.pdf. 16 December 2009.
Tynan, Maeve. '"Everything Is in the Way the Material Is Composed": Joseph O'Connor's Star of the Sea as Historiographic Metafiction.' Eds Maria Belville, Marita Ryan and M. Tynan. *Passages: Movements and Moments in Text and Theory*. Newcastle upon Tyne: Cambridge Scholars, 2009. pp. 79–95. Print.
Ungar, Stephen. 'Against Forgetting: Notes on Revision and the Writing of History.' *Diacritics* 22.2 (1992): 62–69. Print.
Valente, Joseph. 'Race/Sex/Shame: The Queer Nationalism of *At Swim, Two Boys*.' *Éire-Ireland* 40.3–4 (2005): 58–84. Print.
Voyage of the Damned. Distributed by Avid Home Entertainment, Van Nuys, CA, 1992. DVD.
Voyage of the St. Louis. United States Holocaust Memorial Museum. n.d. www.ushmm.org. 8 October 2009.
Wells, Warre B. and N. Marlow. *A History of the Irish Rebellion of 1916*. New York: F.A. Stokes, 1917. Print.

Whelan, Kevin. 'The Revisionist Debate in Ireland.' *boundary 2* 31.1 (2004): 179–205. Print.

———. *The Tree of Liberty: Radicalism, Catholicism, and the Construction of Irish Identity, 1760–1830.* South Bend, IN: University of Notre Dame Press, 1996. Print.

White, Hayden. *The Fiction of Narrative: Essays on History, Literature, and Theory, 1957–2007.* Ed. Robert Doran. Baltimore, MD: Johns Hopkins University Press, 2010. Print.

Williams, Trevor. 'Mr. Leopold Bloom, Staunch Britisher: The Problem of Identity Under Colonialism.' *Joyce, Imperialism, & Postcolonialism.* Ed. Leonard Orr. Syracuse, NY: Syracuse University Press, 2008. Print.

Williams, W.H.A. *'Twas Only an Irishman's Dream.* Urbana, IL: University of Illinois Press, 1996. Print.

Wills, Claire. 'The Aesthetics of Irish Neutrality During the Second World War.' *boundary 2: An International Journal of Literature and Culture* 31.1 (2004): 119–145. Print.

Worton, Michael. '*Waiting for Godot* and *Endgame*: Theatre as Text.' *The Cambridge Companion to Beckett.* Ed. John Pilling. Cambridge: Cambridge University Press, 1994. pp. 67–87. Print.

Yeats, W.B. 'Easter, 1916.' *The Collected Poems of W.B. Yeats.* 2nd edn. Ed. Richard J. Finneran. New York: Scribner, 1996. pp. 180–182. Print.

———. 'The Statues.' *The Collected Poems of W.B. Yeats.* 2nd edn. Ed. Richard J. Finneran. New York: Scribner, 1996. pp. 336–337. Print.

Yeats, W.B. and Lady Augusta Gregory. *Cathleen ni Houlihan. The Yeats Reader.* Ed. Richard J. Finneran. Rev. edn. New York: Scribner, 2002. Print.

Young, Robert. *Postcolonialism.* Oxford: Oxford University Press, 2003. Print.

Index

abortion 101
Act of Union (1800) 124n27
'The Aesthetics of Irish Neutrality' (Wills) 71
ambiguity 44, 68
ancestor worship 57
Anderson, Benedict 70
Anglo-Irish Treaty (1921) 89n12, 169
Apes and Angels: The Irish in Victorian Caricature (Curtis) 24
apparition of the inapparent 3
Arata, Stephen 132–133
Arnold, Matthew 107
Arnold-Forster, Katherine 181n38
At Swim, Two Boys (O'Neill) 97–112
   as coming-of-age narrative 106, 108
   Hellenistic ideals and 105, 107, 108, 109
   myth-building in 103, 105
   narrative parallelism in 104
   national identity issues in 101–102, 105, 109, 111
   secularization of morality and 100
   spectrality in 13
   temporal fragmentation in 102, 106, 112
   warrior ideal in 107
Attridge, Derek 15n6, 69

Backus, Margot Gayle 98, 116, 130, 149
Baldick, Chris 158n25
ballad construction 54–55
Banville, John 37, 99, 130
Barry, Sebastian 5, 13, 53, 67–93, 166
   see also The Whereabouts of Eneas McNulty

Beckett, Samuel 164–182
   Celtic Revival and 166
   cosmopolitanism and 169
   Famine imagery used by 169, 171, 172
   on *Finnegans Wake* 4, 167, 179n4
   French Resistance and 168, 169, 174
   Ireland's neutrality in World War II and 167, 170
   on Jewish displacement and persecution 173, 175, 176
   temporal fragmentation in works of 166–167
   see also Waiting for Godot
Behrens, Peter 25
Belfast-Derry march (1969) 159n36
Benedict XVI (Pope) 123n12
Benjamin, Walter 39
Bentley, Eric 171
Bentley, Michael 176
Bhabha, Homi K. 45
Bishop, John 3
Botting, Fred 133
Bourke, Angela 28
Bowen, Elizabeth 70
Breakfast on Pluto (McCabe) 133
Brennan, Edward 81
Brennan, Timothy 62n12, 125n47
Brown, Terrence 69–70, 100
Bruhm, Steven 140, 161n70
Burning Your Own (Patterson) 149
Burns, Anna 14, 130, 134, 148–156, 161n77
   see also No Bones

Campbell, Joseph 2

Index

Canada, Irish immigrants in 80
Caruth, Cathy 40
Casement, Roger 110
Castle, Gregory 5
The Castle of Otranto (Walpole) 131
Castle Rackrent (Edgeworth) 131
Cathleen ni Houlihan (Yeats & Gregory) 28, 107
Catholic Association 122n8
Catholic Church
  Easter Rising narratives and 97, 105
  gender inequalities and 113–114
  national identity and 14, 86–87
  Northern Ireland Troubles and 129
  sexual abuse scandals and 99–100, 101, 123n12
  unchecked authority of 86, 99
Catholic Emancipation Act (1829) 122n8
Celtic Revival 4–6, 9, 107, 116, 146, 166
Cheng, Vincent 15n6
child narrators 130
Children of The Troubles: Our Lives in the Crossfire of Northern Ireland (Holliday, ed.) 129
Cleary, E. J. 131
Cleary, Joseph 68
Collins, Michael 89n12
colonialism 45–46, 71, 83, 131
'Colonial Policing' (Cullingford) 77
coming-of-age narratives 106, 108, 113, 149
Commission to Inquire into Child Abuse (CICA) 122–123n10, 123n12
conjuration of specters 6, 36, 140, 154–155
Conley, Thomas 32
Connell, Desmond 123n12
Connolly, James 116
Connolly, Sean 99
contamination theme 3
Coogan, Tim Pat 136
Coppola, Francis Ford 133
Corish, Marguerite 100–101
Cork Multitext Project on Modern Irish History 80
cosmopolitanism 71, 169
Criminal Law Amendment Act of 1885 100, 123n17

Cromwell, Oliver 8
Cronin, Michael G. 104
Culler, Jonathan 1
Cullingford, Elizabeth 76, 77, 78, 81
Cumann na mBan 115, 116, 119
Curtis, Liz 24
Curtis, L. Perry, Jr. 24

Daly, Mary 24
Damned to Fame (Knowlson) 171
Dante 174
Davey, Maeve 142
Davis, Thomas Osborne 126n49
Dawn (Gonne) 25, 28
Deane, Seamus 14, 130, 132, 134, 138–148
  see also Reading in the Dark
Department of Justice and Law Reform 123n12
Derrida, Jacques
  on characteristics of a specter 3, 11, 15n6, 143
  on historical spectrality 73, 90n21, 165
  on historical writing 29
  on 'logic of the ghost' 29, 32
  on Marx's *Eighteenth Brumaire* 6
  on spectrality 1–2, 16n15, 68, 102, 120–121, 134, 137
  on temporal fragmentation 10, 71–72, 102, 134, 146
  theory of repetition 71
Deschevaux-Desmesnil, Suzanne 168, 172
de Valera, Éamon
  Celtic Revival and 4
  Ireland's neutrality in World War II and 67, 70–71, 75, 79, 170
  role in Ireland's independence struggles 17n32
Devlin, Anne 137
dispossession themes 29, 31, 33, 46–47, 58, 61
distancing mechanisms 40
divorce 101
Doing My Bit for Ireland (Skinnider) 116
Donoghue, Emma 130
'Don't talk about the Troubles' (O'Doherty) 156
Dowling, Linda 107, 108

Doyle, Richard 93n56
Doyle, Roddy 13, 97, 98, 112–121
   see also *A Star Called Henry*
Dracula (Stoker) 132, 133
Dracula (film) 133
dual possession 7
Dufferin, Lord 24
Duffy, Eoin 98, 111
Dugan, John P. 89n6
Dust: The Archive and Cultural History (Steedman) 85
dysfunctional families 139

Eagleton, Terry 24, 81, 132
'Easter, 1916' (Yeats) 110
Easter Rising (1916)
   feminist discourse in narratives of 97, 98, 112–121
   historical repetition and 8
   queer discourse in narratives of 104–112, 165
   spectrality in narratives of 13, 97–128
Edgeworth, Maria 131
Edwards, Ruth Dudley 24, 136
Eighteenth Brumaire of Louis Napoleon (Marx) 6, 102–103, 121
Ellis, Peter Beresford 136
Ellmann, Maud 15n6
Ellmann, Richard 2
emasculation 118
emigration due to Famine 23, 48, 79–80, 174
Endgame (Beckett) 171
Esslin, Martin 173
estheticization 32, 40, 42–43, 137, 166
Evans, Ruth Dudley 122n4
'Everything is in the Way the Material is Composed' (Tynan) 47
exceptionalist ideology 70–71, 75

falsification 57, 84
Famine
   allegorical uses of 52
   de-allegorization of narratives 45
   emigration due to 23, 48, 79–80, 174
   as founding myth 75
   Ireland's neutrality in World War II and 167
   persistence in postcolonial Ireland 23–66
   politicized uses of 50
   spectrality in narratives of 12, 21–93
   in World War II narratives 67–93
Famine (O'Flaherty) 25
The Famine in Ireland (Daly) 24
Fanon, Frantz 46
feminist discourse
   in Easter Rising narratives 97, 98, 112–121, 165
   intersectionality in 122n3
Fennell, Desmond 136
Fianna Fáil government 67, 69, 75, 167
Fianna myth 144–145, 148
Finnegans Wake (Joyce) 1–12
   apparition of the inapparent in 3
   Celtic Revival and 4–6, 9
   conjuration of specters in 6
   cyclical framework of 2–3
   dual possession in 7
   historical authenticity and 10
   imaginative reconstruction and 6
   national identity issues in 4–5, 11
   performative interpretation and 3, 11
   reconstructive nature of spectrality in 10
   return and repetition patterns in 8
Fitzgerald, Garret 136
Fitzgerald-Hoyt, Mary 34
Flanagan, Tom 136
Foster, Roy 24, 73, 136
framing devices 44
Freccero, Carla 156
French Revolution (1848) 6, 102–103
Freud, Sigmund 72, 137–138
From Burke to Beckett (McCormack) 170

Gaelic League 119
Galveston, Texas, Irish immigrants in 79–80, 92n47
gender inequalities
   in Easter Rising narratives 97, 104, 113
   in Famine narratives 34, 38, 40
George, David Lloyd 89n12
Gibbons, Luke 104
Glenn, Jeffrey 129

Gloria SMH (French Resistance) 168
Gluck, Barbara Reich 173
Goldman, Peter 90n21
Gonne, Maud 24–25, 28, 32
Good Friday Agreement (1998) 41, 63n30, 129, 159n39
Gordon, Lois 169–170
Gothic (Botting) 133
The Gothic Family Romance (Backus) 130
Gothic narratives 129–163
  Celtic Revival and 146
  child narrators in 130
  colonialism and 131
  coming-of-age themes in 149
  conjuration of specters in 140, 154–155
  conventions of 157n13
  dysfunctional families in 139
  mistrust of public officials theme in 148
  mythological heroes in 144
  national identity issues in 130
  psychological trauma in 130, 139, 150–151
  retributive violence in 130, 136, 145, 149
  Second Wave Gothic 132
  spectrality in 72–73
  transgression themes in 131
Gould, Matilda 135
Gráinne, Henry 174
The Great Famine: Studies in Irish History 1845–1852 (Edwards & Williams) 24
'The Great Hunger' (Kavanagh) 25
The Great Hunger: Ireland 1845–1849 (Smith) 23–24
The Great Irish Famine: Impact, Ideology and Rebellion (Kinealy) 30
Greek influences *see* Hellenistic ideals
Gregory, Lady 28, 107
Griffith, Arthur 89n12
Grosse Île, Canada, Irish immigrants in 80
Grossman, Judith 149

Hamacher, Werner 1
Hand, Derek 72
Hansen, Jim 155
Hardwick, Susan 92n47

Harker, Jonathan 133–134
Harris, Eoghan 32
Haslam, Richard 157n13
Heathcliff and the Great Hunger (Eagleton) 24
The Heather Blazing (Toíbín) 133
Hellenism and Homosexuality in Victorian Oxford (Dowling) 107
Hellenistic ideals 105, 107, 108, 109
heroic-aristocratic stage of history 2
historical authenticity
  elasticity of facts and 56
  Famine narratives and 29, 37, 43, 53, 54–56
  historical fiction vs. historical writing 31–32
  Joyce's challenge to claims of 10
historical revisionism 159n40
historical stages 2–3, 8
History of the Great Irish Famine (O'Rourke) 23
Hofheinz, Thomas 15n6, 18n46
Holland, Jack 136
Holocaust 81, 173
homosexuality
  criminalization and decriminalization of 100, 124n18
  Hellenistic ideals and 105
  national identity and 98
  secularization of morality and 100
  see also queer discourse in Easter Rising narratives
Howes, Marjorie 69
human-democratic stage of history 2
humanism 173
humanitarian assistance 31, 83, 178
Humphreys, Helen 25
Humphries, Steve 122n10
Hurley, Kelly 130–131
Hutcheon, Linda 33, 47
Hyde, Douglas 4, 67

identity *see* national identity
'Imaginary Homelands' (Rushdie) 65n62
imaginative reconstruction 6
In a Glass Darkly (Le Fanu) 132
Ingelbien, Raphael 132
Inghinidhe na hÉireann 28, 117
Inglis, Thomas 99–100

'In Love with Hiding: Samuel Beckett's War' (Perloff) 171
intersectionality 122n3
In the Name of the Father (film) 162n92
'Ireland, Island of Saints and Sages' (Joyce) 166
Irish Citizen Army 115, 117
Irish Civil War (1922–1923) 169
Irish diaspora 29–30
Irish Emigration and the Tenure of Land in Ireland (Dufferin) 24
Irish Free State 10
Irish Republican Army (IRA) 135, 159n39
isolationism 69, 73
The Italian (Radcliffe) 131

Jameson, Fredric 52
Jewish displacement and persecution 68–69, 77–81, 88–89n4, 173, 175–176
Joyce, James
  Celtic Revival and 5, 166
  on *Finnegans Wake* 2
  spectrality in works of 1–12, 141
  see also specific works

Kavanagh, Patrick 25
Keating, Patrick 69
Kenner, Hugh 170, 171–173, 175–176
Kenny, Mary 100
Kiberd, Declan 9, 10, 18n49, 73, 174
Kilfeather, Siobhán 133
Kinealy, Christine 25, 30
Kitcher, Philip 7, 18n47
Klein, Richard 1
Knowlson, James 168, 171
Knudsen, Suzanne 122n3

Lanters, José 119
layering of historical moments and spaces
  in Easter Rising narratives 112
  Famine narratives and 26, 77, 81
  in *My Dream of You* 37–38, 51
  in *Star of the Sea* 51, 53
  see also temporal fragmentation
Le Fanu, J. S. 132
Lennon, Peter 67, 73
Leventhal, A. J. 180n17

Lewis, Brian 98
Lewis, Matthew 131
Lloyd, David 14, 116, 121n1
The Long March (Devlin) 137
loyalist perspective
  on Easter Rising (1916) 97
  Famine narratives and 23, 47, 51
  historical authenticity and 37, 38, 43
Lynn, Kathleen 98–99, 111
Lyotard, Jean-François 33

MacEntee, Sean 180n14
Magdalene laundries 100–101
The Magdalene Sisters (film) 122–123n10
Mahaffey, Vicki 2
Mahon, Peter 15n6, 161n71
Mallin, Michael 116
Markievicz, Constance 113, 115, 116, 119
Marx, Karl 6, 102–103, 121
The Master (Tóibín) 53
Maturin, Charles 72, 132
McCabe, Patrick 130, 133
McCann, Eamonn 136
McCormack, W. J. 167, 170–171
McGahern, John 181n38
McGarry, Fearghal 114, 118, 126–127n72
McGill, Meredith 1
McGlynn, Liam 100
McGurk, John 174
McNamara, Kevin 123n12
McQuaid, John Charles 123n12
Medd, Jodie 104
Melmoth the Wanderer (Maturin) 72, 132
Mill, J. S. 107
Miller, Scott 91n41
mistrust of public officials theme 148
Mitchel, John 23
Modern Ireland (Foster) 24
Moloney, Ed 159n39
Moloney, Helena 99, 111, 114–115
The Monk (Lewis) 131
Moynihan, Sinéad 48
Mullan, Peter 122n10
Mullan, William 34, 36, 39
Murphy, James 146
Murphy Report (Department of Justice

and Law Reform) 100, 123n12
My Dream of You (O'Faolain) 25–46
  colonialism and 45–46
  conjuration of specters in 36
  de-allegorization of Famine narratives in 45
  dispossession themes in 29, 31, 33, 46–47
  distancing mechanisms in 40
  gender inequalities in 34, 38, 40
  historical authenticity and 29, 31–32, 37, 43
  layering of historical moments and spaces in 26, 37–38
  national identity issues in 28–29, 38
  spectrality in 12–13
The Mysteries of Udolpho (Radcliffe) 131
myth-building 103, 105
mythic-theological stage of history 2
mythological heroes 2, 144

Naficy, Hamid 63n35
narrative parallelism 104
national identity
  authenticity of 38, 84
  Catholicism vs. Protestantism and 14, 86–87, 130
  Celtic Revival and 4–5
  Famine narratives and 28–29
  feminist discourse and 101–102
  individual identity and 63n35
  Joyce's challenge to conceptions of 11
  malleability of 87
  as product of dislocation 29
  queer discourse and 101–102, 105, 109, 111
nationalist perspective
  Barry's resistance to Irish identity defined by 74–75
  on Easter Rising (1916) 97, 98
  Famine narratives and 23, 47, 51
  historical authenticity and 37, 38, 43
  on Northern Ireland Troubles 136, 137
National Theatre Society 28
Nation and Narration (Brennan) 62n12
'A Nation Once Again' (song) 108–109, 126n49

Nazis 88–89n4, 179n5
'The Necessity for De-Anglicising Ireland' (Hyde) 4
New Orleans, Irish immigrants in 79–80, 92n47
No Bones (Burns) 148–156
  as coming-of-age narrative 149
  conjuration of specters in 154–155
  Fianna myth in 148
  psychological trauma in 150–151
  retributive violence in 149
  spectrality in 14, 130
Norman conquest (1171) 8
Northern Ireland Civil Rights Association (NICRA) 159n36
Northern Ireland Troubles 129–163
  colonialism and 131
  coming-of-age narratives and 149
  conjuration of specters and 140, 154–155
  dysfunctional families and 139
  estheticization and 137
  Fianna myth and 144–145, 148
  historical repetition in 8
  historical revisionism and 159n40
  mistrust of public officials and 148
  national identity and 130
  psychological trauma and 130, 139, 150–151
  retributive violence and 130, 136, 145, 149
  see also Gothic narratives
Nothing but the Same Old Story (Curtis) 24

O'Brien, Conor Cruise 32, 136
O'Connell, Daniel 122n8
O'Connor, Joseph 12–13, 25, 46–61, 80
  see also Star of the Sea
Ó Corráin, Donnchadh 80
O'Doherty, Malachi 156
O'Faolain, Nuala 12–13, 25–46
  see also My Dream of You
O'Faolain, Sean 178
O'Flaherty, Liam 25
Ogilvie, Sarah 91n41
O'Halloran, Claire 136
O'Hehir, Andrew 161n75
Oh Play That Thing (Doyle) 116
O'Kane Mara, Miriam 34, 38, 40, 45

The Old English Baron (Reeve) 131
O'Malley, Ernie 127n76, 127n85
omnipresence 3
On Canaan's Side (Barry) 53
O'Neill, Jamie 13, 97–112
   see also *At Swim, Two Boys*
O'Neill, Terence 135
'On the Concept of History' (Benjamin), 39
O'Rourke, John 23
Owenson, Sydney 132

Paddy and Mr. Punch: Connections in Irish and English History (Foster) 136
Paget, John 42, 43
Parker, Andrew 1
Partition and the Limits of Irish Nationalism (O'Halloran), 136
Partridge, William 119
Pater, Walter 107, 125n45
Patrick Pearse: The Triumph of Failure (Edwards) 136
Patterson, Glenn 149
Pearse, Pádraig 98, 110, 116, 122n4
performative interpretation 3, 11
Perloff, Marjorie 171, 175
The Picture of Dorian Gray (Wilde) 132
PIRA (Provisional Irish Republican Army) 30, 63n30, 135
Platt, Len 9, 15n6
The Playboy of the Western World (Synge) 17n32
A Poetics of Postmodernism (Hutcheon) 47
A Portrait of the Artist as a Young Man (Joyce) 5, 141
post-Catholic era
   feminist discourse in 97, 98, 112–121
   identity construction in 87
   queer discourse in 104–112
   sexual abuse scandals and 99–100
   spectrality in narratives of 97–128
postcolonialism 7, 46
The Postmodern Condition (Lyotard) 33
Prendergast, Christopher 71
Protestantism
   gender inequalities and 113–114

national identity and 14, 86–87
Northern Ireland Troubles and 129
Provisional Irish Republican Army (PIRA) 30, 63n30, 135
psychological trauma 130, 139, 150–151
Punter, David 132, 134–135
Purgatory (Dante) 174

queer discourse in Easter Rising narratives 97, 104–112, 125n36, 165
Quinn, Owen 89n6

Radcliffe, Anne 131
Raftery, Mary 122n10
Rambo, Shelly 1
Raymond, James 182n49
Reading in the Dark (Deane) 138–148
   Celtic Revival and 146
   conjuration of specters in 140
   dysfunctional families in 139
   Fianna myth in 144–145, 148
   mistrust of public officials theme in 148
   mythological heroes in 144
   psychological trauma in 139
   retributive violence in 145
   spectrality in 14, 130
Reeve, Clara 131
Reid, Alec 176
reinvention 85
religion see Catholic Church; Protestantism
The Renaissance: Studies in Art and Poetry (Pater) 125n45
Renan, Ernest 57, 62n12
repetition 71, 76, 85, 137
Resistance (France) 168, 169, 174
resurrection themes 3
retributive violence 14, 130, 136, 145, 149
'Return of the Gunman 1966–1969' (Holland), 136
return patterns 8
revolutionary history of Ireland 12
ricorso stage of history 2
Riquelme, Jean Paul 131, 134
Roach, Joseph 172
Robinson, Mary 27–28, 29, 30–31, 46
Rocky Road to Dublin (film) 67

Index

Roman Republic and Roman Empire 6
Ross, Daniel 141
Royal Irish Constabulary (RIC) 148
Royal Ulster Constabulary (RUC) 137
Rushdie, Salman 65n62
Ryan, Dermot 123n12
Ryan Report (CICA) 100, 123n12

St. Louis cargo ship 67–68, 77–80, 82, 91n41
Samuel, Raphael 57
Schröder, Gustav 77
Second Wave Gothic 132
The Secret Scripture (Barry) 53, 69, 74, 85, 86
secularization of morality 100
self-invention 6, 103
Self/Other binary 9
Sex in a Cold Climate (documentary) 122n10
sexual abuse scandals 99–100, 101, 123n12
The Shadow of the Glen (Synge) 28
The Shan Van Vocht: A Story of the United Irishmen (Murphy) 146
Sheridan, Jim 162n92
silence 57, 59
Skinnider, Margaret 115–116, 119–120
slavery 48
Smith, Cecil Woodham 23–24
Socialist Feminist agenda 117, 118
Somalia, famine in 28, 30
Spartan 300, 109, 125n36
Specters of Marx (Derrida) 3, 6, 10, 29, 71–72, 102
spectrality as theoretical lens
  awareness of cultural factors and 47, 165
  for Easter Rising narratives 97–128
  for Famine narratives 23–66, 164–182
  framework for 11
  for Gothic narratives 129–163
  for Irish history and identity 33, 38
spectral recurrence 85, 90n21
Spivak, Gayatri 1, 45
A Star Called Henry (Doyle) 112–121
  emasculation in 118
  gender inequalities in 113
  layering of historical moments and spaces in 112
  Socialist Feminist agenda and 117, 118
  spectrality in 13, 97
  suffrage movement and 113, 116
  warrior ideal in 119
Star of the Sea (O'Connor)
  ancestor worship in 57
  colonialism themes in 45–46
  dispossession themes in 46–47, 58, 61
  Famine ships depicted in 80
  historical authenticity and 53, 54–56
  layering of historical moments and spaces in 51, 53
  motivation for writing 25
  silence in 57, 59
  spectrality as theoretical lens for 12–13, 25, 46–61
States of Fear (documentary series) 122n10
States of Ireland (O'Brien) 136
Steedman, Carolyn 85
Stephen Hero (Joyce) 5
Stevenson, Jonathan 8, 135, 162n91
Stewart, Bruce 132
Stoker, Bram 132
Studies of the Greek Poets (Symonds) 125n45
suffrage movement 113, 116
Symonds, J. A. 107, 125n45
Synge, J. M. 4, 17n32, 28
Szeman, Imre 52

Talbot, Marianne 34, 36, 39
Talbot, Richard 34, 39, 42
tapestry metaphor 5, 166
Taylor-Batty, Mark and Juliette 168, 173, 174
temporal fragmentation
  Derrida on 10, 71–72, 102, 134, 146
  in Easter Rising narratives 102, 106, 112
  in Famine narratives 166–167
Theatres of Memory (Samuel) 57
Tóibín, Colm 53, 133
Tong, Rosemarie 118
Towards a New Ireland (Fitzgerald) 136

Transformations in Irish Culture (Gibbons) 104
transgression themes 131
trauma 40, 130, 139, 150–151
Troubles in Northern Ireland *see* Northern Ireland Troubles
Tynan, Maeve 47

Ulster Volunteer Force (UVF) 135
Ulysses (Joyce) 9
Ulysses and Us (Kiberd) 18n49
uncanny (Freud's conception) 72, 137–138
Unclaimed Experience (Caruth) 40
Uncle Silas (Le Fanu) 132
Ungar, Steven 32
United Irishmen Rebellion (1798) 103, 124n27
Urquhart, Jane 25

Valente, Joseph 104, 105–106, 125n36
van Boheemen, Christine 15n6
Vanderpyl, Fritz 2
Vico, Giambattista 2
violence *see* retributive violence
voting rights 113, 116

Waiting for Godot (Beckett) 164–182
  Celtic Revival and 166
  cosmopolitanism in 169
  Famine imagery in 169, 171, 172
  French Resistance and 168, 169, 174
  Ireland's neutrality in World War II and 167, 170
  Jewish displacement and persecution and 173, 175, 176
  temporal fragmentation in 166–167
Walpole, Horace 131
warrior ideal 107, 119
Weaver, Harriet Shaw 2
'We Wrecked the Place': Contemplating an End to the Northern Irish Troubles (Stevenson) 135
Whelan, Kevin 130
The Whereabouts of Eneas McNulty (Barry)
  ambiguity in 68
  colonialism in 71, 83
  cosmopolitanism in 71
  exceptionalist ideology and 70–71, 75
  Gothic aesthetic in 72–73
  humanitarian assistance and 83
  isolationism and 69, 73
  Jewish displacement and persecution in 68–69, 77–81, 88–89n4
  layering of historical moments and spaces in 77, 81
  national identity issues in 84, 86–87
  repetition of history in 71, 76, 85
  spectrality in 13, 67–93
  spectral recurrence in 85, 90n21
White, Hayden 31
Wilde, Oscar 106, 107, 110, 111, 124n18, 125n45, 132
The Wild Irish Girl (Owenson) 132
Williams, T. D. 24
Wills, Clair 71
women
  in Famine narratives, 34, 38, 40
  political roles of 34
  voting rights for 113, 116
  in workforce 101
  see also feminist discourse
Woolf, Virginia 181n38
Work in Progress (Joyce) 2, 3
  see also Finnegans Wake (Joyce)
World War I 58
World War II
  Ireland's declaration of neutrality 67–68, 70–71
  Jewish displacement and persecution 68–69, 77–81, 88–89n4, 173, 175–176
  spectrality in narratives of 67–93
  see also The Whereabouts of Eneas McNulty (Barry)
Worton, Michael 174, 175
Wyse-Power, Nancy 127n85

Yeats, W. B. 4, 17n32, 28, 107, 110
Young, Robert 159n40